A BAG
OF MARBLES

A BAG
OF MARBLES

Joseph Joffo

Translated from the French
by Martin Sokolinsky

*With a new Afterword
by the author*

The University of Chicago Press

The University of Chicago Press, Chicago 60637
Copyright © 1974 by Houghton Mifflin Company
All rights reserved. Originally published in French under the title
Un sac de billes, © 1973. J. C. Lattès/Edition spéciale.
English translation of Afterword, "Conversations with My Readers,"
© 2000 by The University of Chicago
University of Chicago Press edition 2000

Printed in the United States of America
14 13 12 11   8 7 6

Library of Congress Cataloging-in-Publication Data

Joffo, Joseph.
    [Sac de billes. English]
    A bag of marbles / Joseph Joffo ; translated from the French by Martin Sokolinsky ;
    with new transcript by the author.
        p. cm.
    ISBN 0-226-40069-7 (pbk. : alk. free)
    1. Joffo, Joseph.   2. Joffo, Maurice.   3. Holocaust, Jewish (1939–1945)—France—
    Personal narratives.   4. Jewish children in the Holocaust—France—Biography.
    5. Jews—France—Biography.   6. France—Biography.   I. Title.
    DS135.F9 J64513 2000
    940.53′18′092—dc21
    [B]   00-062900

To my family

PREFACE

This book isn't the work of a historian.

I've drawn on my childhood recollections to tell my adventures during the Occupation.

Thirty years have gone by since I was that ten-year-old boy. Not only do we forget things, but our memory often plays tricks on us, altering the things that we remember. But the important part, the true part, is still there — that mixture of tenderness, comedy, and anguish.

To avoid hurt feelings, the names of many people who appear in this story have been changed. It is the story of two children in a world of cruelty, absurdity, and, at times, helpfulness of the most unexpected kind.

A BAG
OF MARBLES

I

THE MARBLE ROLLS AROUND in my hand at the bottom of
my pocket.

It's my favorite marble — one I take with me everywhere. The funny part is that it's the worst-looking one
of the lot: it doesn't come anywhere near the aggies or the
big glassies that I stare at in the window of old Ruben's
shop at the corner of the rue Ramey. The one I love is
made of clay, and the glaze has chipped off here and
there, leaving rough spots and crackled designs. It looks
like a scale model of the globe in school.

I love that marble. It's nice to have the earth tucked
away in my pocket, with the mountains and oceans and
everything.

I'm a giant, and I have all the planets in my pocket.

"Well? Can't you make up your mind?"

Maurice is waiting, sitting on the sidewalk right in front
of the delicatessen. His stockings are always getting
twisted. They're so full of wrinkles that Papa calls him
"the walking accordion."

Between his legs is a pyramid of four marbles: one on top of the triangle made by the other three.

Granny Epstein watches us from the doorway. She's a shriveled-up old Bulgarian, wrinkled like a prune. Strangely enough, she has kept the coppery complexion that comes from the wind of the steppes. There in the recess of the doorway, on her straw-bottomed chair, she's a living piece of the Balkans that the gray sky of the Porte Clignancourt can't tarnish.

She's there every day, smiling at the kids on their way home from school. They say that she walked across Europe, fleeing from one pogrom to another, finally ending up in this part of the 18th *arrondissement* where she was thrown in with other fugitives from the East: Russians, Rumanians, Czechs, comrades of Trotsky, intellectuals, craftsmen. In the twenty years or more that she's been here, her memories must have faded, even if the color of her brow and cheeks hasn't changed.

She laughs when she sees me waddling around. Her hands rumple the worn serge of an apron that's as black as my smock. In those days all the schoolboys wore black — a childhood in mourning. It was a foreboding in 1941.

"What the hell are you up to?"

Naturally, I can't make up my mind. Maurice is great. I've shot seven times already and missed everything. His pockets bulge like balloons with what he won at recess. He can hardly walk he's got so many marbles. I'm down to my last one, my beloved.

Maurice growls, "You think I'm going to sit here on my ass till tomorrow?"

All right, here goes.

The marble in the palm of my hand trembles a little. I shoot with my eyes open. Missed!

Well, that's that. Miracles don't happen. We have to go home now.

Goldenberg's delicatessen looks funny — you'd swear that it's in a fish tank and the storefronts along the rue Marcadet are all wavering crazily. I look to the left, because Maurice is walking to the right of me. That way he doesn't see me crying.

"Quit your blubbering," says Maurice.

"I'm not blubbering, damn it!"

"When you look away like that, I can tell you're blubbering."

A wipe of my sleeve and my cheeks are dry. I don't answer, and I speed up. We're going to get a scolding — we should have been home over half an hour ago.

Here we are. There on the rue Clignancourt stands the shop with the painted lettering on the front — big, broad letters printed with downstrokes and upstrokes as neat as the ones the teacher makes on the blackboard. They spell out *Joffo — Coiffeur*.

Maurice gives me a dig with his elbow.

"Here, idiot."

I look at him and take the marble that he hands me.

A brother is someone who gives you back your last marble after he's won it from you.

I get back my miniature planet. Tomorrow, in the schoolyard, I'll win a pile of marbles with that one and I'll do him out of his. He'd better not go around thinking he's the boss just because he's two years older than I am. After all, I'm ten now.

4

I remember going into the barbershop then and being greeted by those familiar smells. No doubt every childhood has its own particular smells, but I had them all — the whole range from lavender to violet. I can still see those jars on the shelves again, still smell the clean scent of the towels, and still hear the snip-snip of the scissors too. That was the first music I ever heard.

When Maurice and I came in, the place was really busy; every chair was taken. As usual, Duvallier tweaked my ear when I went by him. I swear he spent his whole life in the barbershop. He must have loved the atmosphere, the conversations. It's not hard to understand why. He was old and a widower, living in a three-room apartment on the rue Simart, a fourth-floor walk-up that must have been awfully dingy. That's why he'd go downstairs and spend the afternoon with the Jews. He'd always take the same chair — near the cloakroom. When all the customers had gone, he would stand up and move into his regular barber chair. "Just give me a shave," he used to say.

It was Papa who used to shave him. Papa with his wonderful stories — the king of our street — Papa who went to the gas chamber.

We did our homework. I didn't own a watch in those days, but it couldn't have taken more than forty-five seconds. I always knew my lessons before doing the homework. We hung around in the bedroom so Mama or one of my older brothers wouldn't catch us and send us back to the books. Then we'd go out again.

Albert was working on a big customer with curly hair and was sweating blood over an American-style cut; he still managed to look over his shoulder as we went by.

"All done with your homework?"

Papa looked at us too, but we lit out of there while he was making change at the register. Then our fun started.

Porte Clignancourt 1941. The neighborhood was a paradise for kids. I'm always astounded nowadays by the "child-oriented play areas" that the architects talk about. In the plazas of modern housing projects there are sand-piles, sliding ponds, seesaws, and all kinds of stuff. It's all been designed especially for kids by experts with a zillion degrees in child psychology. And it still doesn't work. The children are bored to tears.

So I wonder if all those specialists wouldn't do better to ask themselves why we — the kids of my day — were happy in that section of Paris. A gray Paris with the lights of shops, the high roofs and the bands of sky above them, the ribbons of sidewalks choked with trash barrels to be climbed, hallways to hide in, and doorbells — we had everything. There were the voices of bustling *concierges*, there were horse-drawn carriages, the florist's shop, and the sidewalk cafés in summer. And it all extended as far as the eye could see — a maze of streets, an endless maze of intersecting streets. We even used to make discoveries there. I remember that one day we found a river. It lay at our feet, after we'd turned down some dirty street. We felt like explorers. I learned much later that it was the Canal de l'Ourcq. We used to watch waterlogged corks drift by and the strange forms of oil slicks; at nightfall we'd head for home.

"Where to?" Maurice is the one who asks the questions — almost always.

I'm about to answer when my eyes wander up the avenue, all the way up.

And I saw them coming. You couldn't miss them. There were two of them, dressed in black — big men with their chests crisscrossed by leather belts. They wore high boots that must have been polished for days on end to get such a shine.

Maurice turned to me.

"SS," he murmured.

We watched them come. They weren't going fast; they moved slowly and stiffly as if they were on an immense square full of trumpets and drums.

"How much do you want to bet that they're coming to get haircuts?"

I don't think the idea dawned on one of us before the other. We glued ourselves together in front of the shop window as if we were Siamese twins, and the two Germans went in.

That's when we started to laugh.

Hidden by our two bodies was a little notice posted up on the windowpane. It had a yellow background and black lettering:

JUDISCHES GESCHAEFT *

Inside the shop, in the most intense silence that could ever have reigned in a barbershop, two SS men from a Death's Head unit sat with their knees pressed together. Among the Jewish clients they waited — waited to entrust the napes of their necks to my Jewish father or to my Jewish brothers.

Outside, two little Jews doubled up with laughter.

---

* Jewish shop. *Translator.*

II

HENRI BRUSHED the bits of hair from Bibi Cohen's collar.
With that, the man got up from the barber chair and
moved toward the cash register. Maurice and I were behind it, waiting to see what would happen next. There
was an uneasiness in the pit of my stomach: maybe we've
done something crazy. It really was a wild idea to lure
these two bruisers right into the heart of the Jewish section. We'd gone a little too far.

Henri turned to the German.

"I believe you're next, monsieur."

The SS man got up, seated himself in the barber chair
with his visored cap on his lap. He looked at himself in
the mirror as if his face weren't the least bit interesting
and maybe even a bit repulsive.

"Shall I make it fairly short?"

"*Oui, la raie à droite, s'il vous plaît.*"

I thought I would choke behind the cash register when
I heard that. A German who speaks French! What's

more, he's got a better accent than many of the people from the neighborhood.

I look at him. He has a tiny pistol in a highly polished holster. You can see that the pistol butt has a ring on it like the one on my cap gun. In a few minutes, he's going to realize where he is and he'll pull out the gun and start shouting and massacre all of us — even Mama upstairs; she's cooking and doesn't even know there are two Nazis in the shop.

Duvallier is reading the newspaper in his corner. Next to him sits Crémieux, a neighbor who works for the insurance company; he's bringing his son for the monthly shearing. I know that Crémieux kid — he goes to my school and we play together at recess. He doesn't move: he's small, but right now he looks as if he wishes he could make himself even smaller.

I don't remember the others any more. I must have known them all right, but I've forgotten. I was getting scared. I only know one thing: it was Albert who took the offensive while sprinkling tonic on his client's new-mown hair.

"The war's rotten, isn't it?"

The SS man gave a start. It must have been the first time that a Frenchman had spoken to him, and he jumped at the opportunity.

"Yes, it's rotten all right."

They went on talking; the others joined in the conversation and it became friendly. The German translated for his buddy who didn't understand and who was trying to join in with nods and shakes of his head that Henri tried to control. It wouldn't have been a good idea to gash the cheek of the lord of the Germanic race; the situation was complicated enough as it stood.

I could just see my father — my backside burned already from the hiding that wouldn't be long in the coming. No sooner would the two guys go out the door than I'd be over Albert's knees and Maurice over Henri's. And we'd just have to wait until their hands hurt too much for them to go on.

"It's your turn now, monsieur." My father took the second one.

It was when Samuel came in that I couldn't help laughing even though I was scared. He used to come by in the evening, just to say hello, as a good friend. He ran a secondhand furniture stall two hundred meters away. His specialty was old clocks, but you could find just about anything near his sign at the flea market; Maurice and I used to go there and rummage around.

He was smiling when he entered.

"Hello, everybody."

Papa had the towel in his hand. He unfolded it with a snap before putting it around the SS man's neck. Samuel had just enough time to see the uniform. His eyes grew rounder than my marbles and three times bigger.

"Oh, oh," he said. "Oh, oh . . ."

"Looks like we're a bit crowded today," said Albert.

Samuel stroked his mustache.

"Oh, that doesn't matter," he said. "I'll come back when everything quiets down."

"Good. Give my regards home."

Flabbergasted, Samuel still hadn't moved, staring at the strange customers.

"I'll do that," he murmured. "I'll do that."

He stood there a few seconds longer. When he left, he seemed to be walking on eggshells.

Thirty seconds later, from the rue Eugène-Sue to the Saint-Ouen quarter, from the backs of Yiddish restaurants to the storerooms of kosher butcher shops, everybody knew that old Joffo had become the Wehrmacht's official barber.

He had performed the feat of the century. In the shop, the conversation grew friendlier and friendlier.

In the mirror, the SS men saw our two heads sticking up.

"Are those your boys?"

Papa smiled.

"Yes, they're little hooligans."

The SS man nodded his head fondly. "Oh, the war is terrible," he said. "The Jews are to blame."

The scissors didn't stop; then came the clippers.

"You really think so?"

The German nodded with a certainty that you felt was unshakable.

"Yes, I'm sure of it."

Papa gave the last two snips just over the temples; he did it with one eye closed like an artist. A flick of the wrist to take off the towel; then the mirror was brought out.

The SS man smiled with satisfaction.

"Very good. Thank you."

They went to the cash register to pay.

Papa went behind the cash desk to make their change. Squeezed against my father, I saw his face high above me, beaming.

The two soldiers put their caps back on.

"Do you like your haircuts?"

"Absolutely."

"Well, before you leave," said my father, "I ought to tell you that all these people are Jews."

He'd been an actor in his youth: when he told us stories at night, he used Stanislavsky-like mime with sweeping gestures. At that instant, no actor could have had greater majesty on the stage than old Joffo behind his cash desk. Time stopped in the barbershop. Then Crémieux was the first to get up; he squeezed his son's hand and he got up, too. The others followed.

Duvallier said nothing. He put down his newspaper, slipped his pipe into his pocket, and François Duvallier, son of Jacques Duvallier and Noémie Machegrain, baptized at Saint-Eustache and a devout Catholic, got to his feet. We were all standing.

The SS man didn't waver. Suddenly his lips seemed thinner.

"I was talking about rich Jews."

The change clinked against the plate glass on the cash desk; there was the noise of boots.

When they had probably reached the corner, we were still frozen, petrified; for a second it seemed to me that a bad witch from the fairy tales had changed us into statues of stone and we would never come back to life. When the spell finally broke and we all began to sit down again, I knew that I had escaped a thrashing.

Before going back to work, my father allowed his hand to stray over Maurice's head and mine, and I closed my eyes so that my brother wouldn't be able to say that he'd seen me cry twice in the same day.

As she does every evening, Mama comes to inspect our teeth, our ears, our nails. Plumping up the pillow with a blow of her fist, she tucks us in, kisses us, and leaves the room. And, as on every other night, no sooner has the door closed behind her than my pillow flies through the darkened room, hitting Maurice who curses like a taxi-driver. We fight often. Especially at night, trying to make as little noise as possible. Generally, I'm the one who does the attacking.

I listen with my ear cocked. I hear the rustling of sheets to my right: Maurice has left his bed. I can tell from the wheeze of the springs that he's preparing to pounce on me. I expand my string-bean biceps, panting with terror and joy: I'm ready for a savage battle and . . .

The lights.

Dazzled, Maurice throws himself into his bed and I try to look like I'm fast asleep.

It's Papa.

No use faking — he's never taken in by our tricks.

"The next part of the story," he announces.

That's the greatest thing that can happen.

Of all my memories of childhood (which, as we shall see, was short) this is one of the best.

Some nights, he came in and sat on my bed or Maurice's and began the stories about Grandfather. Children love the stories that you read to them, the ones that you make up for them; but I had something special. The hero of the stories was my own grandfather, whose daguerreotype in an oval frame I could see in the parlor. With time, the stern and mustachioed face had acquired the faded pink color of a baby's blanket. You could tell that under the well-trimmed suit there was a muscular torso, accentuated by the stiff pose that the photographer had required. Grandfather leaned against the back of a chair that seemed ridiculously frail and ready to collapse under the giant's weight.

His stories have left me with the confused memory of a series of interlocking adventures against a backdrop of deserts white as snow, winding streets in cities sprinkled with gilded cupolas.

My grandfather had twelve sons; he was a rich and generous man, respected by the inhabitants of a large village to the south of Odessa, Elysabethgrad in Russian Bessarabia. He lived happily and reigned over the tribe until the pogroms began.

I was weaned on those stories. I saw rifle butts smash in doors, breaking windows; the wild flight of peasants, flames racing over the beams of *izbas*. My eyes saw a whirlwind of saber blades, the breath of charging horses, the glint of spurs and, towering over the whole scene, standing out in the smoke, the gigantic figure of my grandsire, Jacob Joffo.

My grandfather wasn't the kind of man to allow his friends to be massacred without doing something. At night he put aside his beautiful robe with its floral design, went down into the cellar and, by the light of a dark lantern, drew on the boots and outfit of a *muzhik*. He spat into the palms of his hands, rubbed them on the stone walls and then on his own face. Black with dust and soot, he used to go out alone in the night, headed for the area of the barracks and soldiers' dens. In the shadows, he lay in wait; when he saw three or four of them, he knocked them senseless. Without haste and without anger, with the clear conscience of the righteous, he would knock their heads against the walls, then go home, satisfied, humming a Yiddish air.

But then the massacres intensified and Grandfather understood that his punitive expeditions were no longer effective and, with regret, gave them up. He called together the family and sadly informed its members that it was impossible for him to knock out, all by himself, the three battalions that the Czar had sent to the region. For that reason, they would have to flee — and fast.

The rest of the story is a spirited and picturesque cavalcade across Rumania, Hungary, Germany; there were stormy nights, revelry, laughter, tears, and death.

We listened that night as we usually did: our mouths agape. Maurice's twelve years didn't stop him from being fascinated. The lamp threw shadows on the wallpaper and Papa's arms waved on the ceiling. The walls were peopled with refugees, terrified women, and trembling children. They left dark, rainy cities with strange, ornate architecture; there was an infernal series of tortuous passes and glacial steppes, and then, one day, they crossed the last border. The sky brightened and the band of refugees found a beautiful plain basking in sunshine. There were the songs of birds, wheat fields, trees, and a whitewashed village with red rooftops and a steeple. Sitting on chairs before their houses were old women with their hair drawn back in buns.

Over the doorway of the biggest house, they saw the inscription: *"Liberté–Egalité–Fraternité."* Then all the refugees set down their bundles or let go of their little wagons and the fear left their eyes, for they knew that they had arrived.

France.

I've never been surprised by the love of the French for their own land. It's so easy to understand, it's so natural. There are no doubts, no problems. But I know of no one who ever loved that country as much as my father — born 8000 kilometers away.

We never went past the town hall of the 19th *arrondissement* without Papa squeezing my hand a little in his own. With his chin, he gestured to the letters on the façade of the building.

"You know what those words mean up there?"

I learned to read very early; at five, I could tell him the three words.

"That's it, Joseph. You've got it. And as long as they're written up there, we'll be all right here."

And it was true that we were all right, that we had been all right. One evening at the supper table, when the Occupation had begun, Mama had raised the question.

"Don't you think we'll have trouble now that they're here?"

We knew what Hitler had already done in Germany, Austria, Czechoslovakia, and Poland; race laws were coming in one after another in those countries. My mother was Russian. She owed her freedom to forged identity papers. She had been through the nightmare and didn't have my father's optimism.

I washed the dishes, Maurice dried. Albert and Henri tidied up the shop — we could hear them laughing through the partition.

Papa had a certain way of moving his hands; it was a gesture intended to allay fears, a gesture befitting a member of the Comédie Française.

"No, not here. Not in France — never."

But that confidence of his had been considerably shaken for some time now — ever since they put through the law requiring identity cards and, most of all, since two men in long raincoats came around to stick up a notice on the shop window without saying a word. I can still see the taller one: he had a beret, a mustache. They posted the sign and ran away into the night like thieves.

"Good night, children."

Papa closes the door again. We're in the dark. We're nice and snug under our blankets; muffled voices reach us, then fall still. It's a night like any other night, a night in 1941.

III

"ALL RIGHT, it's your turn now, Jo."

I come up to the table, my jacket in my hand. It's eight o'clock in the morning and still pitch dark outside. Mama is sitting on a chair on the far side of the table. She has a thimble, a spool of black thread, and her hands are shaking. She's smiling with just her lips.

I turn around. Under the lampshade, Maurice stands motionless. With the flat of his palm he smoothes something down on his left lapel: a yellow star, and embroidered on it in big stitches:

JUIF

Maurice looks at me.

"Don't cry. You'll get your medal, too."

Yes, I'm going to get one. Everybody in the neighborhood is going to get one. This morning when the people step out it'll be like spring in midwinter, a spontaneous blooming — everyone with a big daffodil in his buttonhole.

Once you've got one, there isn't much you can do: you

can't go to the movies or take the train; maybe you won't have the right to play marbles anymore. Maybe you won't have the right to go to school either. That kind of race law wouldn't be so bad.

Mama pulls on the thread. She nips it with her teeth, nips it down close to the material, and it's done. I'm branded. With two fingers of the hand that has just done the sewing, she gives the star a little thump — just like a real seamstress who's finished a tough stitch. She couldn't resist that.

Papa opens the door as I pull on my jacket. He's finished shaving and the scent of soap and rubbing alcohol comes in with him. He looks at our stars, then at his wife.

"Well, well, well," he says.

I've picked up my school bag; I kiss Mama. Papa stops me before I reach the door.

"Do you know what you've got to go and do now?"

"No."

"Be the best pupil in your school. Know why?"

"I know," Maurice answers. "To give Hitler a pain in the ass."

Papa laughs.

"All right," he says. "That's about the size of it."

It was cold outside; our wood-soled shoes echoed against the cobblestones. I don't know why, but I turned around. Our apartment windows looked out over the barbershop and I saw the two of them watching us from behind the windowpanes. For a few months, they had been haggard-looking.

Maurice walks fast, puffing hard so he can see his own breath. The marbles click in his pockets.

"Are we going to have the stars on for a long time?" I ask him.

He stops to look at me.

"How should I know? Why — does it bother you?"

I shrug. "Why should it bother me? It doesn't weigh much. It doesn't stop me from fooling around, so . . ."

Maurice snickers.

"If the star doesn't bother you, how come you've got your muffler over it?"

That guy always has to see everything.

"I don't have my muffler over it. The wind blew it that way."

Maurice laughs. "Sure, pal, it's the wind."

Less than two hundred meters away stands the iron fence around the school, the courtyard with its chestnut trees black in the winter. Actually, the chestnut trees of the school on the rue Ferdinand-Flocon have always seemed black to me. Perhaps because they've been dead for a long time, dead from having grown under the asphalt, from being squeezed by iron gratings — that's no life for a tree.

"Hey, Joffo!"

It's Zérati calling me. He's been my pal since first grade. At the rate of three pairs of short pants a year, we've worn out a good two dozen between us sitting in those classrooms.

He runs to catch up with me. The flaps of his fur-lined hat are down so all you can see is a nose, red with the cold. He has mittens on and he's all bundled up in the hooded cape that he always wears.

"*Salut.*"

"*Salut.*"

He looks at me, stares at my chest, and his eyes grow round. I swallow.

Silence seems like forever when you're a kid.

"Jesus, you're lucky," he murmurs. "That star sure is a beauty."

Maurice laughs and so do I. What a feeling of relief! All three of us walk into the school courtyard.

Zérati can't get over it.

"You know, it looks like a medal or something," he says. "You're a lucky son of a gun."

I feel like telling him that I didn't do anything to earn it, but it's plenty reassuring to see his reaction. Actually, it's the truth: it *is* just like a big medal. Maybe it doesn't shine, but you sure can't miss seeing it.

There are groups of kids in the courtyard; other kids are running wildly in and out of the columns that hold up the roof.

"Hey, fellows! Seen Joffo?"

Zérati didn't mean any harm. He only wanted to show me off a little, to make me shine in the other boys' eyes, as if overnight I'd performed some act of heroism and he wanted everybody to know about it.

They formed a ring, and I was in the middle.

Kraber smiled right away; you could see his face in the light.

"You're not the only one — some of them in the other grades got stars too."

Behind the ring, in the shadows, there's a stir and two faces push through — not smiling at all.

"Hey, you a kike?"

It's hard to say no when it's marked on the lapel of your jacket.

"It's on account of the kikes that we're in the war."

Zérati is beside himself. He doesn't weigh more than thirty-five kilos, and in our muscle-flexing contests he always comes in last. No matter how hard he tries to make a muscle, he can never manage to produce more than a slight swelling. But that doesn't stop him from turning to the big boy.

"You're a real idiot, you are. You think it's Jo's fault that there's the war?"

"That's right. Got to throw all the damned yids out."

Murmurs of voices.

What was happening? I was a kid like any other — with marbles, games, clouts on the ear, lessons to learn. Papa was a barber, and my brothers too. Mama did the cooking. On Sunday, Papa took us to Longchamp to see the horses and get some fresh air; on the other days, there was school — and that's all there was. Now all of a sudden they stick a few square inches of cloth on me and I turn into a Jew.

A Jew. What does that mean anyway? What the hell is a Jew?

I feel anger welling up in me, along with the helpless rage of not understanding.

The ring tightens around me.

"You seen the beak on him?"

There was a big colored poster over the shoe store on the corner of the rue Marcadet. It had a picture of a spider crawling over the globe — a black widow with a human face, an ugly, hairy one with bulging eyes, cauliflower ears, liver lips, and a hideous nose like the blade of a scimitar. Underneath, it said: "The Jew trying to take over the world." I used to go past it a lot with Maurice. The poster didn't bother us one way or another: the monster wasn't us. We weren't spiders and, thank God, we didn't have faces like that. I was almost blond, with blue eyes and a nose like everybody else. It was simple: I wasn't the Jew.

And then all of a sudden that moron told me that I had a beak like the one in the poster. Just because I had a star.

"What's the matter with my nose? It's the same as yesterday, isn't it?"

That big oaf couldn't think up an answer; I could see him trying to come up with something when the school bell rang.

Before getting into line, I saw Maurice at the other end of the courtyard. There was a bunch of boys around him and it looked as if they were arguing; when he got into line behind the others, he had an angry face. It was a good thing that the bell rang just when it did, because a fight was brewing.

I took my time for once and got at the very end of the line. We went inside, by twos, past old Boulier; I managed to get alongside of Zérati.

The first hour was geography. Monsieur Boulier hadn't called on me for a long time, and I was a little scared. I was sure that he was going to get me. His eyes moved over us as they did every morning but they didn't stop at me; his eyes slid over. It was finally Raffard who went to the board and got a zero. That really bothered me: perhaps I didn't count anymore; perhaps I was no longer a pupil like the others. A few hours before, the idea would have delighted me, but now it upset me. What did they all have against me anyway? Either they try to beat me up or they ignore me.

"Take out your notebooks. The date in the margin. The heading: 'The Rhone Trench.' "

Like the others, I obeyed, but it drove me crazy that he didn't call on me. I had to have it out with him; I needed to know if I was still in the class or if I just didn't exist anymore.

Old Boulier had a mania for silence. He always wanted to be able to hear a pin drop. When he heard talking, the fall of a pen, or anything else, he didn't beat around the bush. His index finger pointed to the guilty party and the sentence came down like the guillotine: "You will stand in the corner during recess. Conjugate 'to make less noise from now on' in the perfect tense, past perfect, and future perfect thirty times."

I laid my slate down on the edge of the desk. It was a real slate and a rarity in those days; most of us had black cardboard rectangles that couldn't be sponged too much. It was hard to write on them.

I had this real one with a wooden frame that had a hole drilled in it for the string that held a sponge. With my fingertip, I pushed it. The slate teetered on the edge a second, then fell with a crash.

He was writing on the blackboard and turned around. He looked at the slate on the floor, then at me. All the others stared at us. It's unusual for a pupil to try to be punished. Perhaps it had never happened. That morning I would have given a lot for the teacher to stretch his finger toward me and say, "You're going to stay in after school." It would have been proof that nothing had changed, that I was still the same, a schoolboy like the others who could be praised, punished, called on for answers.

Monsieur Boulier looked at me and then his gaze became vacant, completely vacant, as if all his thoughts had suddenly flown away. Slowly he took the big ruler from the top of his desk and placed the end of it on the map of France that hung on the wall. He pointed to a line that went from Lyon to Avignon and said, "The Rhone Trench separates the ancient mountain masses of the Central Massif from the younger mountains . . ."

The lesson had begun and I knew that, as far as I was concerned, school had ended.

I wrote the summary like an automaton and then I heard the bell for recess. Zérati nudged me with his elbow.

"Come on, hurry up."

I went out and found myself in the courtyard and suddenly I was in the center of a whirlwind.

"Kike! Kike! Kike!"

They were all around me. One shoved me from behind and I bounced off someone else's chest; then there was another jolt and I went sailing backwards. I managed to keep from falling and plunged ahead to break through the chain. I made it and could see Maurice fighting twenty paces away. They were shouting around him too: "Kike! Kike! Kike!"

I threw a punch and took a violent blow on the thigh; I thought that the whole school was piling on me, that I would suffocate under the charging horde.

My smock was ripped, and a punch landed square on

my ear. The teacher who supervised the recess blew his whistle and stopped everything.

"All right, what's going on here? Get the devil out of there!"

I felt that my ear was swelling so fast that you could see it. I went looking for Maurice. He had his handkerchief knotted around his knee. The blood had already begun to dry, leaving brown splotches. We couldn't talk; it was time to go back to the classroom.

I sat down. Before me, over the blackboard, was a portrait of Marshal Pétain. A handsome, dignified face topped by a visored cap. Underneath was a sentence with his signature: "I keep my promises — even those made by others." I wondered whom he could have promised to make me wear a star. What good was it? And why did the other boys want to beat me up?

What I remember of that morning — more than the blows, more than the indifference of the adults — is that feeling of not being able to understand. I was the same color as they were, my face was the same. I'd heard of different religions, and they told me at school that people used to fight over that a long time ago, but I didn't have any religion; on Thursdays I even went to the church club with the other kids from the neighborhood. We played basketball behind the church; I used to love that, and when teatime came the priest would give us a big snack: whole-wheat bread filled with chocolate. It was the kind of chocolate they had during the Occupation — with a white dough in the center, a bit on the sticky side and just slightly sweetened. Sometimes he even threw in a dehydrated banana, or an apple . . . Mama felt better knowing that we were there; she preferred that to seeing us roam the streets, wandering in and out among the secondhand furniture stalls of the Porte St.-Ouen or stealing wood from buildings under demolition to build cabins or make swords.

So, what then was the difference?

Eleven-thirty. My ear still aches. I put on my coat and go out. It's cold: Maurice is waiting for me. His scraped knee isn't bleeding anymore.

We don't say anything: there's nothing to say.

We go up the street together.

"Jo!"

Somebody's running after me. It's Zérati, all out of breath. In his hand, there's a drawstring bag made of canvas. He offers it to me.

"I'll trade you."

I don't understand.

"For what?"

With an eloquent finger he points to the lapel of my coat.

"For your star."

Maurice doesn't say anything. He waits, knocking the wooden heels of his shoes one against the other.

I make up my mind abruptly.

"Okay."

It has been sewn on with loose stitches and the thread isn't very strong. I work one finger underneath, then two — and I rip it off.

"Here you are." Zérati's eyes shine.

My star. For a bag of marbles.

That was my first business deal.

Papa hangs up his shop apron on the coatrack behind the kitchen door. We don't eat in the dining room anymore — to save heat. Before sitting down at the table, he inspects us. My ear swollen, my smock torn, Maurice's knee and his eye slowly turning purple.

Plunging his spoon into the noodles, he gives himself a shake and makes a smile that barely manages to reach his lips. He chews, swallows with difficulty, and looks at my mother, whose hands tremble on each side of the plate.

"No school this afternoon," he orders.

Maurice and I drop our spoons. I'm the first to pick mine up.

"Really? But what about my school bag?"

Papa's hands show me that it doesn't matter.

"I'll get it; don't worry about it. You're free this afternoon, but be home before night. I have something to tell you."

I remember the joy, the flood of relief that washed over me. A whole afternoon to ourselves, while the other boys worked! It served them right; they didn't want us, so now it was our turn to put one over on them. While they sweated over math problems and past participles, we would paint the town red, intoxicating ourselves with the choicest streets, the streets of our Kingdom.

We ran up the streets leading to the Sacré-Cœur. There are incredible staircases over there, with handrails made especially for children to slide down on at top speed, burning their backsides on the cold metal. There are also squares, trees, starved-looking cats, the ones that still haven't been turned into stew by the *concierges* of the buildings.

And we roamed through all that, crossing empty streets where an occasional taxi or a few bicycles roved. Before the Sacré-Cœur stood German officers wearing long hooded capes and little daggers on their belts. They laughed; they took photos. We made a detour to avoid them and came racing back toward the house.

At the boulevard Barbès, we stopped on the square to catch our breath and sat down under the portico of a building. Maurice touched the bandage that Mama had put on for him.

"Want to crack the safe tonight?"

I nod.

"Fine."

We used to do that every now and then. When everybody was asleep. With infinite precautions, we would open our bedroom door and glance into the corridor; encouraged by the silence, we would go downstairs to the shop, barefoot, without making the steps creak. It takes real practice. You have to probe with the tip of your toe, then, gradually, with the sole — without letting your heel touch. Once we reached the shop, we slid past the barber chairs. Then came the most exciting part.

Not a glimmer of light from the street filtered through the iron shutters. In total darkness my fingers would find the counter, the boxes of razor blades, the plate glass hollowed out where my father made change; then my fingers would reach the drawer of the cash desk. There were always piles of small coins in it . . . We'd take them and go back upstairs to bed.

We would be safe-crackers again tonight.

During these hours of roaming we forgot what had happened that morning; we loved to wander this way through the city, smoking eucalyptus cigarettes. In a France deprived of tobacco, they were hard to come by. I would go into a pharmacy and look up sadly at the proprietor.

"I'd like eucalyptus cigarettes, please. They're for my grandfather. He has asthma."

Sometimes it took a lot of fast talking but more often than not it worked. I used to come out triumphantly with my pack and we would open it ten steps further down the street. Then, with butts plastered in our mouths, hands in our pockets, wreathed in clouds of fragrant smoke, we would swagger around under the furious glances of deprived adults. We often gave one to Duvallier, to Bibi Cohen, and to the secondhand furniture dealers of the neighborhood. They accepted them gratefully, but from the first drag they missed their gray domestic tobacco. The eucalyptus ones were awful.

On the square, Maurice got up suddenly.

"We'd better get home — it's getting dark."

It was true. Behind the dome of the Sacré-Cœur rose the first mist of the evening. At our feet the city lay spread out, already graying, like the hair of a man growing old.

We looked for a moment without saying a word. I loved those rooftops, those monuments growing faint in the distance. I didn't yet know that I wouldn't be seeing that familiar landscape anymore. I didn't know that, within a few hours, I would no longer be a child.

Rue Clignancourt. The shop was closed. For quite some time, many of our friends had been leaving. Papa and Mama used to confer privately, and I overheard a few names in the middle of their whispering; the names were of regular customers, the ones who used to come to the barber shop, the ones my father used to meet for coffee in the evening. Almost all of them were gone.

There were other words that cropped up frequently: *Ausweis, Kommandantur,* demarcation line . . . The names of cities, too: Marseille, Nice, Casablanca.

My brothers had left at the beginning of the year. I hadn't really understood. There began to be a long time between customers. Sometimes, in the shop that used to be packed, there might be only the eternal Duvallier, the ever faithful.

But this was the first time that Papa had pulled down the iron shutters in the middle of the week. At the foot of the stairs his voice reached us; it came from our room.

He was stretched out on Maurice's bed, his hands clasped under his head, and he was looking at our kingdom as if trying to see it through our eyes. He roused himself when we came in, and sat up. Maurice and I sat down across from him on the other bed. He then began a long monologue that was to echo in my ears for a very long time — in fact, I still hear it. Maurice and I listened to him as we had never listened to anyone before.

"Many evenings," he began, "since you've been old enough to understand things, I've been telling you stories, true stories that members of your family played a part in. Today I realize that I never told you about myself."

He smiled and went on.

"It's not a very interesting story, and it wouldn't have entertained you for many nights, but I'm going to tell you the main part. When I was little — a lot smaller than you — I lived in Russia. There was a very powerful leader in Russia called the Czar. This Czar was like the Germans today. He liked to make war, and he came up with the idea of sending emissaries . . ."

He stopped and frowned. "Do you know what emissaries are?"

I nodded even though I didn't have the slightest idea what they were; but I was sure that they couldn't be anything nice.

"So he used to send emissaries to the villages. They rounded up little boys like me and they took them away to camps where they became soldiers. They were given uniforms; they were taught to march in step and obey orders without question and kill enemies. So, when I was of the age to go, when those emissaries were going to come into our village and take me away with friends as young as I was, my father spoke to me as . . ."

His voice grew hoarse and he went on.

"As I'm doing, in my turn, tonight."

Outside, night had almost fallen: I could hardly make him out against the window, but none of us made a move to light the lamp.

"He made me come into the little room in our farmhouse, the little room where he liked to shut himself up to think, and he said to me, 'My son, do you want to be a soldier of the Czar?' I said 'No.' I knew that I would be mistreated and I did not want to be a soldier. People often think that all boys dream of being in the army. Well, you see that it isn't true. In any case it wasn't true with me.

" 'So you don't have much choice,' he said. 'You're a young man, you're going to leave, and you're going to manage for yourself very well because you are not stupid.'

"I said 'Yes,' and after kissing him and my sisters, I left. I was seven years old."

While he was telling this, I could hear Mama walking; she was setting the table. Beside me, Maurice seemed to have changed into a statue of stone.

"I earned a living while staying out of the hands of the Russians; believe me, it wasn't always easy. I plied all the trades: for a crust of bread I shoveled snow with a shovel that was twice as big as I was. I met good people who helped me and I met others who were bad. I learned to use scissors and became a barber. I walked a great deal. Three days in one town, a year in another, and then I came here where I have been happy.

"Your mother's story is a bit like mine; when you get right down to it, it's all quite ordinary. I met her in Paris, we fell in love, we got married, and you were born. What could be simpler?"

He stopped and I could just make out that, in the shadows, his fingers were playing with the fringes of my bedspread.

"I opened this shop — it was quite small at the beginning. Any money that I earned came from my own hands . . ."

He gave the impression of wanting to go on but he stopped short and his voice suddenly became less clear.

"You know why I'm telling you all this?"

I knew why, but didn't dare say it.

"Yes," said Maurice. "It's because we're going to go away too."

He took a deep breath.

"Yes, boys. You're going to go away. Today it's your turn."

His arms moved in a gesture of restrained tenderness.

"You know why. You can't come home every day in this condition. I know that you can defend yourselves and that you aren't afraid, but there's one thing to bear in mind: when you're not the strongest, when you're two against ten, twenty, or a hundred, the bravest thing to do is to swallow your pride and run away. But there's something worse I have to tell you."

A lump was rising in my throat, but I knew that I wouldn't cry; maybe even the day before my tears would have flowed, but now things were different.

"You've seen that the Germans are getting harder with us all the time. There was the census they took, the notice stuck on the shop window; today there was the yellow star, tomorrow we'll be arrested. So we've got to run."

I gave a start.

"But what about you — you and Mama?"

I could just barely see his hands trying to reassure us.

"Henri and Albert are in the free zone. You're leaving tonight. Your mother and I are settling some business and then we'll leave."

He laughed a little and leaned forward so that he could place a hand on each of our shoulders.

"Don't worry — the Russians didn't get me when I was seven, so the Germans aren't going to do it when I'm fifty."

I relaxed. We were going to be separated, but we were going to be together again after the war, which could not last forever.

"Now, you'd better remember what I tell you," my father said. "You're leaving tonight; you'll take the Métro as far as the Gare d'Austerlitz. You'll buy a ticket there for the town of Dax. From there you'll have to cross the line. But you won't have the papers to get you across, so you'll have to do it the best way you can. Just outside of Dax is a village called Hagetmau; there are men there who can guide you over the line. You're safe as soon as you get on the other side. You'll be in the free zone, in Unoccupied France. Your brothers are in Menton — in a few minutes I'll show you where it is on the map. It's right near the Italian border. You'll find them."

Maurice piped up, "How do we get on the train?"

"Don't worry. I'm going to give you money — make sure you don't lose it or let somebody steal it. You'll each have five thousand francs." *

Five thousand francs! Even on nights when we'd cracked the safe, I'd never had more than ten francs in my pocket. What a fortune!

Papa hadn't finished. I could tell from the tone of his voice that the most important part was still to come.

"Look, there's one final thing you'd better get straight," he said. "You're Jews but you must never *ever* admit it, do you understand? *Never!*"

Our two heads nodded together.

"Don't even let on to your closest friend. Don't even whisper it under your breath — always deny it. Hear me? *Always!* Joseph, come here."

I rose and went up close to him, so close that I could hardly see him.

"Are you a Jew, Joseph?"

* The equivalent of fifty francs today, or approximately ten dollars. *Translator.*

"No."

With a sharp crack, his hand landed on my cheek. He had never struck me before.

"Don't lie. Are you a Jew, Joseph?"

"*No!*"

I had shouted without realizing it; my answer was sure, final.

My father got to his feet.

"All right now," he said. "I think I've told you everything. You know what you're up against."

My cheek was still smarting, but a question kept running through my mind — I had to have an answer.

"Papa, could you tell me — what is a Jew?"

He turned on the little lamp with the green shade on Maurice's night table. I loved its cozy light — that light I wouldn't see anymore.

Papa scratched his head.

"Well, it's kind of embarrassing to say this, Joseph, but the fact is that I'm really not very sure."

We were looking at him and he must have felt that he had to go on or we might think he was trying to wriggle out of explaining.

"Long ago," he began, "we were living in a country and they drove us out, so we scattered all over. This happens every so often — just the way it's happening now. You might say that the hunting season is on again, so we've got to go away again and hide. We've got to wait till the hunter tires himself out. Come now, it's time for supper — you're leaving as soon as you're done eating."

I don't remember that meal anymore. The only things that stick in my mind are the clink of spoons against the rims of the bowls, the murmur of voices asking for something to drink, to pass the salt, that sort of thing. On a straw-bottomed chair near the door were our two knapsacks, filled to bursting with underwear, our toilet articles, folded handkerchiefs.

The clock in the hall struck seven.

"Well, then, you're all set," Papa said. "In the zipper pouch of your knapsacks there's money and a little paper with the address of Henri and Albert. I'm going to give you two tickets for the Métro; then say goodbye to Mama and leave."

She helped us get our arms into our coatsleeves, then tied our mufflers around our necks. She gave our stockings a few last tugs. All the while she smiled, and all the while her tears streamed down. I felt her wet cheeks against my forehead, and her moist and salty lips.

After helping Mama to her feet, Papa broke into badly faked laughter.

"Come now!" he exclaimed. "You'd think they were going away forever and were just little babies. Go along now, boys. See you soon!"

A brief kiss, and his hands pushed us toward the staircase. There was the weight of the knapsack on my shoulders and then Maurice opened the door on the night.

My parents stayed upstairs. I learned afterwards, when everything was all over, that my father had gone on standing there, rocking gently back and forth with his eyes closed, nursing a grief as old as time.

In the night without lights, in streets deserted at the hour when the curfew would soon ring, we disappeared into the darkness.

Our childhood was over.

IV

"NOT HERE — take it easy!"

Maurice catches me by the sleeve and yanks me out of the crowd. I scale a pile of suitcases, knapsacks; we thread our way through baggage and sweating men.

"Come on, there's another entrance."

We're at the Gare d'Austerlitz. There are hardly any outbound trains and the platforms are mobbed. Who are these people? Are they Jews, too? Maurice weaves, feints, runs; he looks like a soccer player pushing an invisible ball in a forest of motionless players. I follow him, my knapsack bouncing up and down.

"That way — it's longer but it's less crowded."

Under the glass roof, the bells of the baggage wagons ring. Bicycles are tied together in stacks. Through the dirty windows we can see the vague outlines of the quays; the Seine is like a black chasm with the white line of the bridge spanning it. Further on against the sky stands the Notre Dame; still further on, our home. But we mustn't think about that. Right now we've got to take the train.

We position ourselves behind a charging porter who plunges into the crowd, pushing his handtruck before him as if it were a machine designed to throw people to each side. This is a good move for us because, a second later, our heads ringing with shouts, calls, whistles, loud-speakers, there's the ticket window before us. The line twists like a snake.

"Of the first five people in line, which one looks the nicest?" Maurice asks.

I look at the faces. Tense, irritable faces. A woman wearing a light-colored coat tries to tuck her locks into place under her hat. There's something stern about her lips, a set line that I don't like. Not her.

The big man looks nice, but we can't be sure.

"The young fellow in the third place — the one with the collar turned up."

Maurice goes up to him; he hasn't been hesitating much so far — now he moves right in.

"M'sieur, it's for my little brother . . . He's got a bad foot . . . We come from far away . . . Would you please. . . ?"

The fellow looks us over. For a split second I'm afraid he's going to refuse. Then he makes a weary gesture, a gesture mingling generosity and resignation.

"Go ahead, boys," he says. "My train isn't due in for a long time anyway."

Maurice thanks him and it's his turn almost right away.

"Two one-ways to Dax, third class."

I take the tickets while he gathers up the change. What's odd is the fact that nobody pays attention to us — two bewildered kids alone in the crowd. All these people have lots of worries of their own and they must think that our parents are with us somewhere.

Maurice leads the way and points to the signs.

"Track seven," he says. "We've got over half an hour; we'll try to get seats."

As the train comes in, billows of steam fill the vast hall. The tops of the iron columns are lost in the smoke.

Maurice curses. He's got good reason to swear: all the cars of our train are jammed with passengers. Everywhere — in the corridors, the vestibules between cars. We'd never be able to get aboard. Through the open doors we glimpse piles of suitcases and bags. I see a man stretched out on a baggage rack; he's arguing heatedly.

"Let's try further up."

We walk up along the train in the hope of finding seats closer to the locomotive, but there's the same mob everywhere, the same human conglomeration. I give a start: there are three empty compartments but they're reserved for German soldiers. Those vacant seats are really enticing, but we'd better not tempt the devil.

"Come on, let's get on here."

The steps are very high. I work my way between the compartment partition and the people pressed against the windowpane. There are arguments about reserved seats; two men confront each other waving the same seat number. The tension mounts. It's hopeless to look for seats.

"Here we are," says Maurice. "This won't be too bad."

It's a little corner; on one side, it's walled in by a suitcase, a huge suitcase made of maroon cardboard with a metal handle. We'll be able to set our knapsacks on the floor and sit on them, with our backs resting against the partition that separates the compartment from the corridor.

We settle ourselves side by side. I inspect my knapsack and come up triumphantly with a package. There's an enormous sandwich with butter and ham, a real wonder. Maurice checks and finds that he has the same kind.

"You'd better hide when you eat it, otherwise you'll make people envious."

After two mouthfuls I'm thirsty. I'd give ten years of my life for a glass of ice-cold *grenadine*. For the first time, I have a fortune in my pocket and I can't even treat myself to a *grenadine*. Our fortune has been considerably chipped away by the price of the tickets. Soon there won't be much left of our ten thousand francs. We're going to have to live on it for quite some time. But money can be earned: when we reach free France we'll find a way to live.

There's another train on the track across from us. That one is almost empty — no doubt a suburban train. Very gently, without a jolt, the empty train starts up. It's headed for the station, toward Paris. I open my mouth to share my stupefaction with my brother when I understand my error: the other train isn't moving — we're the ones who've started up. This is it. I stand up and glue my forehead to the windowpane.

There is a tangle of rails; we go under footbridges made of iron. Piles of coal gleam in the moonlight. We're still inching along. The wavy lines of the track bed rise and fall. People are talking all around us. Sitting on the big cardboard suitcase, an elderly lady looks at us; she is nice-looking, like the grandmothers from the illustrations in my reader. It's all there: the white hair done up in a bun, the blue eyes, the wrinkles, the lace collar, the gray stockings.

"Are you going far, children?" She is still smiling, looking at each of us in turn. "Are you traveling all alone? Don't you have any parents?"

I get the feeling very fast that, from now on, I've got to be distrustful of the whole world — even this nice grandmother from the school reader. She must know nothing, absolutely nothing.

Maurice stifles the answer in his sandwich.

"Yes, we do. We're going to meet them when we get there. They're sick. I mean, my mother is sick."

She looks sad. I'm almost angry at Maurice for lying to her, but he's right — for the time being we're condemned to lying. I remember old Boulier's lessons in ethics: "You must never lie." "Nobody ever believes a liar." Darned old Boulier can't ever have had the Gestapo chasing him to say things like that.

"And what's your name?"

"Joseph Martin. And he's Maurice Martin."

She's still smiling; she leans toward a wicker basket that she keeps pressed against her skirt.

"Well, Maurice, I bet you're thirsty after that piece of bread."

She has a bottle of lemon soda in her hand.

Maurice loosens up. "A little," he says.

Her eyes turn to me; she smiles.

"And I'll bet you're thirsty too . . ."

"Yes, madame."

She has everything in her basket; she has just taken out a celluloid drinking cup wrapped in a napkin.

"All right, now, we're going to have a drink, but just a

little because the bottle has to last us until the end of the trip."

It's good. It tickles my tongue and palate, a million bubbles explode against the inside of my mouth. The liquid rocks in the drinking cup with each lurch of the train. Now we're moving fast. I see myself in the window; beyond it lies the countryside, flat land that rolls at every curve.

She is the last to drink; she dries the cup with the towel and puts everything back into her basket.

Maurice has closed his eyes; his head is resting against the door of the compartment and wobbles with the vibrations. Further on, behind the grandmother, there is laughter; snatches of songs come through the din of the wheels and rails. We're nice and snug. There's nothing to worry about until we reach Dax. There's a German checkpoint in Dax that we'll have to get through. I mustn't think about it — not yet. I'm going to sleep, or try to at least, so I'll be in shape for tomorrow.

I turn around. There are eight people in the compartment on the other side of the window — the lucky ones who got seats. In the blue reflection of the night-light, I can just make out the face of a man — he's looking at me.

He must have been staring at me for a long time. There are many things in his eyes — suffering, most of all. He's very serious, with the sadness of people who don't dare to smile. He has an odd-looking collar, stiff and tightly closed. My eyes slide over him. I see his cassock. I don't really know why, but he makes me feel better. I know I'm going to fall asleep on this train carrying me toward life or death under the protection of that old priest. We have never spoken and yet I have the feeling that he knows all about me. He is there, watching over us amid the din. Sleep, little boy.

During the night, the sky is lighter than the earth. The windowpane trembles in its frame and two men are in front of me. They lean forward; they have fur hats, red boots, and baggy pants like Zouaves. Long black mustaches, curving and bristling, divide their faces in half. They are Russians.

"Are you Joseph? Well, you come with us — the Czar wants to see you. You're going to be a soldier."

I race down the corridor to escape them. It's strange — I'm flying over people. It's pleasant — I soar like a bird. They run behind me, drawing their long, razor-sharp sabers. I must have jumped from the train, for I'm running on the platform of a station, but they're not the Russians — it's a child's voice calling me. I stop and there's Zérati, all out of breath.

"Come on, I'm going to show you something . . ."

We run through streets that I don't know. The station has vanished; we're still running along deserted streets. It's night, but a night that will never end. The sun must have disappeared for good; it will never come back to light up those façades, those trees . . . and suddenly I recognize the rue Ferdinand-Flocon, my school, and there's old Boulier in the doorway; there's a big star on his chest. It's all yellow and he's making sweeping gestures with his arms.

"Come on, Joffo. Let's go drink some lemonade."

The courtyard is covered with bottles, thousands of bottles full of mud; they're practically in the classrooms, even on the roofs; the bottles gleam in the moonlight. There's someone behind old Boulier; he stands out from the shadows and I see the luster of his uniform. It's the SS man that came to Papa's shop for a haircut the other day — I recognize him right away.

"Do you have papers for drinking lemonade?" Boulier laughs harder and harder and I don't understand why. The SS man looks fierce. His fingers tighten more and more on my arm. "Show your papers fast. You're in Dax and you've got to have papers."

I've got to run; if I don't, that bastard will take me away. He's going to arrest me. I've got to call for help, so someone will save me; Boulier is rolling on the ground with laughter; Zérati is gone.

My cry must have roused me from my sleep. I look around me: nobody has heard me. Maurice is sleeping, his mouth agape, an arm thrown over his knapsack; the grandmother dozes, her chin propped up on her hands. There are indistinct silhouettes in the corridor; they must be sleeping, too.

I'm terribly thirsty. If only I could get back into my dream and grab one of the bottles and gulp it all down without stopping.

No, I mustn't think about it: I've got to go on sleeping, sleep as long as possible . . .

Dax.

The name lashes my ear. The train keeps going a few more meters, the brakes screech, the blocked wheels go on sliding a little further over the rails and stop.

Maurice is standing. The dismal light, made even more sinister by the windowpane, gives his face the color of aluminum; my face must look the same way.

I look around me, stupefied: the corridor is almost

empty. In the compartment behind me there are empty seats. The priest is still there.

Maurice anticipates my question. "A lot of them jumped while the train was still moving, back there when it slowed down."

I look at the other end of the car; a couple is waiting near the door; they look very pale. I see the woman's hand convulsively squeeze the handle of a suitcase.

The loudspeaker blares; there's a long sentence in German and suddenly I see them: a dozen of them are on the platforms. They cross the tracks and come toward us. They are German policemen. Hanging on their chests are silver half-moons like the ones the knights wore in the Middle Ages. There are civilians in long leather raincoats, too.

The couple has retreated. The man is ahead, he runs, goes past me and I feel his rapid breath.

Maurice grabs me by the arm.

"Get back in."

The compartment door slides open and we go in. There's an empty seat next to the priest. He is still looking at us; he is pale too, and his whiskers have sprouted during the night. Stupidly, I am surprised — I didn't think that priests had beards. All the ones I knew at the church club were so smooth-faced that I thought . . .

Near the window, a gaunt woman is already clutching her *laissez-passer*. I can see the white sheet of the permit trembling. There are round black stamps with angles in the center, signatures; all done in dark ink. How good it must feel to have your hands on so many signatures, authorizations . . .

"*Halte!*"

The shout comes from outside and we rush to the window.

A man is running over there, at the other end!

A group of them fan out across the tracks. A civilian gives orders in German; he also runs, climbs on the footboard of the neighboring car and blows a whistle drawn from his pocket. The shrill blasts pierce my eardrums. Suddenly, a man emerges just below me — he must have gone under the train, between the wheels. He climbs a platform, two platforms; he stumbles.

"*Halte!*"

He stops when they shoot, but he isn't hit; I'm sure that he isn't hit.

Abruptly he raises his arms and two soldiers hustle him off at top speed toward the waiting room. I see him clubbed with a rifle butt. The civilian is still blowing his whistle.

I see the couple from a little while before; they're coming back between two SS men; now they're tiny, and the woman is still clutching her valise as if her very life were inside. They go past us fast and I wonder what she sees through her big eyes, filled with tears.

Others have also been caught over there; the daylight glints on helmets and the bolts of rifles.

I realize then that the priest's hand is resting on my shoulder, that it has always been there — from the very beginning.

Slowly, we go back to our seats. The train is silent now; the Germans are blocking the exits.

The words come to my lips all by themselves.

"Father, we don't have any papers."

He looks at me and a smile stretches his lips for the first

time since Paris. He bends down, and when he whispers I can hardly understand.

"If you go around looking so frightened, the Germans are going to notice without your telling them. Get close to me."

We squeeze against him.

The grandmother is there, too. I recognize her suitcase in the baggage rack over her head. She seems to be sleeping.

"Papers . . ."

They're still far away, at the beginning of the car. It sounds as if there are a lot of them. They're talking to one another, and I understand a few words. Papa and Mama spoke Yiddish quite often and it's a lot like German.

"Papers . . ."

They draw closer. We hear the doors slide when they open and close them.

The grandmother is still keeping her eyes shut.

Now it's the compartment across the way. I have a curious feeling in my stomach: it's as if my intestines had suddenly become independent and wanted to get out of their bag of skin. Whatever I do, I mustn't show my fear.

I plunge my hand into my knapsack and take out the remainder of a sandwich. I bite into it just as the door opens. Maurice glances at them with perfect detachment, full of innocence; I admire the actor's control that my brother has.

"Papers."

The gaunt woman holds out the white sheet. I see the sleeve of a uniform, epaulettes; the boots are a centimeter from my shoes. My faraway heart has a strong, regular beat. The hardest part is swallowing; I take another mouthful.

The German reads the sheet of paper, studies it, then stretches out his hand toward the grandmother, who hands him a green paper, an identity card.

The German scarcely looks at them.

"Is that all?"

She smiles and nods her assent.

"Take your suitcase and go out into the corridor."

Others wait behind the windowpane, talking. Among them is an SS man.

The priest stands, takes down the suitcase, and the grandmother goes out. One of the policemen takes her basket and beckons to her. In the light of day, her white chignon gleams for a split second, then she disappears behind the uniformed backs. Goodbye, grandmother. Thank you for everything; good luck.

The priest shows his papers and sits down again. I'm still chewing. The German looks at the photo and compares it with the original. I go on chewing.

"I've lost a little weight," says the priest, "but it's me all right."

The shadow of a smile flickers across the face of the German.

"The war, all the rationing . . ."

He has no accent, or just a trifle on certain consonants. He returns the paper and says, ". . . but priests don't eat much."

"You're really mistaken there — at least, in my case."

The German laughs and stretches out his hand toward me. The priest gives me a flick of the finger on the cheek.

"The children are with me."

The door has already closed after a quick salute from the jocular German. My knees begin to tremble.

The priest stands.

"We can get off now. And since you're with me, we're going to have our breakfast together in the station buffet. How does that suit you?"

I see that Maurice is more touched than I. You could beat the hell out of that guy without getting him to cry, but just be a little nice to him and he gets all choked up. And this time he had plenty of reason for it.

We were able to get onto the platform. There was still a baggage search to go through and then we gave our tickets to the ticket-inspector. Following our rescuer, we entered the buffet.

It was a gloomy place, high-ceilinged, arched; the benches around the walls were covered with patent leather. The heavy marble-topped tables had elaborately carved legs. Waiters in black jackets and long white aprons stood waiting, leaning their elbows on the massive columns; in their hands were shiny, empty trays.

Now our priest looked very happy.

"We're going to have *café au lait*," he said. "I'm warning you — the coffee is made of barley, the sugar is saccharin, and there isn't any milk. But it will warm us up just the same. As for bread and butter to go with it, we'd need ration stamps. You probably don't have any and neither do I."

I cough to clear my throat.

"Before anything else, Maurice and I would like to thank you for what you've done."

For a moment he is disconcerted.

"But what have I done?"

Maurice is the one who goes on; there's a hint of mischief in his voice.

"You lied to save us by saying that we were with you."

Slowly the priest shakes his head.

"I didn't lie," he murmurs. "You were with me just as all the children of the world are. That's one of the reasons why I'm a priest — to be with them."

Maurice doesn't answer; he stirs his saccharin tablet with a little tin-plated spoon.

"Anyway, if it weren't for you, they'd have taken us away. That's what counts."

There's a moment of silence, then the priest asks: "And now where are you going?"

I can feel that Maurice is hesitant about talking, but I can't bear letting this priest think for even a second that we still don't trust him.

"We're going to Hagetmau and we're going to try to cross the demarcation line there."

The priest drinks and sets the cup down on the saucer with a scowl. It must be that he loved pre-war coffee and can't get used to *ersatz*.

"I understand," he says.

It's Maurice's turn now.

"After that, we're going to meet our parents in the south."

Can he feel our hesitation? Was our situation so common that explanations were unnecessary? In any case, he doesn't ask any more questions now.

He removes a big wallet from his pocket; there's a rubber band around it. He takes a slip of paper from among religious pictures. With a blunt pencil, he scrawls a name, an address, and hands it to us.

"You'll get across," he says. "I'd be glad to hear from you. And if you ever need me — you never know — just write to me."

Maurice takes the slip of paper, folds it, and puts it into his pocket.

"We're going, Father. Maybe there'll be a bus for Hagetmau soon, and we've got to get there in a hurry."

He watches us sling on our knapsacks.

"You're right, boys. There are times in life when you have to go fast."

We wait, embarrassed by that melancholy gaze that goes right through me to the soul. He stretches out his hand and we shake it one after the other.

Maurice goes first and heads for the revolving door at the other end of the hall; but something makes me uneasy. There's something I have to ask the priest.

I turn around and come back to him.

"Father, what did they do to the old lady?"

"Nothing. They didn't do anything to her. It's just that she didn't have any papers, so they made her go home. That's all."

It's true. How come I didn't think of that? I had already imagined her in prison, in an internment camp. They just made her go home, that's all. Nothing bad.

Outside, Maurice is waiting for me. There's a ray of cold sunlight and he's suddenly lost the wan look he had a while ago. I feel better too — as if that light had suddenly washed away the fatigue of the trip.

The bus station isn't far; we have to cross a plaza with its rows of trees with knobby bark, trees whose name I don't know. I never had a chance to see many different kinds of trees between the rue Marcadet, the gas tank at Saint-Ouen, and the Basilica of the Sacré-Cœur.

"The bus for Hagetmau?"

Behind the counter, the guy hasn't even bothered to look up.

"In two hours."

"Two tickets, then."

Here we are again with two tickets in our pockets. We don't have a hell of a lot of money left, but that doesn't matter: we're walking around the streets of Dax — free France isn't far off.

We're going to get across.

V

THE BUS STOPS just outside the village. On the road, a German car filled with officers had passed us. I had been scared for a few seconds, but they kept going without paying the least attention to our rattletrap bus.

The sky is clear and the smell of smoke from the chimneys drifts to us. It's very flat country and the houses are huddled around the steeple of the church.

Maurice hitches up his knapsack.

"Let's go!"

At a brisk pace we cross a narrow bridge over a tiny river, a mere trickle of water that disappears under the stones.

The main street goes uphill a bit. Our wooden heels resound on the uneven cobblestones; we come to a fountain under a portico. There isn't a soul on the streets; an occasional dog crosses our path, then disappears into an alley after sniffing around our legs. The town smells of cows and woodsmoke; there's a tang in the air. The wind doesn't seem to meet any obstacle and comes roaring right down into our lungs.

Two grocery shops face one another on what must be the main street; both are closed.

"Jesus," Maurice growls, "everybody's dead here."

The silence begins to make an impression on me too. After the din of the train, the commotion of leaving, our arrival, we feel as though we'd lost one of our senses, as if someone had stuffed two enormous balls of cotton into our ears.

"They must be in the fields . . ."

Over our heads, the church clock rings and Maurice scratches his head.

"That's right," he says. "It's noon and everybody's eating."

That's a word he should never have mentioned, for the sandwiches have been gone a long time, the morning coffee seems way in the past, and the fresh air is sharpening my appetite. If I closed my eyes, I'd see a steak and fried potatoes.

We wander aimlessly around the village; there's a path that opens on the deserted fields where the forests begin. We turn around and go back and then we're on another square, smaller than the first. Across from a building that must be the town hall stands a café-restaurant.

We spot it together and I look at Maurice anxiously.

"Maybe we could get something to eat . . ."

Maurice hesitates a little; he's certainly even hungrier than I am. At home, he never used to stop; he could eat continuously from lunch to our four o'clock snack and non-stop to the evening meal.

"Let's go," he says. "We don't want to collapse from hunger."

We open the door and stand on the threshold. The roads may be empty but not the café. At the end of the long room stands a counter topped by an antique coffee machine; a hundred people are jammed around the tables. Three waitresses run through the aisles carrying plates, pitchers of water, silverware. The place is heated by an enormous terra-cotta stove, its pipe zigzagging across the room halfway between floor and ceiling. There are three overloaded coatracks behind the door.

"What do you want, boys?"

One of the waitresses, red-faced and disheveled, tries to catch a curl at the top of her head, a curl that's falling down over the others. She struggles with it for a moment, then gives up.

Still bewildered, Maurice replies, "We'd like to eat."

"Come this way."

She pushes us along and we cross the room; there is an intense clacking of forks and knives. Against the counter is a bare wooden table on which she places two glasses.

"We've got lentils with bacon and stuffed eggplant. For dessert, there's cheese and a piece of fruit. That all right? I can give you radishes with salt to start."

"That'll be fine."

She's already running toward the kitchen, where another waitress is emerging with a plate of lentils in each hand. It doesn't look as if there's much bacon on them.

I look at the other diners. They aren't country folk: they represent the mixture that you find in train stations

or waiting rooms; they're men and women from the city.
There are children too — even very young ones.

Maurice bends over his plate.

"We're going to bump into everybody from rue Marcadet in this place."

"They're like us — running away. They're Jewish and they're waiting to cross the border. But what are they waiting for? Maybe it's harder than we thought."

Our waitress comes back with three radishes at the bottom of a bowl. She places the salt shaker between us.

"*Bon appétit,* boys."

Maurice thanks her and I add, "You're always as crowded as today?"

She raises her arms. "Every day for six months or more! Believe me, when the Fritzes put that line a kilometer from here, they helped a lot of people in this town to get rich."

I follow her gaze and see the *patronne* delicately drying a coffee cup behind the bar. She is wearing jewelry and her hair is dyed red and glossy.

"For her it's nothing to get a permanent every couple of weeks. With what she makes here, she could spend her whole life at the beauty parlor."

She makes another attempt at putting her curl back in place and takes away our empty dishes. Nothing goes down faster than three radishes when you're hungry. And all the more so when two out of three are hollow.

"What about . . . Is it easy to get across?"

She shrugs. "Yes, it's easy enough. Most of the time they get across without trouble . . . only you've got to wait till night because it's too dangerous during the day. Excuse me."

She comes right back with lentils, sets them before us, and goes off again so fast we can't ask her any more about crossing the line.

Maurice looks at the people around him.

"The real joke," he says, "would be if we meet somebody from our neighborhood."

The eggplant that comes next is stringy and the stuffing nonexistent. The cheese is flat and dry. The apples are withered but our waitress makes the mistake of leaving the basket near our table: all the apples are going to wind up at the bottom of my knapsack.

Maurice folds his napkin and declares, "If we stay in this town too long we'll end up being skeletons."

Little by little the café empties out. A few stragglers still huddle around cups of coffee made from barley or chicory, but the others are gone.

We pay our bill, which looks outrageously high, and then we're back on the streets of Hagetmau lugging our knapsacks, our hands in our pockets. Now the wind is bitter and unpleasant.

"Listen," says Maurice, "we're going to try to cross tonight — there's no sense hanging around here. So what we have to do first is find out where we can get a *passeur* * and how much they'll charge to take us across the line."

That seems sensible to me. Fifty meters away, a fifteen-year-old boy rides a huge black bicycle. There's a wicker basket on the baggage rack. He stops in front of a house, rings the doorbell, hands over a package from his basket, and greets the person in a loud voice.

"Good morning, Madame Hudot. Here's the order."

*A person who aids others to cross a frontier clandestinely. *Translator.*

Hidden from view, Madame Hudot murmurs her thanks, goes back inside, then returns. I see her hand placing a coin in the delivery boy's hand.

"Thank you, Madame Hudot. Goodbye, Madame Hudot. See you next time, Madame Hudot." Whistling, he gets back on the bicycle and watches us come toward him. His cheeks are full and hard, his red hands covered with blond down; his fingernails are filthy.

"We'd like a little information."

He laughs and shows me that he has magnificent cavities in most of his teeth.

"I'll tell you even before you say what it is. You'd like to know where the *passeur* is, right?"

Maurice stares at him. He never lets himself be intimidated by grownups.

"Yes, that's right."

"Well, it's easy. You leave the village by the main road, go three hundred meters and, at the first farmhouse on your right, ask for old Bédard. Only I'm warning you, it's five thousand francs each."

I turn pale. Maurice is stunned too. The delivery boy looks at us, laughing.

"Now, there's another way out if you want. I can get you over the line myself for five hundred francs. Like that better?"

We laugh with relief. There's something nice about this delivery boy.

"Look, I'll make you a deal. I give you my basket and you finish my route. It's just some meat and there's addresses on the packages. You'll find the houses and they give you tips. While you're doing that, I'm going to take a look at my traps and tonight at ten we'll meet under the bridge, near the arch. You can't get lost — there's only one bridge."

Maurice hands me his knapsack. I sling it over my shoulder fast and he gets the basket.

Relieved of his load, the delivery boy climbs on his bicycle and smiles with all his mottled teeth. When he reaches the curve, he turns around and yells, "Hey, you really have your five hundred francs each, right? 'Cause I'm warning you — you've got to pay me first."

I'm the one who answers.

"Yes, yes. We've got it."

The delivery boy rides away as fast as he can go. I turn to Maurice.

"You've got the thousand francs, right?"

He nods, worried.

"Sure I have it, but just about. Once we pay him, we'll be almost broke."

I bounce the knapsacks enthusiastically.

"That doesn't matter! Once we get to the free zone, we'll manage all right. Just think — if we hadn't stumbled over that guy, we never would have made it across, not at five thousand francs apiece. We'd be stuck here!"

"Meanwhile," Maurice breaks in, "we've got meat to deliver."

And that was the beginning of one of the most curious and happy afternoons of my life. We went from one farmhouse to another. There were hens, ducks in ponds black as ink; the sky was blue and clear with just a fringe of clouds right at the bottom of the horizon.

We were intoxicated. Two kids from the gutters of Paris suddenly breathing the fresh country air, while Maurice gave the farmer his roast of mutton, his rib of

beef, his beefsteak — which made us think that the black
market was flourishing in that area. I looked at the rab-
bits in their hutches while the farmers' wives went to get
change; I played with puppies, piglets in their litters of
rotting straw. And then there were horses. Not many
were left — most of them had been requisitioned at the
start of the war, but there were still one or two — huge
old plow-horses, standing motionless, nuzzling the
wooden trough in search of feed that wasn't there. I went
into the stalls and scratched their foreheads. I moved the
coarse hair of their long tails, which were tangled, speck-
led with bits of hay. And then we went on our way
again . . .

In a cottage near the church, an old codger showed us
into a low room with smoke-blackened beams. Over the
fireplace hung a photo that showed him as a soldier in the
other war with helmet, puttees, gas mask. He showed us
his ducks, a brood of yellow chicks squawking and hesitating as they advanced in single file . . . I was fascinated.

The basket was almost empty. Coins jingled in
Maurice's pocket. The people were surprised not to see
their regular delivery boy, Raymond, but they gave us
money anyway.

After we brought a joint of mutton to the game warden,
there was only a single delivery left to make: a half-joint
of lamb to bring to the schoolteacher's house, which was
out of the way, behind a little woods.

Maurice and I were talking. My legs were beginning to
feel heavy, but we were moving at a good pace when we
came abreast of the trees.

"Psst . . ."

The whistle froze the blood in my veins. Maurice stopped in his tracks.

Behind a tree, a man motioned to us, but seeing that we were petrified at the side of the road, he smiled and clambered up a short bank and came toward us.

By the look of his clothes, by the look of his face, I knew that he wasn't somebody from this part of the country, but a fugitive like ourselves. His frightened eyes, his nervous hands, everything about him said that he was a man trying to cross into Unoccupied France.

He was a thick-set, balding man with the physique of a boxer. He looked at us for a moment.

"Excuse me, are you from around here?"

"No."

He gulped, scrutinizing us as if searching for something on our faces.

"Are you Jewish?"

Maurice shifted the basket to his other hand.

"No."

His jaws tightened instantly.

"I am. I've got my wife and my mother-in-law hiding in the woods. I'm trying to get across."

With the flat of his hand, he slapped the knees of his trousers that were green with moss; the whole side of his jacket was covered with dry, crackled earth.

"What happened to you?"

He struck the air in a hopeless gesture.

"Yesterday I was about thirty kilometers from here if you follow the banks of the Adour. I had the address of a *passeur* that they'd given to me in Bordeaux. I found the guy; he charged twenty thousand francs for the three of us and took us out at night. We walked for a long time and then he squatted down and said, 'Wait for me here — I'm going to see if the coast is clear.' I told him that I was going to go with him — that we'd manage better if we both went. Just then he hit me with his cane and started to run away. I tried to catch him but I fell down. We spent the whole night in the woods and we've been walking since daybreak."

Maurice seems to be weighing the pros and the cons. Two women come out from behind a tree; they look exhausted.

"Listen," says Maurice, "we're going to cross too, but we don't know if the guy who's showing us the way will agree to take you. Come along with us and ask him. Ten o'clock under the bridge at the other end of the village."

"Thanks. Thanks from the bottom of my heart. We're so tired that . . . anyway, I hope this time we'll make it across the line and . . ."

He mumbles words that don't make sense and then shakes our hands and goes back into the woods, where we hear him telling the news to the women who are with him.

Maurice has started up the road again and turns to me frowning. "We'd better be careful — people around here have some funny ways of earning a living."

"You think this Raymond could pull . . . ?"

He shrugs.

"I don't know and because I don't know, I'm going to watch out."

We walk in silence for a few minutes.

"First of all," he says, "we have to stick right on top of him."

"Okay, and then if he tries to get away, we jump him. Think the two of us can fight him?"

Maurice looks dubious. "We'll see. If we can lick him, he'll get us across without any tricks. Hey, want to race?"

"Wait till I put down the knapsacks."

We kneel like sprinters before the start.

"Up to the yellow tree — the big one, the one at the corner."

"Okay. On your mark, get set . . . you ready? Go!"

Our legs pound the road; I feel my tongue hanging out of my mouth. I fall behind a few steps, a few meters. I catch up; I lose ground again. I lunge — too late.

Sitting on the road, my head between my knees, I struggle to get my wind back.

"Naturally you won — you're bigger than me."

Maurice pants.

"That's no excuse — I know smaller guys than you that can run like hell."

At a slow walk, we go back to get the knapsacks and the basket that we left on the road.

"Aren't you hungry?"

"Yes, it's no joke lugging meat the whole afternoon when all we had were lentils." He searches his pockets. "With the money left over from the bus, maybe we can treat ourselves to something."

We knock at a door. An old guy with a flat cap opens it. There aren't any young men left around here.

We speak for a few minutes and finally manage to get two eggs that we gulp down outside the house.

Night is falling by now. The grass is wet and the leather uppers of our shoes gleam in the moonlight. Soon the clock in town will strike ten. I can't make out the hands of the clock on the steeple anymore, but the pit of my stomach tells me that the time has come.

To think that a few days before I would have been wildly excited to be in a situation like this! It's got everything: the night, the rustle of leaves, the waiting, the Indians across from us with their moccasins, and me, the unarmed cowboy who's going to sneak through the outer boundary of their camp. And my life at the mercy of their rifles . . . I'm almost sorry not to hear the slow beat of war drums. The night is clear. Good or bad? I don't know.

I move my legs slowly, very slowly, to avoid snapping a dry branch; you never know — the slightest sound carries a long way and can give us away to sharp ears. Close beside me, Maurice holds his breath.

On the other side of the arch, I can make out the three cowering silhouettes of the Jewish people that we met on the road.

The Germans are across the way on the other side of the woods. Funny that they haven't already fired at us — I feel terribly exposed.

"Listen . . ."

At night bicycles make noise. It's the friction of the little headlight dynamo against the tire. But what we can really hear now is the cyclist whistling, a happy tune . . . I know it — it's a Tino Rossi song.

What a stupid break — this cyclist in the dark is going to give us away to the Germans; we mustn't . . . He stops, right near us. I hear the handlebars and a pedal scrape against the low stone wall. The man gets off the bicycle, still whistling; he comes toward us. I make him out against the sky. He stops — it's Raymond.

He looks happy — not at all the way a Comanche scout should look. His hands are in his pockets and he makes no effort to keep his voice down when he speaks to us.

"Well, ready to go?"

Maurice holds out our money and Raymond stuffs it in his shirt. Maurice points to the silhouettes a few yards away.

"These people want to get across, too. They're all tired out and they've got money."

Raymond looks their way. "All right, tell them to come along. How many are there?"

"Three."

Raymond rubs his hands.

"I'm having a good night. Usually the other *passeurs* don't let me have this many. Well, let's get going."

Carefully, I stand up, trying hard not to let a single joint creak. I hear Raymond snicker.

"Take it easy, kid. You don't need to play Indians. Just walk behind me and do what I do and don't worry about the rest."

We started off. I was sweating like crazy under my coat and it seemed to me that, when we crossed the fields, our column could be spotted thousands of kilometers away. A bad genie had put the noisiest possible stones under our heels and I was sure we were making an awful racket. Hitler himself must have heard us in his Berlin apartment. We finally entered the forest. Raymond moved through the ferns making the brittle stalks crack. From the moment we were under the trees, I had the feeling

that we weren't alone, that there were other people near
us, walking on our left. I tried to peer through the darkness between the tree trunks, but saw nothing.

Raymond stopped. I plowed into his back and held my
breath. He must have heard it, too, but I couldn't help
warning him.

"There's somebody to the left of us."

Raymond didn't turn around.

"I know, a dozen. It's old Branchet taking them across.
We'll let them get ahead of us and then we'll follow. We
can sit down for a minute."

Brambles and bark cracked under our rumps and, motionless, we listened to the wind in the upper branches.

"We still have far to go?" whispered Maurice.

Raymond moved his hands in a vague gesture.

"If we went straight, we'd be there in no time at all, but
we've got to go around the clearing."

The hike starts up again and we don't stop anymore.
The sand seems finer now and rises in gradual hills.
There are pine cones on the ground and several times my
wet soles slip.

How long have we been under way — two minutes or
three hours? It's impossible to tell — I've lost all means
of estimating.

The woods grow lighter ahead of us; the trees spread
apart and form a pale lane. Motioning to us, Raymond
groups us about him.

"See the lane over there? You follow it — not even two
hundred meters. You come to a ditch. Watch out because
it's plenty deep and full of water. You pass the ditch and
you hit a farmhouse. You can even go in if there's no

lights — the farmer knows what's going on. You sleep in the straw and you won't be cold."

Maurice speaks.

"You mean . . . that's the free zone over there?"

Raymond turns and laughs softly.

"The free zone? You're in it already!"

I was overwhelmed by a feeling of frustration. We had crossed the line and I hadn't even noticed it! That was the goal we were to reach; we ran away just for that; everybody talked about it; it was at the other end of the earth and, unsuspecting, I had passed it like a flower, completely unaware, across that pencil line dividing the map of France Papa had shown us one evening.

The line! I had imagined it as a wall, a space crammed with sentry boxes, cannons, machine-guns, barbed wire, with patrols creeping through in the dark and floodlights searching every blade of grass. In watchtowers, officers with faces like vultures look through their field glasses, the lenses of which cover their ferocious eyes. And instead of all that — nothing, absolutely nothing. Not one second did I have the feeling that there was even a single Apache after me — it was enough to make you disgusted with the Far West.

Near us, three Jewish people congratulate one another, and thank Raymond who takes on a modest air.

I'm happy anyway. I'm now safe, but a little of my bitterness remains. I can't help asking Raymond if it is always this peaceful.

"Usually it goes pretty smoothly. I'm lucky there. The guard posts are far apart and there are blind corners where neither the post on the road nor the one in the village of Carmot can see us. It would be dangerous if they sent out patrols, but if they did, they'd have to go by the ford, near the Badin farm. They couldn't make it anywhere else. They'd have to go through forests of brambles, but as soon as Badin sees them, he sends his son who knows the shortcuts and he comes to warn us.

Raymond hitches up his trousers and shakes hands with us.

"But don't start thinking that it's going to be this easy the whole way — there's a spot not twenty kilometers from here where people were killed not so long ago. And they're getting tougher all the time. Well, I'll be seeing you — and good luck!"

He has already vanished, the trees hiding his silhouette; he goes back up toward the village.

We continue on our way — alone this time. Maurice holds my hand; we can't risk getting lost. A night in this forest wouldn't be very pleasant — not with the temperature dropping every minute.

"Watch out!"

It was a good thing he warned me: we've come to the ditch. It's down there, the surface of the water smooth as silk. We hear it slap-slap among branches and fallen rocks.

"Take my knapsack."

Maurice climbs down first. When I hear his soft whistle, I hand down our packs. Then it's my turn to go down clutching at tufts of grass. The barbs of a bramble bush catch me by one sock. I work myself free, climb up the far side of the ditch, and there's the farmhouse before us: massive, a block of granite set on the naked back of the earth.

We go on helping the three Jews who have caught up with us and now we're in the courtyard of the farm.

I give a start.

There's a man, motionless, in the dark. He looks very tall; he's got a fur collar that hides his ears and the wind coming down from the plain ruffles his hair.

With a mechanical stride, he moves toward us. His voice is gravelly and raucous — like the actors who play the role of the *gendarme* at puppet shows.

"This is the place, boys. You'll find straw in the shed over there behind you. You've got blankets behind the door; they aren't much to look at, but they're clean. You can sleep as long as you want. I only ask one thing: if you've got any matches or a lighter, give them to me right away, because I wouldn't want to see my crops go up in smoke with you inside."

I shake my head and so does Maurice.

"Good, then. If you need anything, you can just tap on the little windowpane — you see it? The one right after the hen house. That's where I sleep. All right, then. Goodnight."

"Can you tell me the time, monsieur?"

He has to struggle to fish out the pocket watch from under his old sheepskin coat; it seems buried under a dozen vests and sweaters. Finally the dial shines in his hand.

"Eleven-fifteen."

"Thank you. Goodnight, monsieur."

The wooden door creaks on its old hinges and the warm odor rushes to my nostrils. The mere smell of clean dry hay makes my eyes grow heavy.

I climb up a bale of hay and bury myself in another that

flattens out. I haven't got the strength to go after the blankets. Gray light enters through a skylight. Our three companions are whispering, huddled together at the other end of the barn.

I hear Maurice coming back and a rough fabric grates my cheek.

"Roll yourself in this."

I can just about make the effort. Up to now, anxiety and overexcitement have kept me awake but, with the relief of reaching safety, the tension has fallen away all at once and the weight of my eyelids pulls me down; two unrelenting burdens pull me into a heavy, black world where I plunge dizzily, ever further, ever deeper. One last effort and I can make out the lighter-colored rectangle of the skylight over my head. I even see that it is decorated at each corner with silvery, tenuous cobwebs, and I fall asleep at once, snoring like a lumberjack.

I won't sleep long — an hour, perhaps two. I open my eyes again and my hand doesn't need to feel the place beside me: I know already that my brother isn't there anymore.

Ever since Mama decided that there was no need to have my cradle near her, Maurice and I have shared the same room. And a strange phenomenon has always occurred; I can't say if it is the same for him, for I've never discussed it with him. It seems that without his making the slightest sound, without the creaking of a floorboard to rouse me, I've always sensed when he's away. Every time he went downstairs to the kitchen to drink a glass of water, every time he slipped out of his bed for any reason whatever — I was perfectly aware of it.

What told me? What hidden instinct was at work?

But at this moment, I wasn't wondering about which conscious or unconscious mechanism had alerted me to my brother's leaving. The fact was that just a few hundred yards from the line of demarcation, as tired as I was from those last twenty-four hours, at a time when he should have been deep in well-earned sleep, Maurice Joffo had gone away.

No panic. He can't be far off. The most plausible explanation when somebody gets up during the night, ninety times out of a hundred, is that he's gone to the toilet. So there's nothing to worry about — Maurice just had to piss.

As brilliant as my reasoning is, I'm not comfortable for long. We pissed together against the farmhouse wall before coming in here, after the farmer went away. And if you have a good bladder, you just don't piss anymore until morning if you've pissed before going to bed. So where has he gone? Where has he gone without telling me?

That, more than anything, is what I don't understand — why did he go off secretly, without telling me?

Either he went to ask the farmer for a drink or else . . . My head spins at the thought of all the possible explanations.

The sound of whispering. I cock my ear and throw back the blankets, making the straw rustle. That voice is coming from outside.

One thought chills my blood. What if it's the Germans? No, that couldn't be — we're in Unoccupied France; they couldn't come here . . . What about thieves? It's said that gangs of hooligans attack refugees and steal everything they have — jewels, suitcases, money . . . Perhaps Maurice has heard them and is spying on them in the dark at this very moment.

In my stocking feet, I steal noiselessly across the floor of beaten earth that's covered with a dust of dry straw. My fingers recognize the wood of the door, the heavy latch that I raise cautiously. I look through the crack and leap backwards: the whispers are coming toward me, their mingled shapes approach me.

Their breathing grows louder; they all seem to be puffing on invisible cigarettes. I recognize one of the men who had been near us in the restaurant at noon. There are two children in the group, a little one being carried and a young girl in white stockings. What a mistake to wear those stockings — they can be seen a good distance away. They brush past me in the dark and collapse in the hay. There are the stifled murmurs of a conversation.

Still no Maurice. What can he be doing?

My anxiety grows; I must do something before it turns into a panic that could make me call out his name or go off looking for him in the dark. That wouldn't get me anywhere, except to attract the attention of the other people.

I go out. The night is growing clearer and colder.

I plunge my hands into the pockets of my coat.

A slip of paper. My fingers have just touched a paper that wasn't there before. Touching it, I recognize the torn perforations of a spiral notebook. It's the one Mama gave to Maurice before we left.

A wise precaution: at times a notebook and pencil can be the most useful things in the world. He must have written in the dark and slipped his message into my pocket before going away.

The moon is bright enough for me to read the lines scrawled diagonally:

I'll be back. Don't say anything to anybody.

M.

He wrote *M.* like the spy stories where the characters are identified by a code or an initial.

I feel relieved. I still don't know where he is, but I know he's coming back — that's all that counts. I go back to my place in the hay, find the blanket, and roll myself up in it again, delighted by the fragrant warmth that's waiting for me. A few meters away, a sleeper whimpers softly, a weak, musical sound that is almost pleasant; it helps me fall asleep.

"Oh, excuse me."

A body straddles me and buries itself right next to me. I smell a mixture of eau de cologne and sweat. It's a woman; she's wearing a thick woolen coat that covers my hand.

It looks like day is breaking. I must have slept for several hours.

I raise myself on one elbow; it's light enough now for me to see that the barn is full of refugees. I can't count them but they're all over the place, sprawled out in every position. I make a very hasty count. There are fifty of us, maybe more. The *passeurs* have been bringing groups across all night. Perhaps even more will come — and still no Maurice.

They're all sleeping. Near me, the woman with the coat can be seen under the skylight. A tear trembles on her cheek. She's crying in her sleep. Perhaps she hasn't stopped crying since reaching the farm.

And here come new ones. This time there's a big

group. I snuggle up in my own warmth and, through one half-open eye, I watch the visitors bedding down in the hay. I hear someone swear softly in Yiddish and, very quickly, the barn falls still again.

"You asleep?"

Suddenly he's there; I hadn't seen him loom up. I sit up all at once.

"Where the hell have . . ."

He places his finger on my mouth.

"Not so loud. I'm going to explain."

It's very hard to bawl someone out when you've been reduced to nearly inaudible whispering. Besides, I'm completely dumfounded as I listen to Maurice.

What he had done was very simple. He told me about it, very pleased with himself, with stifled laughter. It can be summed up in a few words. He had gone back the way we had come and made eight trips across the line. He'd brought forty people through and made himself twenty thousand francs.

It's broad daylight now. Just a little cloud that's going to go sailing off toward the west and then the sun will be on us. The grass is still a bit wet but we're sitting on our bags. Twenty thousand francs! That's a fortune! We'll be able to buy food and have enough money for the trip to Menton.

But there's something about his escapade that upsets me.

"Maurice, what if you'd been caught?"

He runs his fingers through his hair.

"You heard what Raymond told us — there isn't the slightest danger. When I crossed the first time, I got a good idea of the way: keep going straight, circle to the left around the clearing, the little bridge and then you're over. It's easier than going from the Porte de Clignancourt to Ornano. There's less chance of getting lost."

I'm not quite satisfied.

"One more thing: don't you think it's kind of mean to take the people across for money?"

Maurice stares at me.

"First of all, I didn't make anybody come with me. Second, at five hundred francs instead of five thousand, I don't think they can say that I robbed them. I showed them the right way and it went without a hitch. There was a woman who lost her shoe and we had to go looking for it in a thicket, but aside from that, it was really easy. And then there's something you forget, old friend — we're going to need money if we want to get there safe and sound."

"But we could have . . ."

But he's all wound up and when he's like that nothing can stop him. "You think that because we're in the Unoccupied Zone we're going to be well off? You think people are going to feed you for free? And what if the police ask us for our papers and we don't have any money — you think they're going to pat us on the back?"

I can see that he's right — once again.

". . . And I've got to think about earning money. Tonight it's me, but next time it'll be up to you to figure out something . . . Don't think that just because you're younger you're going to sit around twiddling your thumbs while I work like . . ."

"Stop yelling like that, for Christ's sake. I get it! I get it!"

But Maurice is really screaming now. "You think it was fun crossing the line eight times with that bunch of people behind me? Don't you think I would rather have had a good night's sleep? And now you put on airs and tell me I shouldn't have done it!"

I jump to my feet.

"Look, I never said that! You don't understand anything!"

He yanks the wad of crumpled bills from his pocket.

"Here, go ahead — give them their money back if you want to."

Confused, I stare at the money that's now in my hands. The money that he made by risking his life — money that's going to enable us to continue our journey, money that an exhausted boy has just handed to me.

I smooth out the bills and give them back to him without a word. He has calmed down now. His chin on his knees, he stares into the sun which has just appeared.

There is an endless silence, then I ask him: "Are we going to take the train again?"

He must sense from my voice that I'm trying to make conversation and get him to forgive me.

"Yes, that's the best thing to do. I talked it over with a guy I took across last night. The nearest station is at Aire-sur-l'Adour. We've got to be careful because the police are all over the place and they've got orders to arrest any Jews."

That news takes my breath away. Why have we made this journey if we're right back in the same mess?

Maurice senses that the news has given me a jolt. He shakes his head and goes on: "It isn't exactly the same thing: these guys are French. Some of them even let you get away and some take bribes. There are others who do carry out their orders but, from what that man told me on the path, we should be able to get through with our eyes shut."

I'm hungry. It's been a long time since the lentils. Even longer since we had the radishes.

"Don't you think we could ask the farmer to give us some milk and bread? Can't we afford that now?"

Maurice's legs are so stiff he has to struggle to his feet.

"All right, I guess we could use something."

Ten minutes later we were in the low room used for a kitchen, bedroom, and dining room all at the same time. Two thick earthenware bowls filled with milk were set on the table, which was covered with oilcloth full of pinkish stains made by wine glasses and bottles. There were also two long loaves of bread, sliced lengthwise and covered with that luxury of luxuries — a layer of butter a quarter of an inch thick. We were alone with the farmer, for all the others had left at dawn or even before.

The owner of the farm watched us eat. He was still wearing his sheepskin coat and I was wondering if he ever took it off. Maybe in the springtime. But he really must have slept in it. He looked older in the light of day, a few wispy strands of hair lay on top of his skull and the hairs of his mustache followed the wrinkles at the corners of his lips.

"You going far?"

With my mouth full, I reply, "We're going to take the train as far as Marseille."

I trust him. He's undoubtedly a good man, but I've already gotten into the habit: the less you say, the better.

He nods. "Well, you're really going to get around!"

He looks at us a bit fondly and adds, "When I went to school as a little fellow . . . it was more to the south, a little village in the province of Hérault, where my father owned chestnut trees . . . The teacher made us read a book called *Tour de France* . . . It was about two children on a journey through France and there were drawings at the beginning of each chapter. You look like them a little."

Maurice swallows.

"What happened to them in the end?"

The farmer makes a vague gesture with his hand.

"I don't remember anymore — all kinds of adventures. I only remember that there was a happy ending."

He pauses and then adds, "But there weren't any Germans in the story."

We have finished, and Maurice stands up. The man takes a knife from his pocket — a jackknife with a wooden handle. The blade is all worn down and as thin as a little saber. He takes the loaf from the table, carves two big chunks by rotating the bread around his knife, and hands them to us.

"Put them in your packs — it's for the journey."

Once more we start on our way.

It's a back road that winds even when the land is flat. The fields are empty, the earth is still gray, and the bushes make darker spots. There is a sprinkling of farmhouses, but far away. A dog has emerged from a sunken road and follows us. It's a mongrel coated with mud to the shoulders; he seems especially grateful for our company and his tail wags when — after getting a lead on us — he waits, motionless, for us in the middle of the road.

Vingt-sept kilomètres à pied, ça use, ça use . . .
Vingt-sept kilomètres à pied, ça use les souliers . . .

We haven't done any twenty-seven kilometers on foot, barely three, but we sing the song over and over. If it weren't for the pain in my heel, I'm sure I could walk all the way to Marseille and even further, but I can feel a blister forming. It's been a long time since I've taken off my shoes — too long.

And there's another marker by the roadside: *Aire-sur-l'Adour 19*. Still nineteen more markers to pass.

"You want a piece of bread?"

Maurice shakes his head.

"Not in the middle of an event. Any athlete knows you mustn't eat in the middle of an event — you won't have any wind."

"We're no athletes!"

He shrugs. "No, but we've still got a long way to go, so we'd better not eat."

We go on hiking while the sky clouds up little by little. Clear and black just a while ago, our shadows have now become indistinct, then gradually they disappear.

Vingt-huit kilomètres à pied . . .

It isn't so bad as long as my heel doesn't touch the ground. I have to walk on the toes of my left foot. You have to get the knack.

"Are you limping?"

"Don't worry about it."

The white marker stones driven into the shoulder of the

road every hundred meters seem to be getting further and further apart. My shins begin to ache. From walking tip-toe, the muscles have to work like the devil and it's too much for me — my heel drops to the ground again. My leg is trembling up to the thigh. At once I feel the sharp pricking of the blister as it rubs against my sock.

I won't stop — that's out of the question. I may come in on bloody stumps, but nobody will say that I slowed us down. I grit my teeth and whistle.

Aire-sur-l'Adour 17.

Suddenly Maurice heads for the shoulder of the road and sits down at the foot of the marker. He rests his pale face on the top of the stone.

"I've got to stop. I'm all knocked out — I didn't get enough sleep."

I never expected a break like this. "Sleep for a while — you'll feel better. There's no rush."

I sense that he doesn't even have the strength to answer. His face is drawn and he curls up on the grassy bank at the side of the road.

I take the opportunity to loosen the laces of my shoe. When I pull on the lace, it jams; as usual, I have to struggle to untie the knot.

It's just what I was afraid of: the wool is stuck to my flesh; there's a little rosy circle at the spot where the shoe rubbed — a circle as big as a one-franc piece. If I pull the stocking free, I'm going to bleed even more. I'd better not do it.

I gently move my toes to drive away the pain. We're in great shape: one of us exhausted and the other with a big blister. We'll never make it to that damned town. Things were going too smoothly.

I take a handkerchief out of the knapsack. Neatly folded, carefully ironed, it has pale green and brown squares around the edge. I use it to put a makeshift bandage over the stocking, packing it down against the wound. That way, I won't feel the rubbing so much. I have trouble putting my shoe back on, but finally manage to do it. I take a few timid steps down the road. It looks as if it's going to be better that way.

With his muzzle on his paws, his tongue drooping, the dog watches me. He looks like a Parisian mongrel — the kind you find at the foot of lampposts between the rues Simart and Eugène-Sue. Maybe he's a refugee too; maybe he crossed the line the way we did. Maybe he's a Jewish dog.

There is the creak of a wagon wheel behind me. On a path perpendicular to the road, a cart comes along pulled by a horse. I take a better look: it isn't a cart — it's much more elegant. It looks like an open hackney carriage — the kind you see in movies about the old days.

Maurice is still asleep.

If the wagon is going toward the town, we've got to grab the opportunity. Still seventeen kilometers to go and that's hard on the legs.

I don't let the wagon out of my sight. It's going to turn. If it turns left, we're sunk. If it makes a right, we've got a break.

It makes a right. I scramble to my feet and walk toward the wagon. The driver has a whip beside him but he isn't using it. With the old horse that's pulling the wagon, the whip couldn't do much good. Each step looks like its last, and you begin to wonder if there isn't a family in mourning clothes walking behind a hearse.

A few meters from me, the man draws in the reins.

I go limping up to him.

"Pardon me, monsieur, you aren't going to Aire-sur-l'Adour by any chance?"

"Yes, as a matter of fact, I am. To be exact, I'm going to within two kilometers of there."

This is a distinguished-looking gentleman; he seems to have come from another era. If I knew how to bow, I'd try it on him.

"And would you . . . I mean, could my brother and I ride with you in your hackney?"

The man wrinkles his bushy brows. I must have said something I shouldn't have said. Or maybe this guy is a policeman or a collaborationist. I start imagining the trouble that I've gotten us into. I should have warned Maurice so that we could hide.

"Young man, this vehicle is not a hackney — it's a barouche."

I stare open-mouthed.

"Oh, yes. Excuse me."

He seems touched by this politeness.

"That's all right, young fellow, but it's good to learn as soon as possible to call things by their proper names. I find it ridiculous to say *hackney* when you're looking at a genuine barouche. But that's not really so important, and you and your brother can share this carriage."

"Thank you, monsieur."

Hopping on one foot, I run toward my brother, who's sound asleep, his mouth open. I wake him rudely.

"What's wrong?"

"Hurry up, your barouche is waiting."

"My *what?*"

"Your barouche. You don't know what that is?"

He rubs his eyes, picks up his knapsack, and stares stupidly at the waiting carriage.

"Jesus," he murmurs, "where did you find that?"

I don't answer. Maurice greets our driver respectfully. Smiling, he looks at us as we climb in. The springs groan. Here and there, the upholstery has worn out, letting the springs show, but it's really very pleasant.

The man clacks his tongue to the horse and we start up. He turns to us.

"As you can see, we go rather slowly; it's not very comfortable but it's certainly better than walking. I used to own a car but it was requisitioned just six months ago. It's surely gone to some German officer in the Occupied Zone. That's why I had to resurrect this antique, which my tenant farmer has kept in fairly good shape."

We listen fascinated, without saying a word.

"Let me introduce myself — I'm the Count de V——."

Jesus Christ, a count. I had imagined them rather with plumed hats and rapiers. But if he says so, it must be true. In any case, it's the first time I've ever seen a count.

"As for this horse," he continues, "if I may use the term so loosely, it's the only one that hasn't been taken by the *commune*. He's very old for a horse and I won't be able to harness him much longer."

Aire-sur-l'Adour 16.

We're hardly going faster than we would on foot. Now our coachman-count is talking without a stop. We take turns speaking, giving monosyllabic answers so he doesn't get the feeling that he's talking to himself.

"You see, boys, the fact is that when a country loses a war as decisively as we lost this one, it's because the leaders of that country weren't equal to their task. And I make no bones about it: the Republic wasn't equal to its task."

A hill. That's all we need. We slow down to something under the speed of a hearse. One finger pointing skyward, the count is still making speeches.

"France was only great during the time of the kings. Under the monarchy, we never experienced such a catastrophe. No king would have ever consented to see his people colonized from within by all kinds of foreign elements, sects, races, which have never stopped leading the nation closer to the brink of the abyss . . ."

I had figured he would say something like that.

He goes on orating; I stop listening to him.

Aire-sur-l'Adour 7.

"France lacked a great national movement which would have enabled her — after a return to the sources of her true spirit — to rekindle her faith and find the strength that would have enabled her to repel the Teuton beyond our borders. But this time, we lost."

His voice drops off melancholically; I have the feeling that he's like an actor playing a role, one that he really doesn't believe in.

"Words came along, new words — *'liberté, égalité, fraternité'* — and they helped to blind the eyes and minds of the succeeding generations. Those words lulled the people into a mad hope, concealing the true values of the French spirit: the values of grandeur, sacrifice, order, purity . . ."

Out of the corner of my eye, I see Maurice yawning. I follow a flight of crows circling over a field. What prey have they found there? I wonder if crows eat corpses.

How can I find out? I'd like to ask the count, but he seems to have other concerns.

Aire-sur-l'Adour 2.

The count is going to drop us off here. I'm ready to get out, but he turns to us again.

"Young fellows," he says, "all the way here you've listened to me attentively and courteously, and I don't doubt that those words will have repercussions on your young minds before very long. By way of thanking you, I'm going to take you all the way to town — that'll give me a longer drive. Don't thank me."

With a regal air, he turns back on his seat and shakes the reins against the protruding ribs of his old horse.

I'm afraid I'll break out laughing if I look at my brother, so I go on staring at the horizon. There are more houses now. In the courtyard of a house, a woman watches us go by; she's holding a baby in her arms.

And that's how Maurice and I, born near the Porte de Clignancourt, Paris, 18th *arrondissement,* reached the square in front of the train station at Aire-sur-l'Adour in a barouche from the last century with a count as our coachman.

VI

BLUE, WHITE, AND PINK. It wouldn't take much for the town to be the color of the French flag. Blue — the sky that covers the city, white — the hills surrounding it, and pink — the sprawling, overlapping rooftops that begin at the bottom of the stairs before the Gare Saint-Charles. And rising supreme above all that, the distant gold figure of the Virgin standing guard over the city.

Marseille.

I scarcely remember anything about the train ride other than the fact that it had nothing in common with the trip from Paris to Dax. We slept like logs and, in the middle of the night, we ate veal cutlets in sliced, buttered loaves of bread. A woman passenger gave them to us. Then for dessert we were rewarded with hard-boiled eggs and crackers. I remember standing there for a good ten minutes with my lips glued to the faucet of the sink; the trickle of insipid, lukewarm water couldn't quench my thirst. We had to change trains and there were long waits on the platforms of unknown stations where clerks chalked up the delays on large blackboards. It was a slow journey, but I felt lost in a kind of pleasant lethargy. We had money and time, nobody thought of asking us for anything: two children in the midst of the din made by adults. I had the feeling of being invisible, of having free access everywhere: the war had turned us into elves that nobody cared about, elves who could come and go as they pleased.

I remember lying on a bench under one of those great glass roofs that have disappeared from the platforms of the main stations; I saw policemen go by. They were all over. Listening to the conversations, we were able to learn that they, too, had been ordered to arrest Jews and ship them off to special camps.

And on that clear winter morning, when the clouds had been swept aside by the *mistral*, we found ourselves in a great city — but how different from our own!

We stood at the top of the great, dazzling stairs, already dazed by the wind and sun, deafened by the loudspeakers over which the voices pronounced the vowels that we were accustomed to omit. The city sprawled at our feet: it swarmed under the plane trees and the antennae of trolley cars gouged the leaves of trees. We went down and entered the great circus, Marseille, by its main entrance: the Boulevard d'Athènes.

I later learned the big seaport was a center of gangsterism, drugs, vice — a European Chicago. That's what the films said, and books and articles. They must have been right, but I never liked to hear it said. Marseille, for Maurice and me (who held hands, so we wouldn't get lost), was that morning, that day, a great, riotous, windy festival — my most beautiful promenade.

We weren't going to get back on the train until evening, as the departure scheduled for noon had been canceled. That way we had plenty of time.

Gusts of wind hit us at an angle and we were blown sideways, laughing. All the breezes blew up or down; the town ran from the surrounding hills like soft cheese. We stopped at a huge intersection and walked on down a very big boulevard full of people, shops, and moving-picture houses.

We weren't lured in. Two kids from Paris who knew their way around the 18th *arrondissement* weren't going to become starry-eyed over a few moving-picture marquees. But there was something — a gaiety, an animation — that took our breath away.

At one corner stood a huge blue moving-picture house that had portholes like an old ocean liner. We went closer to look at the billboards: it was a German film, *The Adventures of Baron Munchausen*, with Hans Albert, the big star of the Third Reich. In one of the photos, we saw him riding through the sky on a cannon-ball. In another, he was having a sword-fight with a gang of cutthroats. My mouth was watering.

I elbowed Maurice.

"Hey, look, it doesn't cost much."

He looked at the ticket window and the sign below it.

"It doesn't open until ten . . ."

That meant he was willing to go. I was dancing with impatience on the sidewalk.

"We'll take a walk and come back."

We kept going down the wide boulevard. There were immense glassed-in sidewalk cafés where men in gray felt hats read newspapers and smoked cigarettes as if there weren't any rationing, and then, abruptly, the street opened up. There was a great gust of wind, one that took our breath away, and we stopped in our tracks. Maurice was the first to speak.

"Jesus, it's the sea."

We had never seen it before, and we never imagined we'd find it like that — so suddenly. The sea emerged before us without warning, catching us unprepared.

The sea dozed among the rocking boats in the great basin of the Vieux Port, and we could see it between St.-Jean and St.-Nicolas, where it stretched as far as the eye could see, dotted with tiny white islands that were bathed in sunlight. Before us rose the great suspension bridge that spanned the Vieux Port, and we saw flotillas of small craft and the ferry making one of its first crossings of the day.

We went as close to it as possible, right up to the edge of the quay. Below us the water was green despite the fact that it was so blue in the distance. It was impossible to tell the exact spot where the blue turned to green.

"What do you say, boys? Want to see the Château d'If? Just get aboard and we're on our way."

We lifted our gaze.

He was trying to look like a real sailor, all bundled up in a pea jacket, a black cap with a gold-braid anchor, and skinny legs that were lost in white duck trousers much too big for him.

Tourists weren't very plentiful at that time. He showed us a yellow boat pitching gently, with red seats and topsides that really needed a paint job.

There were so many things to do in Marseille! The movies, boat rides; they ask you just like that, point blank, to go on trips. I sure would have liked a ride to the Château d'If, a castle in the sea. That would have been a marvel!

Slowly, with regret, Maurice shook his head to say no.

"Why don't you want to come? It's half-price for children. You're not going to tell me you don't have that much money? Come on, hop aboard."

"No, it rolls too much; we'll be seasick."

The man laughed.

"You know, I think you might be right."

He had clear, good eyes. He looked at us more attentively.

"From the way you speak," he said, "I can tell you aren't from these parts."

"We come from Paris."

In his excitement, he took his hands out of his pockets.

"Paris! I've been there. My brother moved up there. He's a plumber around the Porte d'Italie."

We chatted for a while. He wanted to know what was going on there, if things weren't too bad with the Germans. Here, the worst was the food shortage. There wasn't anything on sale at the outdoor markets along the rue Longue, behind the Réformés; at the Plaine, all you could find were winter squash. People lined up for lettuce; the artichokes were grabbed right up.

"Look, just look at my trousers."

He showed us the slack in his belt.

"In a year I've lost twelve kilos. Say, if you feel like it, I'll show you the motor of my boat."

Delighted, we went aboard. The very slow pitching was pleasant. The motor was up forward in a kind of little garden-house. He explained what everything was for — from the propeller to the carburetor. He was crazy about boats and talked a blue streak. We had trouble breaking away from him.

We walked along the docks around the Quai de Riveneuve. There were barrels and coils of rope, a salty smell, the smell of adventure: from the rue Fortia, from the Place aux Huiles, I expected to see legions of pirates emerge. I had to admit that it beat the canals of the rue Marcadet where we sailed our ships made from sheets of notebook paper.

"Should we take the boat across the harbor?"

"Yes!"

It was a flat-bottomed launch. The passengers hurried behind the windowpanes, sheltered from the wind. We stayed out in the open, whipped by the wind, with the smell of salt that got into our skin.

It was a short trip, no more than two or three minutes, but we could see the city rising over us. The great boulevard was a straight line splitting the rooftops in two.

Across the quay, that was something else again. There was a jumble of tiny alleys with clotheslines stretched from one window to one across the way, despite the fact that the sun could not ever have reached these places. We went a few steps. The streets there were like stairs, and sewage ran down the middle in a gutter.

I began to feel uneasy. In shadowy doorways women were talking, most of them sitting on straw-bottomed chairs. There were other women in the windows, leaning their arms on the sills.

Suddenly Maurice cries out.

"My beret!"

An enormous woman has taken it from him. She has a

vast, trembling bosom. When she laughs we can see the gold fillings in her teeth. Instinctively I take off my own beret and stuff it into my pocket.

Maurice's beret really made the rounds. Within a few seconds, it had left the head of its owner, the fat woman had thrown it behind her to a second girl who was half-naked in the shadows of a hallway, and suddenly a call made us lift our heads.

In a window on the second floor, a woman even fatter than the first held the precious headgear between her pudgy fingers. She was laughing, too.

"Come up and get it, dearie."

His heart broken, Maurice watches his beautiful Basque beret being twirled on the forefinger of the fat lady.

He looks at me.

"I can't let her have it — I've got to go up there."

I'm not very old, but I know about the world. There are the same kind of girls near Clignancourt and the big boys in school often talk about them during recess. I hold him back.

"Don't go up. Beniquet says they give you diseases and they take your money."

My brother doesn't seem particularly enchanted by these two prospects but he says, "I'm not going to let them have it."

The girls are still laughing. Now one of them starts in on me.

"Look at the little one. Isn't he cute? He's smart, that one, he took off his beret right away."

We stand in the middle of the street and other windows open; we're going to have the whole neighborhood rioting if this keeps up.

A very big woman opens the door of the café nearby. She has red hair, a real flame that hangs down her back. She shouts at the woman holding the beret.

"Maria, aren't you ashamed of starting up with kids? Go on, give it back to him."

Maria goes on laughing, a laugh buried in flesh. Good-naturedly, she throws down the beret.

"Go on, scat, you good-for-nothings!"

Maurice catches the beret in midair and pulls it down over his ears. Then we run through the street as fast as our legs can carry us. It goes uphill almost as steeply as at Montmartre; it is dirtier but there is more color. We get lost in the Panier section and then a clock strikes ten!

What with the sea, the boat, the whores, we have forgotten the movie. We use the sea to help us find our way. As soon as we spy it, we come out at the harbor in front of a cigar store and walk back up the great boulevard called the Canebière.

Minutes later we were sitting three rows from the screen, our knapsacks on our laps, our hands rammed down in our pockets. We were alone, or almost alone, and the immense theater was unheated. There were a couple of hoboes behind us. Around their seats lay a heap of bundles; their sacks tied with twine blocked the aisle. I remember that the newsreels came on first. Seated at a table, a little man with a thick mustache, named Laval, spoke to us. He looked at us with bulging, scolding eyes. After that came tanks in the snow and I understood that they were German tanks awaiting the spring to assault Moscow. The narrator said that it was very cold but that the men's morale was high, and we saw two soldiers on the screen; they waved their white mittens in front of the camera.

Afterwards there was a part on Paris fashions, women turning around. They had black lips, very high hairdos, and high-heeled shoes. They had been photographed in the streets, before monuments like the Eiffel Tower, the Arc de Triomphe and, finally, the Sacré-Cœur.

For a few seconds, lost in that moving-picture house in Marseille, we saw our section of Paris again and that reminded me abruptly that I'd hardly thought about Papa or Mama since leaving home. They had undoubtedly been thinking about us and I would have loved to tell them that everything was all right, that tomorrow — or even that very evening — we would reach our destination safe and sound. The sequence went on and, for a moment, I hoped that the director might have had the idea of photographing his models on the rue Clignancourt, in front of the barbershop. But no such luck — the photographers of the forties avoided working-class sections like the plague; they needed the sublime and the grandiose: Versailles, the fountains of the Place de la Concorde, Notre-Dame, the Panthéon. They never left those hallowed places.

There was an interminable intermission during which Maurice and I played at asking each other riddles, using the words from the advertisements hung on the stage curtain. I told him the first and the last letter and he had to come up with the whole word. When he found the answer, it would be his turn to ask. Finally he got angry because the word I had chosen was one of the shortest in the dictionary; we traded insults, two slaps, a couple of punches, and the fight began.

The heavy tread of an usherette coming down the aisle calmed us instantly. We had just enough time to exchange a few sneaky kicks under the seats and then the film started again.

We saw it three times in a row, as there was a continuous showing. I've seen films since then — some very bad, some very fine ones, some that were ridiculous, others that were touching, but I've never again experienced the bewitchment of that morning. There's one more item to be added to the dossier that cinema-lovers have set up on the Hitlerian cinema: the Nazi film industry succeeded in making a film that gave two young Jews an enchanted morning.

It was four o'clock when we left the theater, our eyes full of dreams; but we also had headaches that the fresh air soon dispelled. We had had a good rest but I was ravenously hungry; without consulting me, Maurice charged straight into a pastry shop.

On a glass shelf stood unbelievable cakes that had been made without eggs, butter, sugar or flour. The result was a pinkish foam at the center of a doughy mass, sticky and tough at the same time. The whole thing was topped off by a currant and a quarter of a glazed cherry. We each gobbled down four of them.

His mouth still full, Maurice looked at me.

"We've got plenty of time before the train. What do you want to do?"

I made up my mind quickly.

"We could go look at the sea again for a while . . ."

We didn't dare go very far. It was out of the question to take the trolley: the few that rolled were overloaded; there were bunches of guys clinging on around the doors.

We just went near the cathedral, where the big harbor begins, where the port looks more like a factory with its cranes, winches, and hoisting machinery. We wandered along the iron fences of the docks like two emigrants trying to stow away. Maurice stretched out his hand.

"That way is toward Africa."

I stare in that direction as if I might see monkeys, a lion, a black woman carrying a burden on her head, African drums, masked dancers wearing grass skirts.

"And where's Menton?"

He points to the left.

"It's way over there — near Italy."

I think, then add, "What about the address? Do you have the address?"

"Yes, we'll be sure to find it. There can't be that many barbershops."

"What if they're doing some other kind of work?"

Now it's Maurice's turn to stop and think. He looks up.

"Why do you always try to complicate things?"

That's the kind of remark from Maurice that bothers me.

"Oh, it's me that complicates everything, is it?"

"Yes, it's you that complicates everything."

I snicker.

"I suppose I'm the one who had my beret swiped?"

Involuntarily he raises his hand to make sure that the thing is still glued to the top of his head.

"Then I suppose it's my fault that she swiped it from me? You could've gone after it — you that talks such a good game!"

"It wasn't my beret. You'd have gone after it yourself if you weren't such a yellow-belly."

We swear at each other for a couple of minutes, then go

on our way again at a swift pace. This kind of squabbling has always done us good. We've kept up our brotherly ties this way and have always felt better afterwards.

Dusk — we've got to get back to the station.

We climb back up the stairs flanked by massive, symbolic statues, and I turn around before entering the great terminal. I already know that a town's train station isn't really the town anymore and that here at the Gare Saint-Charles I'm not really in Marseille any longer. Marseille is there, but she's lost her colors with the passing hours; her hubbub still rises to me, pierced by the plaintive sounds of the trains. I know I'll never forget her. Marseille, a beautiful city, a city of sunlight, the sea, films, whores, boats, and a stolen beret.

I pee in the public toilet in the tiled basement of the station. The place smells of chlorine and my wooden soles make an incredible echo.

I come back up and find myself between the legs of two policemen who are blocking the entrance.

They haven't seen me; their backs are turned.

Should I try going back downstairs, whistling, looking as if nothing had happened? No, absolutely not — they'd hear me.

I slip between them, being careful not to bump into them.

"Excuse me . . ."

They let me go by and I go away taking short steps, with a walk that's serious and impulsive all at the same time, the walk of a boy who's done nothing wrong.

"Hey, kid, where you going?"

I feel the sweat suddenly break out of all my pores. Perhaps my luck has changed abruptly.

I turn to them and go back. Their faces are really mean-looking. I lift my beret politely.

This act, and perhaps the fact that I had washed my hands and face in the sink and wet my hair and combed it with a part down the middle, may have worked in my favor. There are times when little things can decide whether life is to go on or stop.

"I'm going to get on the train."

They are very big — they look like twins. They have their hands behind their backs and rock back and forth on their heels.

"We guessed as much. Do you have your papers?"

"No, Papa has them."

"Where's your father?"

I turn around. It's plenty crowded in the terminal, especially at the other end near the baggage window.

"Over there — he's watching the suitcases."

They are still looking at me. If they ask me to take them to him, I'm sunk.

"Where do you live?"

"Marseille."

"What address?"

"On the Canebière, over the moving-picture house."

It's a good lie, the kind that comes out automatically — and turns out very nicely — provided you don't think too much beforehand. I feel like adding to the story right away; I feel that I could come up with a whole life history. I add, "My father owns the movie house."

If they don't stop me right away, I'm going to tell them that we own all Marseille.

They don't look very impressed but the next question takes on a different tone.

"So you must go to the movies a lot?"

"Yes, I see every new movie. Right now it's *Baron Munchausen*. It's really good."

I wouldn't have believed that they could smile. But they almost do it.

"Go on, get going."

"Goodbye, messieurs."

I put my beret back on and go away. I'm almost disappointed that it's over. But watch out: they may be following me — I've got to trick them.

Maurice is to my right, sitting on a bench outside the waiting room. I walk straight to the place where my father is supposed to be. I weave through trunks and baggage trucks and clusters of passengers and maneuver so that the last car of the train acts as a screen between the two policemen and me.

I make no sign to my brother, who hasn't moved. He must understand that something's wrong.

The best thing to do is to stay as lost as possible in the middle of the crowded station, but without giving the impression that I'm hiding. At the same time, they mustn't see me together with Maurice. I mingle with knots of people and suddenly I see them coming.

My heart stops beating. I should have known that those two bastards wouldn't leave things in suspense. I who was so proud of telling them lies! You've got to watch out at all times. Just when you think you've won — that's always the most dangerous time.

They draw closer, very slowly; as before, their hands are behind their backs.

They go past my brother who's still sitting beside a nice lady. Over there, the man looking at the train schedule can't be more than thirty years old; he could be my father — he's going to be my father. I strike a happy, lively air and ask him for the time.

He looks surprised, for two reasons: one, there's a huge clock just across from us; two, he must wonder why I'm smiling so much while asking such a question.

He looks at me for a moment, a bit amused and sly.

"Can't you tell time?"

I break out into laughter that surprises him even more. He's going to take me for a lunatic. From the corner of my eye I see the policemen have come abreast of us now, a few meters away; but with the noise in the station they can't hear what we're saying.

"Of course I know how to tell time."

"Well, just look up there and you'll see a clock that will tell you the time as well as I can."

They glance at us and go past. The gentleman never knew that, for a few fleeting seconds, he had been — for two *gendarmes* — owner of a big movie house in downtown Marseille and father of a ten-year-old boy.

I turn a little and suddenly there's a hand resting on my shoulder. I give a start — it's Maurice.

"What's going on?"

I quickly lead him behind a column and tell him the news. He too looks uneasy. He's got good reason for that.

"I heard people talking. The police are checking all over the station, right now in the second-class waiting room. Loads of people are being arrested. They're checking everybody."

We look at each other without saying a word.

"What do we do?"

He fusses with the train tickets at the bottom of his pocket.

"We can go out of the station again, but we lose our tickets. They're only good for tonight. I don't feel like staying in Marseille. Where could we sleep? You can always find a hotel, but they probably check your identity there, too." Suddenly he elbows me. "Look, to your left."

I break away from my thoughts. A whole regiment of police has just come in. The officer leading them has a visored cap with gold braid around it; he's at least a captain. Maurice mutters a curse.

The train that we have to take isn't in yet. The platform before us is empty, the rails disappear in the darkness; they come together in the distance, at the spot where the night is the thickest.

I get an idea.

"Listen, if we follow the tracks, we'll come to another station, right?"

Maurice shakes his head.

"No, that's a good way to get ourselves run over. Besides, there are guys working there, the ones that fix the tracks. We'd get picked up even faster that way."

While we debate the issue, the *gendarmes* have been deployed and are asking people waiting on the platforms for their papers. I see some of them going into the waiting room. It's some kind of roundup and we're right in the middle of it.

At just that instant, the loudspeaker announced the arrival of our train. There was pandemonium for a moment, for there were few passenger trains and those were always overcrowded. The passengers had become accustomed to throwing themselves onto the handful of seats that hadn't been reserved in advance. We joined the stampede and were among those leading the charge. Luck was with us: the ticket inspectors had failed to lock the gates and we climbed aboard the train.

In the corridor Maurice told me, "If they come around checking, we hide under a seat — they won't go under there looking for us."

We weren't so sure about that, but they didn't come around.

After a half-hour delay, the train started up with a lurch. We breathed a sigh of relief — we were on the last lap of the journey.

The trip was a long one. We crawled at a snail's pace, making frequent stops in the middle of the countryside without anyone knowing why. Railway workers walked along the track bed beside our car, and, half asleep, I heard their voices, their Provençal accents, their curses.

The sun rose near Cannes and I must have fallen asleep after that. Maurice woke me up. I don't know how we did it, but, after stepping over the bodies of sleepers in the corridor, I found myself standing on a square lined with palm trees that waved their fronds above me. They were the first I had ever seen — unless I count the stunted specimens glimpsed one summer day when Mama took us to the Jardin du Luxembourg.

Four months in Menton.

They say that the town has changed. They've built homes, skyscrapers, new beaches, as they have along the whole Côte d'Azur up to the Italian border and then some. During those wartime months, Menton was still a small town whose fortune had been made by the English, aided by some tubercular billionaires who came there to live out their last days in the sun. The grand hotels and the sanatorium were occupied by the Italian General Staff and a handful of troops who lived there like kings — swimming all summer, roaming the streets, the Biones Gardens and the promenade in front of the old casino in the winter. From the very first hour the town cast a spell over me with its already outmoded charm, its arcades, its Italian churches, its old stairs, and the ancient jetty from whose tip you could see the old town and the mountains, which plunged steeply into the Mediterranean.

As soon as we arrive in Menton, we start out to look for our brothers. It does not take us long.

The barbershop is a smart-looking one on the corner of a broad street leading to the museum.

Maurice sees it first. He elbows me.

"Look."

Despite the reflections on the shop window, I can see inside. That big guy running the clippers over an in-clined neck is Henri, the eldest. He hasn't changed — a little thinner perhaps, but just a trifle. He hasn't seen us.

"Come on, let's go in."

The little bell over the door jingles. The second barber turns around, the cashier looks at us, the customers look at us in the mirrors — everybody stares at us except Henri.

We go on standing in the middle of the shop.

The cashier steps in.

"Have a seat, boys . . ."

Henri begins to turn around and stands there, clippers suspended in midair.

"Well," he says, "well, well, if it isn't the hooligans."

He bends down and kisses us. He smells just as good as ever, the same smell.

"Sit down. I'll be through in a couple of minutes."

His straight razor scrapes over a stubbly cheek; a last touch of the scissors to even up behind one ear, a whisk of the feather-duster on the collar, a quick parading of the mirror, and he whips the sheet off his patient.

"Can I be excused for five minutes, Madame Henriette? I've got to take care of these two."

The proprietress nods her assent and out we go.

He takes our hands in his and pulls us along toward the old town in the wake of his long strides; as we trot to keep up with him, we exchange questions:

"What about Mama and Papa? How did you get across? When did you get here . . . ?"

We both answer at the same time. I manage to ask, "What about Albert?"

"It's his day off; he's at home."

"Where's your house?"

"You'll see."

We went uphill toward the Saint-Michel church through narrow, winding streets, staircases leading down to the sea. We were on the rue Longue, which reminded me of Marseille and the stolen beret because there were clotheslines stretched between the windows. A small arch connected both sides of the street at the level of the second floor.

Almost under the arch, Henri went through a low door. A staircase went down; the steps were steep and narrow.

"Don't make any noise — we're going to surprise him."

He turned the key in the lock and we found ourselves

in a small dining room furnished with a huge Provençal buffet, a round table, and three chairs. Through the half-open bedroom door, we saw Albert reading on his bed.

"I've brought some company home."

Albert, not having seen us yet, was surprised.

"What are you doing home? Aren't you supposed to be in the shop?"

"Guess who's here."

Albert isn't very patient by nature. He jumped to his feet and strode into the dining room.

"Oh, oh," he said, "it's the hooligans."

We flung ourselves around his neck. The family was together again.

They gave us lemonade, bread — and then chocolate. When I was astounded at seeing such a rare delicacy, Henri explained that you could get by quite nicely if you knew your way around.

We told our adventures from the beginning. They couldn't tear themselves away from our story, and Henri's five minutes became a solid hour. They told us how things had gone for them. The German police had checked passports on the train, and a young fellow, very thin, had been the first to show his papers. He wore a big smile, the picture of innocence and geniality.

The German had spelled out his name with difficulty.

"Rauschen . . ."

Politely, the fellow helped him.

"Rauschenberger. Simon Rauschenberger."

The policeman's face twitched.

"You're French, *nicht wahr?*"

The smiling young man nodded.

"From Paris, 14th *arrondissement*, the rue d'Alésia."

The German stroked his chin, perplexed.

"What religion?"

Rauschenberger coughed discreetly.

"Catholic, but of course . . ." — and he raised a sacerdotal finger — "the Orthodox church."

Confused, the policeman had handed back his papers. Meanwhile Henri and Albert had followed in the crowd that surged on by.

"That's not all," Albert said, "but now we've got to put you young fellows up. Until we get something better, you'll sleep on a mattress in the dining room. You'll be snug there. There are sheets and blankets in the closet, and you'll make your own bed."

Henri went back to work and Albert heated some water for us in the kitchen. In a large basin, we washed ourselves with black soap, a sticky mass kept in a tin can. It wasn't exactly perfumed, but it did a fine job of removing the grime we were coated with. It had been a long time since our last bath. We put on clean underwear, a bit creased, from our knapsacks and I have never felt lighter.

"Now," said Albert, "you're going out to do some shopping. Here's the money and a list of things to buy. We're going to celebrate tonight."

There we were, each of us with a shopping net. We flew down the stairs, crossed the street, and ran onto the beach of Les Sablettes, at the foot of the old town.

The sand was hard. It wasn't a very big beach, but there wasn't a soul there — just a few fishing boats with their nets drying and little waves that you could barely hear slapping against the sand. We ran, jumped, danced, shouted — we were drunk with joy and freedom. We'd made it — we'd finally gained our freedom.

With our hair and shoes full of sand, we threw ourselves down on our bellies. Then we went wading. We were sorry to leave that place.

In the small squares of the town, fishermen bowled with iron balls on the beaten earth, cursing in the local dialect, which was like Italian. In the shops, they asked us our names several times and Maurice answered: "We're the brothers of Henri and Albert."

Everything immediately became easier, for everyone seemed to know them and, without asking for a single ration stamp, the butcher handed us a huge steak; the grocer gave us four kilos of potatoes, six eggs, a head of lettuce, and half a kilo of milled flour. My brothers sure seemed to know how to take care of themselves.

We returned to Albert loaded down like mules.

"Let's go, you Joffos. Start peeling those potatoes!"

With knife in hand, we got to work in the kitchen. I was stupefied: through the window I could look straight down at the sea — and we were at least five stories high! Go downstairs to go into your home and then wind up on the fifth floor — that's magic!

All three of us prepared the feast. When Henri came home with a bottle of wine, the table was set, the potatoes were browning in the skillet, and I had taken leave of my senses. My mouth was watering so much I didn't dare part my lips.

I don't remember the meal anymore. Albert gave Maurice and me half a glass of wine to celebrate our arrival, and that must have done me in. After some real

cheese (not the kind people bought in Paris), I heard
Maurice telling about the yellow star, the priest from Dax,
the policemen in Marseille, and then I fell asleep over
the table, my head on my forearms. I slept seventeen
hours straight.

The next three days were delightful.

Henri and Albert would leave early in the morning.
We would get up around nine o'clock and, after breakfast,
we'd go out onto the beach to play soccer. In those days
it was practically impossible to get a soccer ball. The
landlady had lent it to us and my love for soccer dates
back to that time. Maurice was the goalie. We marked
the goals with our coats and I booted the ball till I ran out
of breath, shouting with triumph whenever he couldn't
block a shot. We had the whole beach to ourselves; only
an occasional passer-by looked down at us from the top of
the sea wall.

We did the shopping. Our meals were hasty affairs, for
Henri and Albert used to eat with their employers. I was
the expert on macaroni. After boiling it with a little lump
of margarine and a pinch of salt, I spread *cancoillotte,* a
local cream cheese, over the top. This made a good sub-
stitute for Gruyère and was fairly easy to find in the grocery shops. I used to put the whole thing in the oven to
produce macaroni *au gratin.* It was a real treat.

In the afternoons we used to go out exploring, and the
scope of our investigations broadened constantly. On our
second day, near the Bay of Garavan, we came across an
immense villa that was all boarded up. A long wall surrounded the property, and through the iron gate, which
was locked with a heavy chain, we could see an over-
grown garden — a regular jungle. Tarzan must have

roamed around in there and I was surprised not to see him come swinging out on a vine.

The place was deserted. The owners must have been away. Perhaps the war had forced them to flee, perhaps they were dead. In any case, they weren't around.

Using the lower branches of a pepper tree and then a short ladder, we reached the heart of this paradise. There were statues half-concealed by the climbing plants and, best of all, an empty pool with yellow tiling; its walls were covered with moss. We played inside there the whole afternoon, scaling the pedestals of statues, fighting endless duels, and then the clock in the steeple of Saint-Michel struck six o'clock.

We raced back to the apartment, for we were supposed to set the table each evening and tidy the place up.

After devouring a quick supper, we went to bed. No sooner were we in bed than Maurice attacked.

"Listen, Jo. We're having fun, I know, but don't you think we could try to earn a little money?"

He pointed to our two brothers' bedroom and added, "That would help them out."

Clearly, they were earning their living nicely, but two extra mouths to feed make a difference — especially when appetites are good. Maurice had given them the remainder of the twenty thousand francs, but he was right — we couldn't let them support us until the end of the war. And then there was something else: since leaving Paris, we'd gotten into the habit of counting on no one but ourselves. We had discovered the pleasure that kids like us could experience by fending for themselves in a world of adults.

I don't think that our decision to work came so much

from scruples as it did from the fact that, at our age, earning a living had become a wonderful game, one that was more interesting than soccer games on the beach or exploring deserted villas.

A little after four-thirty, we sometimes met a few boys of our own age. That always meant a razzing: "Parisians, Parisians, ha, ha, ha!" But when you're around ten, ownership of a soccer ball can settle many a problem. I soon made friends with a ten-year-old boy from Menton; his first name was Virgilio and he lived in a decrepit house on the rue de Bréa.

After a few games of jacks in front of his door, he confided to me that during the school vacations he took care of the cows on a mountain farm above Sainte-Agnès. It paid pretty well and the farmer was nice, but he could work up there only when he wasn't going to school.

I decided to talk it over with Maurice that very evening. Bursting with pride at having a plan, I met him on rue Longue. He had a blue apron tied around his waist; his hair and eyebrows were white with flour. That skunk had gotten the jump on me and was already working in the baker's shop at the end of our street.

I borrowed money from Henri and, the next morning at eight o'clock, I went to the marketplace and took the bus for Sainte-Agnès. My forehead against the window, I saw the sea sink down in the distance as the bus rattled and shook, belching smoke from its butane engine, climbing in zigzags at thirty kilometers an hour. The village was half deserted. It was a typical market town of Provence, one of those you see on postcards, the kind that attracts tourists who love old stone.

In alleys even more tortuous than those of old Menton,

I met an elderly man pushing a tiny donkey loaded with dried branches, and I asked him the way to Monsieur Viale's farm — that was the name Virgilio had given me.

He took great pains to explain the way and there I was — following a trail up the side of a hill, completely lost against a background of rocks, steep slopes, and ravines.

I had my trusty knapsack with me and, while climbing slopes that grew steeper and steeper, I nibbled on a hard biscuit that Maurice had brought back from his bakery shop the day before. It looked as though he would take care of all our family's needs for bread, flour, and cakes. I was determined to bring my share back to the house: milk, butter, cheese, everything that could be had on a farm. Clearly, I would not be able to go down the mountain very often. Virgilio had warned me that, if old Viale hired me, I would have to sleep in a tiny room carved out of the side of a mountain and it wouldn't be like sleeping at home.

The mountains spread apart and before me lay a plain that grew wider and wider. The mountainside was farmed with terraces that reached down into the valley and, after hiking an hour or so in complete solitude, I came to some buildings. In the center of them stood an old farmhouse, with Roman tiles that years of sunshine had yellowed; but the owner had built a higher house to one side which reminded me more of the suburbs of Paris than the architecture of Provence. There were also sheds with corrugated iron roofs that must have been used for barns and storehouses.

I moved ahead cautiously, for I was afraid of watchdogs. But I came all the way into the courtyard of the farm and not a single dog appeared. I went up to the front of the high house and knocked.

Madame Viale opened the door.

Even though I was very young, this woman immediately struck me as being out of place. Years later, as I remember her, I realize why she astonished me so much without my understanding the reason why. She had belonged to Parisian high society. On various occasions, she told me that her parents lived in the district of Saint-Germain; her father was a member of the diplomatic corps. She had learned to play golf, ride horses, embroider, play the piano and harpsichord; and she had spent long hours reading the great books over cups of hot chocolate in her sumptuous room with its heavy damask tapestries.

At twenty-two, though she had many suitors, she had yet to make her choice from among the numerous candidates who offered to share her life. During the winter of 1927, she developed a slight cough. After a violent fit of coughing while drinking coffee at Lasserre's, a fit that left a brownish stain on her fine muslin handkerchief, her mother sent her to see a doctor and it was found that her left lung showed signs of tuberculosis.

In such a situation, there was only one thing for a young person of her social standing to do: she left for Menton. Her mother put her in a villa away from the town and away from the sanatorium where the ordinary folks bored themselves to death. After a few months, strengthened by the fresh air, she began going on walks through the countryside.

One day in the spring of 1928, she was following a rough trail and sprained her ankle. She spent three hours sitting on a rock; she thought that no one would ever come by, that she would never be found and that she would die of sunstroke despite her sunbonnet. She began to await the coming of the vultures when she heard footsteps on the stones. It was Monsieur Viale returning to his farm.

He was in his thirties, with a Clark Gable mustache; he took the young woman in his arms and carried her to his home. Fourteen years later, she was still there.

It was a frightful scandal. They married three months later at the town hall of Gorbio, for Viale was a free-thinker at odds with the Church, and her family broke all ties.

She told me this story about four times during the first week that I spent up there. While feeding the chickens, she would listen to a record of Handel, Bach, or Mozart, turning up the volume as high as it would go. In her room there were stacks of records in gray jackets with a big hole in the middle so that you could see the title of the selection. She also read a great deal and lent me the complete works of Anatole France, for whom she had a marked preference.

Before Viale arrived, I already knew that I would stay on and that my main job wouldn't be to scrub the stalls of the few remaining animals, nor hoe out the weeds that sprouted around the vinestocks after a rain, but to listen to the mistress of the house as she sat on a cushioned chair with a cup of tea in her hand.

When the master came in, I explained that I had met Virgilio, that I wanted to work, to perform all the tasks that he asked me to do. He agreed immediately.

I wasn't tall or heavy, and even if I'd swelled my chest,

I doubt that he would have been impressed. But the most important part had been done: I was hired, and that very night I would sleep in the tiny room Virgilio had told me about. My wages had been decided on. I fell asleep happy as a lark: I was working, I wasn't a burden to my brothers, I was earning money. It still wasn't the season for the heavy work and I went off the next morning with my boss to "putter about," as he said. We righted some low stone walls, with me holding the plumb line. I also remember mixing mortar and carrying it to Monsieur Viale, who was perched high up on a ladder, patching the holes in the farmhouse walls. I spent two mornings rinsing bottles with a cleaning brush, my hands covered by rubber gloves so big that they came up to my elbows. I had never seen so many bottles in my life — the cellar was full of them.

I ate with them, and Madame Viale began telling me about a few episodes of her past: her visit to the exposition of Bagatelle in July 1924, her début, her first Vienna waltz with an Italian officer.

Viale listened to her while smoking his pipe; then he got to his feet.

I sat up in my chair, ready to follow him, but he motioned me to stay put.

"Take a rest — you worked hard this morning."

I didn't dare tell him that I would have preferred to be with him in the fields or up on the shed mending the roof rather than listening to the history of fashionable society during the period between the two wars. But I sensed that this too comprised part of my work — he and I were in collusion.

Thus it was that ten days passed among the chickens, ducks, mortar, Anatole France, and the never-ceasing stories of my dear *patronne*. I ate very well and forgot the war — something my employers didn't seem terribly concerned about. He thought that it didn't do any good to talk about it; she considered that the war was something rather indecorous, made for dull-witted, trivial people and that people with good taste had other topics of conversation.

On the tenth day, after the evening soup, I asked Viale if I could go down to town the next day. It was a Monday and my brothers would be off. I would take the morning bus and come back around five that evening.

The following morning, I went down the mountainside as planned. Besides my wages, I carried off eggs wrapped in newspaper inside a shoe box, as well as a kilo slab of lean bacon, both of them priceless. I could already see the enormous omelette that Maurice and I would make for lunch.

I thanked them and left for Sainte-Agnès. I remember turning toward the farmhouse lost in the bottom of the valley, ringed by mountains — that farmhouse where a woman's life had been built, a happy life really, even if it was very different from what it might have been. I saw Madame Viale cross the courtyard — she was the size of a lead soldier — and I thought it would be good to live there until peace returned to the world. There I was sheltered from everything; all I had to do was wait.

It would have grieved me deeply if at that instant I had known that I was never to return to the Viales' house and that I would never see them again.

I was sure to find my brothers at home on Monday. It was the day when all shops closed and they liked to sleep a little later. Maybe Maurice had gone down to the beach with the soccer ball.

As I got off the bus in front of the marketplace fountain, my feet were itching to kick the ball and get a few goals past him. I went flying back up the rue de Paris, holding both straps of my pack so as to keep the eggs from breaking. Then I ran up the rue Longue. The door of our house was ajar; I pushed it open.

Contrary to what I had imagined, they were all awake. Albert and Maurice were in their pajamas and having breakfast. Henri was finishing his coffee near the window. He wore a dark blue suit, a white shirt, a tie; on one corner of the table a closed suitcase waited. Shutting the door behind me, I knew that something had happened.

We embraced and Albert called me "country bumpkin" with a forced cheerfulness. I asked right away, "What's the matter?"

Nobody answered me and Maurice served me a bowl of *café au lait* without opening his mouth. Henri's face was taut, like a man who hasn't slept all night; he was the one who told me about it.

"We've had some bad news."

On the buffet lay a letter covered with postmarks, most of them showing an eagle.

I swallowed.

"Mama and Papa?"

Albert nodded.

"You might as well know right away — they've been arrested."

I had forgotten everything those last few days; I had

lived in my mountains far from men, with an old lady who told beautiful stories and a kindly farmer, and that had been enough to make all the rest disappear. Abruptly I was plunged back into reality and suddenly I had a bitter taste in my mouth.

Henri spoke again, explaining what had happened. Papa and Mama had left Paris, as the situation was growing steadily worse for Jewish people. There had been a huge round-up in our section one evening, and they had barely escaped. They had left everything behind, taking one bus after another, for the trains had become impossible for people without *Ausweis*, identity cards. Finally they landed up in the outskirts of Pau, completely exhausted. They had managed to cross the line after many adventures. But at this point they were caught by the Vichy authorities and thrown into a camp. They had been able to get only one letter out, the letter my brother had just received.

What Henri didn't tell me was the fact that the camp where they were being held was a transit camp from which trains left every day to resettle those prisoners.

I read the letter. Papa had written it; Mama had merely added a line after my father's signature: "I kiss you all. Be brave."

They didn't complain; my father couldn't have had much time to write. At the end he said: "If you meet up with the hooligans, put them in school. It's very important. I'm counting on you for that."

I lifted my eyes to my brothers.

"What should we do?"

Henri pointed to his suitcase.

"Well, I guess I'm going to Pau."

I didn't understand.

"But they'll get you too if you go there. They know Mama and Papa are Jewish, so they'll know you are, too. And they'll keep you there."

Albert smiled weakly.

"That's the same reaction I had yesterday. But we talked it over half the night and finally agreed on one point: we have to try something." He toyed with his spoon, trying to balance it on the rim of his bowl.

"I'll be back as soon as possible," said Henri. "Meanwhile, Albert goes on working at the shop. And this afternoon he signs you two up for school. It was all right working the way you did, but maybe we made a mistake not looking after you enough. Papa had plenty of worries, but he still thought about you. So you're going to do what he said and work hard at it. What do you say? All right?"

Maurice and I weren't very happy about the idea, but we couldn't possibly refuse.

"All right."

Ten minutes later, Henri left.

At noon, we made a superb omelette with my bacon. Albert never stopped praising me for the money and food I had brought home, but his heart wasn't in it.

At one-thirty we entered the courtyard of the school and Albert asked to see the principal.

He asked to see our school record books and I thought with relief how they must be slumbering peacefully under piles of other record books in the closet of the primary school on rue Ferdinand-Flocon, Paris, 18th *arrondissement*, more than a thousand kilometers away. With our arms folded across our chests, we waited for the end of that interminable discussion, secretly hoping that — without identity papers, without record books — it would be absolutely impossible to register for school. I didn't understand everything that was said, but the problems seemed absolutely insurmountable.

Finally, after a lot of beating around the bush, the principal, very obviously from the southern part of the country, with a huge watch that covered his wrist, a watch that particularly fascinated me, tilted his chair back and sighed asthmatically.

He looked Maurice and me over from head to foot, pegging us as potential troublemakers, and said: "All right, they can go to their new classes. I'll take them to their teachers."

Maurice gasped. So did I.

"Right away?" Maurice stuttered.

The principal frowned. For him, that question must have represented the first act of insubordination. Our obvious lack of enthusiasm was an unmistakable breach of discipline.

"Yes, of course right away," he said severely.

Albert felt sorry for us.

"I'll bring them here tomorrow — I've got to buy them school bags and notebooks."

The principal pursed his lips.

"And don't forget slates — they'll need them. The school supplies the books."

We left the office with a respectful "Goodbye, m'sieur." In the courtyard we heard the murmur of a voice making a recitation. I felt right at home.

Maurice was still angry.

"What a mean one! Did you see the way he wanted to yank us in right away, without giving us time to catch our breath?"

Albert laughed.

"I have a feeling that you'd better watch your step with him — he's got your number already."

Thanks to acquaintances he had made at the barbershop, Albert was able to get ration stamps for clothing and my last hope vanished: I found myself before a mirror in the fitting room of a tailor shop in the garb of infamy — a black school smock with fine red piping. Maurice got the same thing, only a size larger. Next came the school bag with pencil box and two notebooks. There was no getting out of it — we were all set for school.

Albert left us to see some friends and, after dropping off our purchases, we went down to the beach and sadly kicked our soccer ball. That wasn't much fun, so we chased each other over the huge rocks of the jetty as far as the esplanade in front of the casino. The building had been closed since the start of the war and the paint was beginning to peel off.

Maurice told me about his work as a baker; I explained to him how we made mortar on the farm and the system we used to wash thousands of bottles as fast as possible. There was something sad about it all.

Furthermore, without either of us speaking about it, we couldn't get the thought of our parents out of our minds. Papa wouldn't be coming in tonight or tomorrow night to tell stories of pogroms that could make our hair stand on end — he was actually going through one, the worst in history.

In the evening we made another omelette — this time with potatoes. Albert wanted us to go to bed early. At eight o'clock he turned out the lights, announcing, "Tomorrow it's off to school!"

I had trouble falling asleep. At that hour I would have been in my farmhouse playing chess with Monsieur Viale. No doubt about it — we couldn't be sure of anything anymore.

My schoolmaster turned out to be a schoolmistress. Pretty nearly all the men had gone to war — for the most part they were now prisoners, and the only teachers left were women or pensioners who had been rehired to teach the French youth of the Occupation years. Maurice got a very old gentleman with a goatee who had retired many years before and who tried — three hundred times a day — to impose silence on a wild mob of thirty-five pupils while spitballs flew from every side.

Every night my brother told stories that led me to believe that he was taking part in the riots. He made paper airplanes, began accumulating marbles again, and learned absolutely nothing.

I wasn't so lucky, but our schoolmistress was young — I thought she was pretty and nice and, without being aware of it, I worked fairly hard.

The Vichy government distributed a four o'clock snack of vitamin-enriched cookies which gave rise to an infinite number of complex dealings. First of all, the nurse assigned to the school arrived at the stroke of ten and handed out acidified, super-vitamin-enriched tablets and spoonfuls of cod-liver oil. At the same instant — all over

France, whether Occupied or not — all schoolchildren from six to fourteen years of age were swallowing the medicine with the same grimace.

As I was without candy, I used to swap four marbles for my neighbor's super-vitamin-enriched tablet, which he received because he weighed less than I did. Later I would win back my marbles at recess, for my aim grew better and better and the boys began to fear those Joffo brothers, who soon earned themselves a reputation as sharpshooters. That's something that always wins respect in a part of the country where bowling is the most popular sport.

Maurice tried every trick; he even lost ten games in a row just to show that he wasn't anything special, but despite that, he couldn't manage to attract any players.

I had met Virgilio again, and we became real pals. We used to stop in front of his house after school and we'd play jacks, a game he much preferred over marbles and which he played throughout the school year — something exceptional among schoolboys, who love to change games with the changing months and seasons.

The days went by — things weren't as bad as I expected, but we still had no word from my brother.

Every evening — for at noon we ate at the school lunchroom — I would look into the old mailbox hung askew on the door, but there wasn't the slightest trace of a letter, despite the fact that Henri had been away for a week.

Albert grew increasingly nervous — he showed it in many ways. He'd smoke ten days' ration of cigarettes in two days and I sensed that he was worrying himself sick.

Determined to stick to the rule that there's always

something to be tried even when it seems as if there's nothing left to do, he announced one evening that if we didn't receive any news by Monday morning (it was now Thursday) he would leave that night. He would provide us with money and we would get by. If he failed to return after nine or ten days, we would have to leave Menton and go to a village in the Central Massif where one of our older married sisters had been in hiding for a longer time than we had.

"Do you understand?"

I only understood that we'd split up, gotten together again, and that we were splitting up all over again. There was no end to it all.

The lamp cast an exact circle on the table and our three faces were in shadows.

I hadn't finished my homework, and I pushed my plate away to make room for my geography book. I had a lesson to learn on water power and had to memorize the summary for the next morning.

Maurice got to his feet without a word and stacked the plates in the sink; it was his turn to do the dishes.

Just as he turned on the faucet, a key rattled in the lock and there was Henri, beaming. Albert grew pale.

"Well?"

"They're free."

There hadn't been any interval between question and answer. Henri put down his suitcase and removed his tie like the hero of a detective novel. He sniffed the air — he could still smell the omelette.

"You fellows have a good time while I chase all over France looking for Mama and Papa."

We still had one egg left over and Albert cooked it

while Henri began to tell his story. He had taken off his shoes and was wiggling his toes with relief.

The story kept us listening for the rest of the evening; that was one time we went to bed very late.

As soon as he reached Pau, Henri had learned about the location of the camp, which he was able to find easily. The municipal stadium was being used to confine Jewish families. They came in by the thousands. Tents sheltered the internees, policemen guarded them. No visitors were allowed to enter; an audience with the commandant of the camp had to be obtained, and these were hardly ever granted. This decision was also based on economic considerations, as the influx of newcomers might seriously upset the prices of foodstuffs in the city. Two hundred meters from the entrance stood a bar where the *gendarmes* came before going on guard duty. There they drank cups of black coffee into which the proprietor poured a stiff jigger of clear brandy for an extra banknote exchanged under the guise of a handshake.

Not knowing where to turn, Henri had a drink at the bar and managed to strike up a conversation with a *gendarme* who advised him to take the next train out of Pau. Henri said that his parents had been arrested by mistake, that they were ordinary folk, that they had never engaged in politics and weren't Jewish, and that his father was just coming to Menton to help him cut hair in the barbershop where he was employed. The *gendarme* sympathized with him. He went out of the café and Henri was also about to leave when the *gendarme* came back with a sergeant who handed him a pair of scissors.

"Do you think you could give me a little trim? I'm on duty and don't have the time to go into Pau. The captain is rough on long hair and I wouldn't want to lose my furlough. François told me you were a barber . . ."

They wound up in the back of the bar. The sergeant had a towel around his neck. Henri, with a scissors and razor borrowed from the proprietor and water from the percolator, gave him the best haircut of his life.

Everyone was delighted. Henri wouldn't accept any money, but he asked the sergeant to speak with the colonel commanding the camp and arrange an audience.

The sergeant hesitated for a second, but finally said, "I can't promise anything, but be at the gate tomorrow morning at ten o'clock and I'll see what I can do."

Henri left his name and spent the night in a nearby hotel — which, he added, was full of cockroaches.

At ten o'clock he appeared at the sentry box. The first time, the sentinels ordered him away; but he came right back, although he knew that he might be imprisoned too. Finally he caught sight of the sergeant from the night before, walking slowly down the center lane between the barracks, each of which bore a huge number painted with tar.

The sergeant had him admitted and led him toward a stone building away from the others. On the way, he told him, "He's willing to see you — but watch out. He's a tough one. He's always pretty mean, but today he's even worse."

Henri thanked him, knocked on the door, entered a first office, where he had to wait for ten minutes, then a second one where a man with an iron-gray mustache, aquiline nose, and bald pate didn't give him time to speak. His message was short and unequivocal.

"Henri Joffo, make it brief and don't forget that, in coming here, you're risking your own freedom and have no certainty of obtaining your parents' release. You doubtless know that we are under orders to turn over all foreign Jews to the authorities of the Occupation."

"But Colonel . . ."

It wasn't going to be easy to get anywhere with him and Henri saw this at once.

"I don't make any exceptions to the rule. I've got at least six hundred suspects here and if I released a single one of them without proper evidence, I might just as well let them all go."

Henri wouldn't give up. It was hard for him to tell this part of the story.

"Colonel, I'm French. I was at Dunkerque, in Flanders, in the Belgian campaign. If I've come here, it isn't to beg for favors or ask you to make an exception, which it would be your duty to refuse — I've come here to tell you that there's been a mistake: nobody in our family is Jewish."

The Colonel's face twitched slightly and he immediately demanded proof. Henri described it all so carefully that I sometimes wonder if I hadn't actually been present when it took place and if I hadn't really seen that man, a career officer — hard, but honest — who seemed to regard favorably Henri's military bearing.

"First of all, anyone can see that my mother is Catholic. You've got her identity papers. Her maiden name is Markoff. I defy anyone to show me a single Russian Jew with the name Markoff. Besides, the Markoffs are direct descendants of the junior branch of the Romanoffs and, therefore, the imperial family. We're still related to them on my mother's side."

Henri didn't stop there.

"I doubt that anyone who knows anything about that period in the history of Czarist Russia would believe that a member of the imperial family could be Jewish — that would have brought all the churches of Orthodox Russia tumbling down."

"What about your father?"

That was the biggest bluff of all.

"As you know, Colonel, all Jewish people have been stripped of their French citizenship by the German authorities. Now, my father is French, just as it's stated in his papers — the ones that you have. If he's French, he can't be Jewish: there's no in-between. To make absolutely certain, just call police headquarters in Paris."

We were hanging on the words of Henri, who was smoking up all of Albert's cigarettes. He dug shamelessly into the pack that had been left on the table. At any other time, the rightful owner would have screamed at the top of his lungs; now he didn't even pay attention.

"I took a big gamble," Henri commented, "but I had a hunch that he would give in, that he wasn't going to risk spending hours on the phone. I thought my arguments had been so solid that he wouldn't bother to dig any deeper. He didn't strike me as particularly keen on hunting Jews; something told me that this prison-guard role disgusted him and that he would release two people if he had grounds for doing so — grounds that he felt warranted such a release. His response wasn't long in coming. He picked up the telephone before I'd even finished the sentence."

Henri mimed the scene, gluing his ear to an imaginary receiver.

"Give me Paris police headquarters. Identity Verification Department."

He assumed his normal voice again and admitted, "It was hard to keep looking sure of myself. I even had to put on this satisfied look — like a guy who's finally going to have his story backed up. Because the whole time he was waiting for the call, he never took his eyes off me; if he'd spotted the slightest sign of uneasiness, he would have made up his mind about me, and I might as well have started walking over to the compound with the new prisoners."

He took another drag on his cigarette and crushed it out in the saucer that doubled for an ashtray; the smoke made my eyes smart.

"While we were waiting, I still had one hope — that his call wouldn't go through, that between Pau and Paris there would be some snag, a short circuit, some switchboard operators who'd forgotten to throw a switch, something like that. Those were the kinds of things I prayed for. And even if the call went through to Paris, I figured that it must be impossible to supply information like that. I imagined rows of file cabinets stretching as far as the eye could see, with dusty dossiers — by the ton — in these manila file folders, so that nobody could ever give out any information . . . We went on waiting and I breathed more easily as the seconds went by. The moment was coming when he would get tired of wasting his time, and would slam the receiver down; he would fume about the incompetence of the department and the case would be closed."

That wasn't what happened. I saw the scene perfectly; in my mind, I could hear the voices — Henri's, the hard, dry

voice of the Colonel and then a far-off nasal twang at the
end of the line, a voice sometimes drowned out by the
static, a voice that would spell life or death.

"Hello, Identity Verification Department?"

" . . . "

"Colonel T. from the transit camp at Pau. I'd like information on a person named Joffo. J as in Joy; Joffo with a
double F, residing at twelve, rue Clignancourt. Occupation, barber. Has he been stripped of French citizenship?"

" . . . "

"His son is right here in front of me and . . ."

" . . . "

"The mother isn't Jewish; he claims that the father isn't
either."

" . . . "

"All right, I'll hold on."

In later years, when people have made phone calls in
my presence, I've often noted the detached way that they
glance at the person in front of them. They no longer
consider you as a partner to the conversation — their
mind is elsewhere. They look at you as if they were staring at a stone, a chair, some inanimate object that surprises them by its presence and form. That's the way the
commandant of the camp must have glanced at my
brother that day.

"Yes, still here."

" . . . "

"Joffo, that's right. Twelve, rue Clignancourt."

" . . . "

"Yes, very well."

" . . . "

"Fine, thank you."

The Colonel hung up. He looked at Henri, who nonchalantly crossed his legs and gazed out at the sky with a detached air.

The Colonel got to his feet.

"Quite so. Your father hasn't been stripped of French citizenship. I'm going to order his release, and your mother's as well."

Henri rose and bowed.

"Thank you, sir."

Half an hour later, the three of them were together. Henri embraced them, took the two suitcases, and they walked toward the bus stop. They didn't give vent to their emotions until they were safely locked in a hotel room.

It was Albert's turn to snatch a cigarette.

"How are they?"

"All right. They had already resigned themselves to the fact that arrest meant deportation. They're a little thinner, of course — and did they ever sleep! They were tickled when I told them that you were with us. They sent you kisses."

"Where are Mama and Papa?"

"In Nice. We're not going to see them yet. They need a little time to get settled. As soon as they're ready, they'll let us know and then we'll go see them."

I broke in.

"How come the guy at police headquarters said Papa wasn't Jewish?"

Henri grew serious again.

"I thought about that a lot. Papa and I talked it over, too. There are several possible explanations.

"First of all, the loss of citizenship might not have been recorded yet . . . some delay in the paperwork . . . an oversight. Any one of these things could happen. Or else . . ."

I saw him hesitate.

"Or else the guy answered the first thing that came into his head because he couldn't find the dossier — or maybe he did it on purpose."

There was a silence that Albert broke.

"I don't go along with that," he said slowly. "The people at police headquarters in charge of registration are hand-picked, and I'd be astounded if there was a champion of the underdog who'd risk his job and his neck to save people he doesn't know. No, as far as I'm concerned, I go along with the first explanation: there was a delay in the paperwork, that's all."

We went on pondering.

"We'll never know why," Maurice said. "But that doesn't matter — the main thing is that everything turned out the way it did."

I had an idea that kept going through my mind. I said timidly, "There might be another reason."

Henri threw me a mocking glance.

"Watch out," he said. "The great detective, Joseph Joffo, is about to reveal the secret of the mystery. Go ahead, fellow. We're listening."

"Maybe it was the Colonel."

They looked at me without understanding.

"Go ahead," said Albert, "explain what you mean."

"I just mean that maybe they did tell him over the phone that Papa was Jewish and he said what he did because he wanted to let them go."

They went on looking at me, but now they wore a different expression. They seemed to be trying to uncover a secret that lay behind my eyes. I began to feel embarrassed by the intensity of their stares.

Henri was the first to reply.

"Well now, fellow," he murmured, "you certainly have given us something to think about."

Albert roused himself and looked at Henri.

"Do you think that guy could have done you a favor like that? Do you think it's possible with what he was? I mean, with his responsibilities, his character?"

Henri leaned his elbows on his knees and seemed lost in contemplating the red tiles covering the kitchen floor.

"I don't know," he finally said. "Frankly, I don't think so. I can't imagine it . . . He looked like a man that went by the book. Didn't the sergeant say that he was very tough and very strict? . . . I don't know . . . It could be . . . You can never know really.

"Jo," he said to me, "if you can't make up your mind about what to do one of these days, you can always earn a living by writing detective stories."

I was very pleased with myself and went to bed feeling absolutely certain that I had found the solution: a hero who hid his generosity under a stern, grumpy mask. That sure sounded better than some file clerk's oversight. Yes, that *must* be how my parents' lives were saved.

Four days after Henri's return, we received the first letter from Nice. Papa was doing all right. He found an apartment in a section that was a bit out of the way, near the church of La Buffa. He had rented two rooms on the floor above and had already got the lay of the land: it would be easy for Albert and Henri to find work in a barbershop there. Of course, he would work too. The season was drawing near — there would be lots of people. Rather bitterly, Papa's letter informed us that, despite the "misfortunes that had swept down upon France," the grand hotels, the casino, and the night clubs were all jammed to the rafters and that, without any doubt, the war was something that existed only for the poor. He closed his letter by asking us to wait a bit longer. He thought that within a month or two we could come there. Then we would all be together again as we used to be in Paris.

Personally, I thought that "a month or two" was much too vague and terribly far off. I was in a hurry to see them again and I also wanted to see that great city, so full of people and palatial hotels. The very name "Nice" set me dreaming; my child's mind confused the great hotels with palaces and I saw Nice as an agglomeration of columns, domes, and sumptuous halls frequented by women bedecked with jewels and furs, smoking long cigarettes in even longer cigarette-holders.

But before going there, I had to go on washing the dishes one evening out of four, do the shopping, my homework, go to school where examinations were coming up — and I was really worried about the one in geometry.

Happily enough, there were soccer games on the beach, matches of jacks with Virgilio, and the movies on Sunday afternoons when our elder brothers gave us permission.

Two more weeks went by. I got a passing mark in composition — which Maurice considered mediocre. That meant another fight. We gave each other a real hiding on the Place Saint-Michel, heedless of the jeers of the townswomen who leaned their elbows on their windowsills.

Good weather set in. The days began growing warmer and the trees in the gardens of the villas were covered with buds and leaves.

The moment when we could swim was drawing near and, so as not to waste any time, we went to buy bathing suits one day after school. Maurice bought a blue one with white stripes: mine was white with blue stripes. Each of us was convinced that he had the best-looking suit. I tried mine on that very evening after supper and did some spectacular somersaults on the bed under the contemptuous gaze of Maurice, who was drying the dishes.

Just then somebody knocked on the door.

That was a frequent occurrence — pals of Albert or Henri came around from time to time; they used to joke with us and my two brothers would go out to play billiards or give a haircut in someone's home.

There were two policemen there.

"Yes, can I help you?"

The smaller one rummaged in his briefcase and pulled out a sheet of paper that I thought he would never finish unfolding.

"Albert and Henri Joffo? Is this the place?"

"I'm Albert, but my brother isn't in."

Albert sure had good reflexes. If they were planning to arrest them, Henri would have a chance of getting away. Henri understood and I saw him back silently toward the bedroom where he waited, ready to slide under the bed.

I was sure the worst had come: they must have picked up the mistake made by Paris and now the commandant of the camp had given the alarm. Now we were going to catch hell. We should have moved as soon as Henri came back. Clearly, we'd been careless.

"What's it all about?"

"Do you have your identity card?"

"Yes, just one second."

Albert went in, took his wallet from the inside pocket of his jacket which hung over the back of a chair. He exchanged a brief glance with us which meant: "Take it easy — we've still got a chance."

Maurice kept on drying the same plate, polishing it with a regular movement of his towel. As for me, I was still in my bathing suit, standing on my bed.

"Here you are."

There was a rustling of wrinkled papers and I heard the *gendarme* say, "Here are two orders to appear, for you and your brother. You've got to report to police headquarters within two days. Tomorrow would be best."

Albert cleared his throat.

"What's it all about?"

"It's for the S.T.O."*

There was a short silence and the one who still hadn't spoken said, "Everybody's being taken, you know . . ."

"Sure," said Albert.

The same policeman replied, "We just bring the orders — we don't write them."

"Sure."

"Well, that's about it," concluded the other. "Good night. Sorry to have bothered you."

"No harm done. Goodnight."

---

* *Service de travail obligatoire.* Under this program, Frenchmen were drafted for work in German war industries. *Translator.*

136

The door closed again and my heart began beating normally.

Albert came back in; Henri emerged from the bedroom.

"What's the S.T.O.?" asked Maurice.

With a taut smile, Henri answered, "That means we're going to Germany to give haircuts to the Fritzes. At least, that's what they think."

I looked at them in horror. Our peace hadn't lasted very long.

Finally, I sat down and listened to what they were saying. Their council of war was brief for the simple reason that their course of action was clear. They weren't going to be taken to Germany. By the same token, they couldn't stay in Menton where the police would certainly come back.

Henri glanced around him at the little Provençal dining room. I could see that he was fond of this place; we had all grown accustomed to living there and we would miss it.

"Okay, it's very simple — we're getting out of here."

"When?" asked Maurice.

"Tomorrow morning. We're going to pack fast, right away, and we beat it tomorrow at dawn. No sense hanging around here."

"Where are we going?"

Albert turned to me with the look of somebody who's about to announce a pleasant surprise or hand you a present.

"You'll like this, Jo. We're going to Nice."

I was pleased about our destination, but I had trouble falling asleep. We only realize that we've become attached to things when we go away. I would miss the

school, the old streets, my pal Virgilio, even the schoolmistress, but I didn't feel sad. I would be on the road
again, I'd sling my knapsack on my back once more and
tomorrow I'd reach the city of a hundred thousand grand
hotels, the city of gold at the edge of the blue sea.

VII

"MARCELLO! MARCELLO!"

I rush after Maurice, who crosses the Place Massena diagonally. I try to keep up, but it's hard to run with a wicker basket on each arm — especially when they're full of tomatoes. The one on my left arm is full of the oval-shaped ones called *olivettes;* on the right are little round tomatoes, the ones I like best and that the local people call "love apples." Four kilos of each; that's eight kilos in all, and it makes a heavy load.

The soldier in front of us has stopped. The sun lights up his face. He laughs to see me running all loaded down. If he didn't have a splendid broken nose and curly hair glossy with brilliantine, he would resemble Amedeo Nazzari, the movie actor. But Marcello had gone too many evenings in the ring of a boxing club in Torino to keep a Grecian profile.

"*Bene,* give me the tomatoes."

He speaks French well, almost correctly, but his accent is catastrophic. He's almost always laughing.

"Follow me, we're going to Tite's."

Tite's is a bistro near the harbor where we often get together. It's a kind of trading post for local pensioners and, most of all, for Italian soldiers. They are Marcello's friends and they sing opera and play the guitar before going on a very relaxed kind of guard duty in the strategic points of Nice.

Here we are. It's a tiny café. Old Madame Rosso leaves the kitchen door open, so the place smells of onions twenty-four hours a day.

Marcello's friends are there — three soldiers who throw open their arms to welcome us. I know them all: there's a tall student from Rome with glasses, who looks more like an Englishman and imitates Benjamino Gigli in *Tosca;* a Parmesan carpenter (before meeting him I thought that all Parmesans had to be cheeses), and a Venetian corporal older than the rest. He had worked in the post office before the war and his buddies call him "the mailman." That fellow is my friend; we often play checkers together.

Triumphantly Marcello moves aside the glasses of white wine on the oilcloth and sets down the two baskets of tomatoes.

"Here's your bargain."

They jabber away together playfully, and Carlo (he's the student from Rome) offers us the liter of olive oil that was hidden behind the bar.

Through the absurdity of the Italian Quartermaster Corps, the various mess halls for the occupying troops were inundated with olive oil in every form. Without letup they received truckloads of tuna in oil, sardines in oil, olive oil in liter cans.

The complaints of the mess officers went unheeded: the

oil kept coming in. The Italians finally got it through their heads that they could use the oil as a valuable commodity for trading purposes. Through a barter system, they obtained vegetables, tomatoes, and lettuce so they could eat something besides their eternal canned fish.

Marcello had talked to us about it. We'd got in touch with a truck farmer who sold his produce near the flower market. He gave us tomatoes; we supplied him with Italian oil, for which he paid us in cash. With that money and packs of cigarettes that my corporal friend used to slip us after pilfering them from the base commissary, we would buy black market rice — which, in turn, was exchanged for sacks of flour that we used to deliver to Tite's café, where the Parmesan, using old Madame Rosso's kitchen, would manufacture a broad pasta. We collected a rebate on that with which we would buy more tomatoes, and, in the two months that this trafficking went on, Maurice and I amassed a secret hoard, one that grew from day to day.

When going past the Negresco and the Ruhl hotels, Maurice nodded at their sumptuous façades and said, rubbing his hands:

"If things keep going the way they're going, we'll buy one of those places."

Life was sweet.

The corporal strokes his short beard and lays his hand flat on the checkerboard.

"What do you say — a game of checkers, bambino?"

I don't have time. It's already eleven o'clock and I've got to bring oil to the truck farmer who's been waiting for me for half an hour.

Marcello is slicing the *olivettes* into a huge salad bowl.

"What you have to do is bring back some little herbs to put in — you know, very green things . . . I don't know how you say it in French . . ."

"Parsley."

"Yes, that's it. Parsley."

I trade glances with Maurice. That's a tall order. The butcher near the docks must carry parsley. I know him casually. He's a smoker.

I turn to the mailman.

"Can you get me two packs for this afternoon?"

"*Si, ma* you gotta come for them. Four o'clock."

"*Va bene.*"

For two packs of cigarettes, I'll get a knapsack full of parsley, a quarter pound of steak, and a tip, if my approach is right.

"*E lucevan le stelle . . .*" Carlo croaks an aria from *Tosca* while stirring the vinaigrette sauce.

I gulp down a glass of *grenadine* paid for by a soldier of the Occupation, and then I go out with Maurice.

The sun is beating down and we cross to the shady side of the street.

"I've got to go up to the barracks," Maurice says. "One of Marcello's pals up there has real coffee, and what he wants is shaving cream."

"You know where to get some?"

Maurice ponders the question. He has turned into a living directory. In times of rationing, he knows where to find butter, eggs, neckties, and, no doubt, shaving cream.

"I think the owner of the hardware store on the rue Garibaldi has some in stock. You know him, right? He's the one who sold us those two kilos of lentils."

He sighs, then mops his brow.

"I'm going to go there. You'll take care of the parsley?"

"Yes. We'll meet back at the house, right?"

"All right. We'd really save time if we had a bike."

That's our old dream. But finding a bicycle isn't as easy as finding eight kilos of tomatoes. And it's not just a matter of finding the bike. There are also the tires to be had, and they cost an arm and a leg — five cartons of cigarettes, ten for a pair of tires, and then they aren't always new ones. A bike would save us time and, above all, save our espadrilles, for the rope-soled shoes don't last long with all the walking we do around Nice.

Anyhow, I don't have a thing to do until one o'clock. I'll have lunch and then go to Tite's to pick up the empty baskets; get the cigarettes at Tite's, carry the baskets into the Old Town, try to get parsley on the rue Garibaldi and come back to the harbor. There'll be plenty to do this afternoon, but from now till then, I'll take a stroll along the Promenade.

The beach is mobbed. It's really crowded in front of the hotels. Lots of Italian officers sitting in the shade of umbrellas at sidewalk cafés. Their uniforms gleam red in the sunlight. What a pleasant kind of war they've got! There are women sitting with them, very elegant ones wearing the kind of dresses that you can't get with ration stamps for clothing. Those are the women that come in to have their hair done by Henri and Albert in the beauty parlor across from the Hôtel Adriatique.

My brothers sure have gone up in the world! They don't work in some dinky little barbershop anymore, like the ones on the rue de Clignancourt or the rue de Paris in Menton. This one is a fancy salon, the most popular in Nice, and Henri and Albert often make house calls for hair-styling in some luxurious apartment or in a suite at the Majestic or the Negresco.

Papa and Mama have settled themselves in their apartment and, if it weren't for the ritual of listening to Radio London each night, I'd swear we were spending a pleasant summer on the Côte d'Azur. For it's our summer holiday — the whole month of August and my dream has almost come true: I'm free in that gleaming, gilded city where money seems easy to come by, where all the deck chairs on the Promenade des Anglais are taken by a crowd of people who protect their faces from the burning sun by covering them with newspapers.

The Nice newspaper is a curious one. It never stops proclaiming German victories. Over there, on the Russian front, the Panzers keep moving ahead; they have reached a town called Stalingrad, which will soon be in their hands.

On the evening radio, despite the jamming of the wave lengths, I also hear plenty about Stalingrad, but this news isn't the same. We hear that lots of Germans have died during the winter, that the treads of the tanks skid helplessly in the mud, and that all armored vehicles are stuck, useless.

So what are you to believe? At night, as I go to bed, I think that the Germans are going to lose — they're really beaten this time. I fall asleep with high hopes. Then, the next morning, at the newsstand on the rue Carnot, I read the headlines and see photos of blockhouses with officers wearing swastika armbands; their faces exude pride and confidence. The dispatches assure me that the Russian front has cracked; that the impregnable Atlantic Wall has ruled out all hope of an Allied landing.

I often talked it over with Maurice on the beach. But it was hard to imagine fields of snow or mud, the night sky full of machine-gun fire and planes, while we were swimming deliciously in a warm, transparent sea. So hard, indeed, that I couldn't believe in the reality of that war anymore; it seemed impossible that elsewhere there could be cold, combat, death.

A dark spot loomed up on the horizon: September.

September would mean going back to school. There was one right near our house on the rue Dante and I went past it every morning before starting my day's roaming. I quickened my pace so as not to see the white lines painted at the back of a narrow courtyard darkly shaded by the leaves of six enormous plane trees.

I leave the seashore and plunge into the town. There's the church, another twenty yards and I'm home.

"That you, Joseph?"

The sizzling of frying fish drowns out my mother's voice.

"Yes."

"Go wash up before you sit down to eat. Is Maurice with you?"

I begin to soap myself with some kind of greenish putty that slips through my fingers without producing any suds at all.

"No, but he's coming. He went to the hardware store on the rue Garibaldi to get shaving cream."

Papa comes in. His hand tousles my hair. He's in a good mood.

"You two and your business deals . . ."

I knew he was really pleased that we could fend for

ourselves. A little further up the street lived two kids about our age. From time to time, the two families invited each other over, but I couldn't stand those two boys. One of them was stuck-up as can be, and Maurice gave the older one a beautiful sock on the jaw — an act that got him confined to the house for twenty-four hours and won him my boundless admiration. Papa's main argument for excusing our wanderings through Nice was to tell Mama: "Would you rather have children like the V——'s?"

She would remain silent a moment, nod with the look of a person who hasn't been convinced in the least, and retort: "You'd better not forget that we're in an occupied country. These Italians may be nice, but the day may come when . . ."

Then did Maurice and I ever speak up.

"The Italians? We know all of them!"

Papa laughed, asking us how much money we had in our piggy bank. He shared our delight over its flourishing health and one day I overheard him saying to my mother, "You don't know they plan to buy the Hôtel Negresco? But the funny part is that sometimes I wonder if they won't actually do it!"

Much later I realized that though he worried about us, and often looked at his watch when we were late, he understood that we were learning about life, that this unique experience must not be spoiled. He knew that we were learning more about life by lugging those liters of oil, sacks of lentils, or packs of cigarettes up and down the dockside streets and the Old Town than we could ever learn in a classroom or by loafing on the beach like two Parisians on vacation.

I gulped down the meal, drank the prune juice right

from the dish, and got out of my seat at the same time as my brother.

"Now where are you headed?"

Maurice began to launch into a complicated explanation. The hardware store man that he had been to see had sold out all his shaving cream, but could get some more in exchange for resoling leather shoes. For that, we had to convince the shoemaker on the rue Saint-Pierre to exchange his services for one or two liters of oil that remained the basic standard of all our trading.

Hearing us, Papa raised his head over the top of his newspaper.

"Speaking of shoemakers, I'd like to tell you a story."

A story — the only thing that could cool our fervor.

"Well, it's that once one man said to another: 'There's a very simple way to get all men to live in peace — you've got to kill all the Jews and all the shoemakers.' The other man looks at him in surprise and, after a moment's reflection, asks: 'But why the shoemakers?' "

Papa looked at us.

There was a rather surprised silence; then Mama began laughing.

I asked, "Why the Jews, too?"

Papa smiled bitterly and, before going back to his newspaper, told me: "That's just what the other man should have asked and that's why the story is funny."

We came out of the house, wrapped in thought. The sun beat down on the cobblestones of the town. Nice was taking its siesta; for us that was out of the question.

On the square we went past the changing of the guard. The soldiers were sweating in their uniforms; they had their rifles over their shoulders. So did the last one in the column, but there was also a mandolin in his free hand.

Yes, the war was indeed far away.

The courtyard is gray and gleams in the rain. It's getting cold already, and the teacher lights the pot-bellied stove in the classroom each morning.

From time to time as I struggle with a geometry problem or drive myself crazy over a map of the rivers (I get the Garonne and the Rhone all right, but the Seine and the Loire keep bumping into each other in my notebooks), the teacher gets to his feet, pokes around in the cast-iron stove, and then a more intense wave of heat envelops us. The stovepipe runs the whole length of the classroom and is hung from the ceiling with baling wire. The ceiling is dotted with spitballs. They're made of blotting paper that we've patiently chewed. Soaked with saliva, the spitballs dry out up there into hard, flattened pellets that come unstuck after a day or two, making us laugh.

In a din of scuffling and the creaking of seats, we stand up. The principal has just come in. He motions us to be seated. He's a skinny man with trousers belted somewhere over his chest. He comes in once a week to give us singing lessons. Behind him, two pupils from an upper grade carry in a harmonium and set it on the desk. It's an instrument like a little piano with a lever on the sides, and out comes a squealing sound, one that's awfully unpleasant.

The principal looks at us.

"We're going to see if you've learned anything. Camerini, go to the board. Make me a stave and a nice G clef."

The lesson begins. I'm not very talented and I mix up the notes: I recognize the ones on the bottom, but as soon as the black or white notes go above the "A" line, I begin to get all mixed up.

"Now we're going to practice our song, and I hope you're going to put some feeling into it. To help you recall the words, I'm going to ask François to sing it alone once."

Without a doubt, François is the worst boy in the school; his hands are one big ink spot right up to the wrists; his eyes tell you that he doesn't care about anything or anyone; he rarely leaves school with the rest of us, for he's almost always kept in, and if he had ever managed to reach the main entrance by four-thirty he would have been the most surprised of all.

Despite all this, François is the principal's pet because François has a wonderful voice. This lord of the rowdies, this shooter of rubber bands, this holder of records for the greatest number of hours kept in had the most beautiful soprano voice that I've ever heard; when he sang in the courtyard it made me forget my soccer match. He readily exploited his talent, singing for us in exchange for penholders, licorice twists, and other gifts.

"Go ahead, François. We're listening."

Amid total silence, the pure voice of François is heard.

"Allons, enfants de la patrie . . ."

We listen to him with admiration; we wish it would last forever, but his voice is stilled.

The principal raises his hands like the leader of an orchestra.

"All right now, all together this time."

We sing all of *La Marseillaise* with great feeling; we know that it isn't just a singing lesson. Through these words the school is trying to communicate to us.

When I told him, Papa was full of admiration that they made us sing things like that. A parent of one of the pupils might complain to the authorities and get the principal in trouble . . . At the time, I didn't know that he wasn't afraid of getting into trouble. That skinny man with his trousers belted too high was a *Résistance* leader in the province.

Four-thirty.

Outside, the rain has stopped.

The principal motions to the two biggest boys in the class.

"Take the harmonium back into my office."

His eyes search me out and he adds, "Joffo, make sure you tear another page off the calendar tomorrow morning. If you forget, I'll give the assignment to another pupil."

"Yes, sir."

I look at the calendar over the desk: November 8.

The eighth of November is an important day. It's Mama's birthday; she'll bake a cake. She'll have presents, too. Maurice has agreed to loosen the purse-strings on our savings to buy her a gold brooch shaped like a seahorse with red stones for eyes.

Since school has started again, business has slacked off — first of all because we have less free time, then because it isn't the tomato season anymore. I know that there are real killings to be made right now in wine. There are triangular exchanges: wine-gasoline-cigarettes, but that's way beyond our means. We went on making a little money in September by selling chocolate bars but since then we haven't run into any bargains and grown-up competition is driving us to more and more paltry dealings. The Italian Quartermaster Corps finally realized its error and stopped flooding the garrisons on the Côte d'Azur with truckloads of oil. This eliminated the main item of barter and made trading more precarious.

We still went to Tite's sometimes, and I would play checkers with the mailman. Carlos was still singing and, after a few glasses of white wine, Marcello would tirelessly act out the last bout he had fought in Cologne. He had opposed a welterweight from Ferrara who was counted out on his feet in the eighth round.

Marcello mopped his brow after acting out the bout and, like all soldiers everywhere, showed his fiancée's photo, asking me for approval.

"*È bella*, Giuseppe?"

While savoring my *grenadine* I squinted at the hazy print, trying to pass myself off as a real connoisseur. The worn photo showed a smiling girl with fair hair — that surprised me, for I thought all Italian girls were dark-haired.

"Very beautiful, Marcello, very beautiful."

Delighted, Marcello burst out laughing and gave me a wallop that nearly knocked me to the floor.

"She's a witch, Giuseppe, a witch. You don't know anything about women, *niente, niente.*"

I was choking; everybody in the bar was laughing at me.

"Then why is she your fiancée?"

Marcello split his sides laughing.

"Because the papa owns the gym, *capito? Molte lire,* lots and lots . . ."

I nodded, heartbroken that Marcello could marry for money, something which seemed completely improper to me, and heartbroken to learn that I knew nothing about women.

Seeing my crestfallen expression, Marcello seized me by the shoulders and then asked old Rosso to give me another glass of *grenadine,* which cheered me up right away.

Mama was enthusiastic about her presents. She immediately pinned the seahorse on her dress and kissed us. Then Mama kissed Papa who, together with my brothers, had given her a Singer sewing-machine. For those days, it was a priceless possession. Henceforth, she would be able to make many more things and not have to tug her needle for long hours before the window. We watched with admiration as she demonstrated the new machine on a scrap of material. It worked very well. It was a machine that you operated by pressing your feet on an iron treadle.

"It's really a present worthy of a Romanoff," Henri commented.

The joke was worn out but we still thought it funny. A good many years before, a poor Jewish woman who became our Mama had gotten out of her country by using forged papers, ones which she had kept and which had saved her life only a short time ago, when she was arrested in Pau.

She slipped out of the room and came back with the cake, a kind of *Kuglof* that even had the traditional almond on top.

Papa swallowed the first mouthful and got up. It was time for the British broadcast. Since we had come to Nice, he had never missed a single evening.

"You tell us the news," said Henri. "I don't have the will power to leave my dessert."

Papa nodded and, while we talked, I saw him glue his ear to the speaker and tune the knobs.

Albert was telling about an annoying customer who claimed that Hitler was actually an intelligent and exceptional being, since he'd not only risen to power in his own country, but in all Europe as well. Just then Papa came back, a little pale.

"They've landed," he announced.

We stared at him, our mouths stuffed with cake.

He leaned toward my mother and took her hands.

"Happy birthday," he said. "The Allies have landed in North Africa, in Algeria and Morocco. This time, it's the beginning of the end. With a new front on their hands, the Germans are finished."

Maurice sprang up from his chair and went for the atlas in our parents' room. We bent over the map of North Africa.

I gauged the distances: from Algiers to Nice, there were only a few centimeters of blue paper, just the sea to cross and they'd be here; we had nothing to fear now.

Henri pondered the situation, knitting his brows. He was the family strategist. His fingernail covered Tunisia.

"I don't understand why they haven't landed there, as well. I'll bet my shirt that the Italians and Germans, bolstered by the Afrika Korps, are about to occupy Tunisia. In my opinion, it's a mistake."

"You ought to call up Eisenhower," remarked Albert.

"At any rate," Papa murmured, "it's a decisive step, and mark my words, this looks very much like the defeat of the Axis. Well, the beginning of it, at least."

I finished the birthday cake, my head full of visions. I saw soldiers with rifles in their hands running past camels and white towns, while the Germans fled, their legs sinking in the desert sand.

From that evening on, there was a ceremony that I suppose most French families observed in those days. On a map of the world hung on the wall, we stuck little flags linked together with yarn. The little flags were straight pins to which we glued a small rectangle of paper. We carried detail to the point of painting these rectangles red for the Russians and making white stripes with one little star in the left corner for the Americans. Radio London reeled off names that we copied down at top speed; on the newly won towns, we planted the flags of victory.

Once Stalingrad had been retaken, there was Kharkov, then Rostov. I felt like sticking up a flag over Kiev to speed things up a bit, but it took a long time to liberate that city.

There was also Africa to take care of, and that gave us trouble. A great battle was taking place at El Alamein, but it was impossible to find El Alamein on the map. I cursed the makers of maps who couldn't foresee the sites of the great events in history. But what really thrilled me was July 10, 1943 — the Allied landing in Sicily.

I remember it all very clearly. There were only three days of school left. Since the vacation would begin on the evening of July 13, we weren't doing much work anymore. From the beginning of the week, the recess time grew longer and longer until, finally, it exceeded actual class time. Oh, the weather was so beautiful then! The winter had been hard for the region, the spring late in coming, and then, all of a sudden, summer came. We were keyed up to the limit. Everything was happening at once: the sun, the vacation, and the Allies. We were out of control.

Each time a pupil knocked at the door to ask for information or the lunchroom menu or a piece of chalk or a geography chart, half the class jumped to their feet shouting: "It's the Americans!"

In the streets the Italians strolled imperturbably, as if all those events had nothing to do with them. The uniforms of officers had begun making their appearance again at sidewalk cafés. Girls even prettier and more tanned than the year before accompanied them once again. As I went past, I dreamt of being one of those handsome soldiers with glossy boots lounging in comfortable rattan armchairs.

With the good weather the tomatoes came back, and we resumed our operations. Through a pal from school, I was able to get a bicycle. It was a bit small for me and my knees bumped against the handlebars but, by sitting all the way at the back of the seat, I could manage. Behind the church of La Buffa, in a niche in the wall that we used for a workshop, we tied a small basket to the bike with baling wire. That made an excellent carrying rack. Then we were ready — our bank would soon be getting fatter.

On the last day of school, prizes were distributed. Books were virtually impossible to obtain so they gave out certificates instead. Having grown a head taller and fast becoming a muscle-man, Maurice won a prize in gymnastics. I got one in reading and came home proud as a peacock. I had a sunny future: two and a half months of freedom, a bicycle, and the certainty that by the end of the summer vacation we would be free. If all went well, I would return to school in Paris next fall.

I ride up the hill standing on the pedals; I brake and jump off.

A turn of the pedal to make the bike stand up against the curbstone and I grab the sack of semolina lying at the bottom of the basket. There are barely two cupfuls in it, but that'll be enough for one of Mama's cakes, giving us a change from the regular menu. I got the semolina by trading cans of corned beef acquired in an earlier deal.

I meet Maurice on the stairs. He stops me, looking excited.

"Come with me."

"Wait, I have to drop off the semolina . . ."

"Hurry up. I'll wait for you downstairs. Make it snappy."

I go up the stairs two at a time, leave the semolina, and come back downstairs four at a time. I do the last part sliding down the banister.

Maurice is already running ahead of me.

"Wait, I'm going to take the bike . . ."

He tells me no with a wave of his hand, and I begin running behind him. The sweat streams down my forehead, stops at the brows, and runs off along my temples.

We're almost at the city limits. He cuts to the inside and, after crossing the field which was once set aside for migrants and is now used as a soccer field by the kids of the section, we finally reach the garbage dump. With the sun, the smell isn't too pleasant and the flies are buzzing. We hike up a trail strewn with dirty papers and rusty springs and we've made it to the top of a plateau of rubbish.

Maurice stops, panting. I finally catch up to him. Ahead of us two boys are squatting. They're pals of Maurice. I've seen one of them around the schoolyard.

"Look."

I bend forward, looking over their shoulders.

Resting on a cushion of detective novels are four rifles. Their varnished stocks gleam in the sun. They're in excellent condition.

"Where'd you find them?"

Maurice's chum Paul turns to me.

"Under a bedspring, and I can tell you one thing — they weren't here yesterday."

"You sure?"

Paul shrugs. "Pretty sure. I come here every day, and if they'd been here I would have noticed. Somebody hid them here during the night."

I feel like touching one, picking it up, but you never know — those things can go off all by themselves.

The boy who still hasn't said anything grabs one of them and yanks the bolt back. A yellowish shell is ejected and bounces off the ground, striking my leg.

"Hey, watch out with that thing!"

All four of us know that they're Italian guns left behind by soldiers.

"What do we do with them?"

I think about the men in the *Résistance* who could really use them. But how do we get in contact with them? As for selling them, that would raise problems, though it could be done.

Maurice takes the initiative.

"The best thing to do is hide them again. Really hide them. Then we'll think about what to do and we won't talk about it to anyone. We'll meet here tomorrow to decide."

I ask him, "Where the devil do these things come from?"

"I heard that the Italian soldiers are starting to desert. People are saying Mussolini was arrested."

I'm stupefied.

"Arrested . . . but who . . . ?"

"I don't know. You know what we should do? We should go to Tite's and find out what's going on. But watch it — not a word about the rifles."

The curtain was drawn in the doorway of the bar to keep the place in the shade. It was cool inside, as cool and dark as a cave. I felt the sweat drying quickly on my face and under my shirt.

Most of the soldiers we knew were gone. Carlo had been sent to Sicily with the Parmesan to help stem the Allied tide. Evidently their assistance was inadequate — Sicily was taken in less than six weeks. They must have been prisoners in an American P.O.W. camp or perhaps they'd had time to get across the Straits of Messina before the rout. I couldn't believe that they were dead.

My friend the mailman had also vanished. Marcello had received a month-old letter telling him that his new regiment was awaiting transfer from a port in Calabria, as they expected an Allied landing on the Italian mainland.

In his letter, he sent his greetings to Giuseppe; when Marcello read me that part, I felt like crying.

As for Marcello, he had become bartender at the officers' mess and seemed determined to be shaking up cocktails on the Côte d'Azur when the fighting came to an end.

The new customers were younger soldiers, but they weren't as happy as the ones before. One of them, a very serious, gentle boy who had studied accounting in Milan became my friend.

That afternoon he was sitting there studying his French with the aid of a grammar book and a dictionary — a certain schoolboy had supplied him with these materials in exchange for cigarettes.

He smiled at us and I sat down at his table. He was hoping to learn to speak French before the end of the war; that would help him find a better job once he was back in his own country. He was an ambitious fellow.

As I didn't really understand it myself, I had trouble teaching him the rule about past participles. I was sweating over the agreement with pronominal verbs when he closed the book with a sigh.

"We've got to stop anyway, Jo. I just won't have the time."

I looked at him in surprise.

"Why?"

Sadly he packed up his books.

"Because we're going away soon."

"You mean they've transferred your regiment?"

"No, no, we're all leaving, all the Italians . . ."

I didn't understand what he meant. Patiently, trying to make a minimum of mistakes, he explained it to me:

"Mussolini isn't running things anymore — it's Badoglio, and everybody expects him to make peace with the Americans. People are saying that they've already had talks; so if there's going to be peace, we're going home."

My hopes suddenly rose.

"If you're going, then we're free!"

He looked at me sadly.

"No, if we go, the Germans will come."

The bar, already in shadow, grew darker still. Maurice had just taken a seat next to mine and joined the conversation.

"Are you sure?"

The Italian's hands and face expressed his resignation.

"Nobody can be sure. But if we make a separate peace with America, we'll be at war with the Germans; so we've got to go and fight in our country."

Maurice went on, "Do you want to fight the Germans?"

He tipped back in his chair, unbuttoning the collar of his tunic.

"Nobody wants to fight. Some of us have already left."

I thought about the four rifles we'd found at the garbage dump.

"Are there any deserters?"

He nodded.

"I didn't know the word for it, but that's it — deserters."

He drank, and when he set his glass down with a weary gesture, I asked him the question that had been bothering me for several minutes: "What about you? What are you going to do?"

His gaze slid over the few bottles remaining on the shelves behind the bar.

"I don't know. I don't like war. I'd rather go back home and stay there, but it's dangerous to run away from the army. They've got police and you can be shot."

"What about Marcello — what's he going to do?"

He coughed and scratched at a little stain on the wooden table.

"I don't know. We've never talked about it."

When we left the bar, I realized that Marcello had undoubtedly left — perhaps he had already crossed the border, perhaps he was back with his blond "witch" whom I had found beautiful, perhaps he was back in training for the ring — anyhow, he could have said goodbye.

In the days that followed, soldiers deserted in droves. On September 8, it became official: Marshal Badoglio had signed the armistice near Syracuse. Units were crossing the border to carry on the war — this time, against the Germans. At the barbershop, an officer came in for a haircut and suggested that my brothers leave with them, as he was convinced that the war had ended in Italy.

One morning Nice awoke and the Italian occupying forces were gone. However, the streets were dreary. Their faces uneasy, pedestrians stayed close to the walls of buildings. London announced that Hitler was sending thirty crack divisions across the Alps and would occupy all of Italy.

On September 10, a train pulled into the station and a thousand Germans got off. Among them were SS troops and civilians — members of the Gestapo.

The second occupation had begun. We all knew that it would have nothing in common with the first one. There would be no more squads going out on guard duty with a careless-looking private toting a mandolin.

VIII

It's six o'clock.

The time really drags when you can't go out of the house. I'd spent the afternoon reading *Michael Strogoff* and helping Mama kill the bugs that got into the last few beans we have left.

Our roaming is over. We're going to watch the hands of the clock until Henri and Albert get home, and every passing minute is a minute of anguish. Three days ago, the Gestapo moved into the Hôtel Excelsior; most of the hotels have been requisitioned. The *Kommandantur* is located at the Place Massena and roundups have begun. Many Jewish people have been denounced by their neighbors, then arrested; it won't be long before they systematically comb each section of Nice.

Papa paces back and forth. Our shutters are closed even though it's still broad daylight outside.

Five after six.

"What can they be doing?"

We don't hear from the V——'s anymore, but we can't

possibly go see if they've left or if they're still at home. They say that when an arrest is made, the Germans station a plainclothesman near the building for several days.

Footsteps coming up the stairs two at a time — it's my brothers.

We rush to meet them.

"Well, what's going on?"

Henri collapses in a chair while Albert goes to the kitchen to get a glass of water. We hear him drinking noisily.

"Well, it's very simple," says Henri. "We've got to leave — and fast."

Papa lays his hand on Henri's shoulder.

"What is it?"

Henri looks up wearily. I can tell that he's had a bad day.

"Albert and I had one German customer after another today, and they were talking among themselves, thinking that nobody understood. It was all mixed up, but the gist of it was that they're arresting all Jewish people, holding them at the Hôtel Excelsior, and every Friday they take them away in special trains to the German camps. They're sealed cars and they even have priority over troop trains. Staying here means a ticket straight to Germany."

Papa takes a seat and lays his hands flat on the tablecloth.

"Boys, Henri is right," he said. "We'll have to split up again. I've had the time to think it all over these last few days, and here's what we'll do: we're going to stick to the method that's always worked for us — we go away by twos.

"First, you two — Henri and Albert. You leave tomorrow for the province of Savoie. You've got to reach Aix-les-Bains. I know an address there, someone who'll hide you. Joseph and Maurice, this is what you're going to do. Listen carefully. You're leaving tomorrow morning for Golfe-Juan; it's not very far. You go to a camp called 'New Harvest.' It's supposed to be a paramilitary organization run by the Vichy government, part of the *Compagnons de France*.* But you'll see soon enough that it's not at all like that."

"What about you two? What are you going to do, Papa?"

My father gets up.

"Don't worry about us. We're old hands at this. And now let's have supper. You've got to go to bed early so you'll be in shape for tomorrow morning."

Once again we sat down to a supper before separating, a meal where little was heard beyond the scraping and clicking of forks and knives against earthenware dishes. The voice of my father or one of my elder brothers occasionally broke the silence when it became too heavy.

When I went into the bedroom, I found my knapsack on the bed. I had forgotten about it long before, and it seemed to me, looking at it, that I wasn't in Nice anymore but out on the road, walking endlessly toward a goal that I couldn't see.

---

* Volunteer work camps, set up by the Vichy government in 1940 as a measure aimed at solving the problem of unemployment among teenage boys. *Translator*.

NEW HARVEST.

That's the big sign over the iron gate. Two *francisques* — the tricolored battle-axes of the Vichy government — have been fastened at the ends of the sign.

Behind the iron gate move teenage boys in blue shorts, shirts, and berets. They carry canvas bags full of water, they chop wood — all very much like the Boy Scouts. It's something that's never appealed to me.

Maurice doesn't look any more excited than I do.

"Well — what do you say? Are we going in or not?"

We've brought along part of our savings and I feel like telling my brother that we should keep on going, make our way to the north. We could hide on a farm, work for a while . . . But, on the other hand, this camp set up by Pétain is certainly the last place that the Fritzes will look for two Jewish kids. So we can't hesitate — safety comes first.

"Okay, let's go."

Together, we push the iron gate open.

A big, gawky boy comes to meet us, his skinny thighs disappearing under shorts much too wide for him. He clicks his heels and gives us a crazy military salute — very elaborate.

Maurice makes one back at him, throwing in a few extra flourishes of his own.

"Are you new boys? Who sent you?"

I take an immediate dislike to this fellow; Maurice doesn't seem particularly charmed by him either.

"We'd like to see the head of the camp, Monsieur Subinagui."

"Follow me."

He pivots and leads us away at a brisk pace toward a

wooden building that rises above the tents. Almost on the threshold stands a white pole, as tall as a ship's mast. The French flag droops for want of wind.

The gawky guy knocks, opens the door, takes a step forward, clicks his heels, and announces in a nasal tone: "Two new boys who want to speak to you, sir."

"Thank you, Gérard. You can go now."

Gérard did an about-face and double-timed out the door, making the thin floor shake with his heavy boots.

We must have looked astonished, for the director motioned us to come closer and be seated.

"Don't get upset," he said. "Gérard is very nice, but his father was a sergeant major in the regular army and he's grown up in a very special atmosphere."

The director was very dark, with a high forehead and something unfathomable in his eyes. I had the feeling that this man knew all about me before I told him anything. Something about him fascinated me. Even in that dimly lit shack, surrounded by metal filing cabinets, old chairs, dossiers, and all sorts of dusty bric-a-brac, he gave the impression of moving as easily as if he were on the stage of the Opéra without any sets on it.

"Your father spoke to me about you. I agreed to take you even though you're not the required age, but you both look big enough. I think you'll be all right here and . . . you'll be safe."

He didn't say another word about that, but it was unnecessary.

"So, you belong to New Harvest, and I'm going to explain how we do things here. You've got several possibilities: you can stay inside the camp and do the work around here — the cooking and cleaning. Naturally, there are sports to take part in after you come off duty. But you have another possibility — that's going out to work and coming back to the camp at the prescribed times. You'll get room and board here in exchange for what you'll be asked to pay. That amounts to roughly three quarters of your wages."

"Excuse me," said Maurice. "What kind of work would there be?"

"I was just coming to that. You can help the local truck farmers or else go to Vallauris where we've set up a pottery workshop. We sell our products, something that makes it possible to keep on supporting the community. It's up to you to decide."

I looked to Maurice.

"I wouldn't mind trying the pottery," I said.

The director glanced at my brother.

"And you?"

"Me too."

Subinagui laughed, hearing the reluctance in my brother's voice.

"It's noble of you to make that sacrifice. I gather that you two don't like splitting up?"

Neither of us would ever have answered a question like that; he didn't push it any further.

"All right, then. It's all settled for Vallauris. You'll sleep here tonight and leave tomorrow. Good luck!"

He shook hands with us and we came out, our spirits high.

Gérard was waiting for us outside. He clicked his heels again, saluted, and gave us the order to follow him.

We crossed the camp. It seemed clean enough; there were already dishes on long wooden tables supported by sawhorses. The scent of sand and pine was in the air.

Inside a khaki tent, Gérard showed us two beds. At the foot of the bed lay two folded blankets and two sheets sewn together that made a sleeping bag.

"Supper's at six o'clock," said Gérard. "Lowering of the colors at seven, showers at eight-thirty, in your bunks at nine, lights out at nine-fifteen."

He clicked his heels for the zillionth time, saluted, and went out, walking like a robot.

A voice came out from under a bed.

"Don't worry about him. He's a little cracked but he's a good-hearted guy."

A head appeared, a mop of wiry hair, two eyes like coffee beans, and a bulbous nose: I had just met Ange Testi.

While I was making my bed, he told me that he was supposed to be peeling potatoes in the kitchen; he had left, claiming that he had a stomachache and that he was going to rest up a bit before the evening meal. He was going to use the same story the next morning at the infirmary where he hoped to be excused from a few days' work.

Pulling on the blankets, I asked him, "Do you like this place?"

"Yes," said Ange. "It's great — there's lots of Jews."

I gave a start, but he had said it innocently, sprawled on his mattress. In fact, try as I may, I can't remember having seen much of Ange in the vertical position. He had a very clear-cut preference for lying down — no matter what the hour — whenever he could.

"You're not Jewish?" he asked.

"No. You?"

He gave a little laugh.

"Don't worry. Baptized, catechism, communion, confirmation, and choir boy on top of that."

"How'd you get here?"

He links his hands behind his head, glancing around like a blissful Buddha.

"Well, you see, I'm on vacation."

He offers me a cigarette that I refuse.

"I'm not kidding. I'm really on vacation. I'm going to explain it all but, if you don't mind, I'm getting back under the bed because if the guy in charge of the kitchen catches me taking it easy, he'll give me hell."

So, with Ange lying on the floor, I sat on my bed and listened to him.

He was from Algiers. He wanted to spend his vacation in France after hearing his father and grandfather boast of its beauty. He was visiting Paris, staying at a cousin's house and sauntering lazily along the Champs-Élysées, when the Americans were landing in North Africa.

He had taken it calmly when he understood, after a day or two, that as long as the war went on he wouldn't be able to return to the white city of Algiers.

He laughed about it under his bed.

"Just think of it — if the war keeps going another ten years, that'll mean a ten-year vacation for me!"

As his Parisian cousin had had the preposterous idea of getting married several weeks after his arrival, Ange found himself out in the street without much money. Like a plant drawn to the sun, he came down to the south of France and stopped at the edge of the sea, the sea that he couldn't cross.

He had begged more or less for a few days and then, by

chance, happened to pass the iron gate of the camp. He had gone in, told them his story, Subinagui had kept him, and ever since he'd been peeling potatoes, sweeping the camp, and, more often than not, taking long siestas.

"Actually," he concluded, "I used to sell shoes all day long in my father's store in Algiers. Here I don't knock myself out as much. Besides, the longer we're split up, the happier I'll be to see them again."

Maurice had taken a walk around the place; he came back while we were busily talking.

"How many are there in the camp?"

"Oh, a hundred or so. It doesn't change much. Some people go, new ones come. But you'll see, it's pretty good here."

I began to regret my decision to go to Vallauris; I felt that Ange and I would have been pals.

At six o'clock a bell announced mealtime. As Ange knew all the tricks, we got seats right away on the bench nearest the chow line. The tureens were gigantic and a fifteen-year-old boy — who I later learned was Dutch — dipped out the soup with a ladle so big he had to hold it with both hands.

The noise was deafening. There were two Belgians next to me; they, too, were waiting out the end of the war to go home. Across from me sat a tow-haired boy named Masso, Jean Masso, whose parents lived in Grasse; I felt that I could have become his friend too.

After the meal everybody assembled in a star formation, facing the flagpole. That gave me a strange feeling; I don't think I had ever stood at attention in my whole life, except when I played soldiers with my friends.

I saw the flag slide slowly down the pole.

After that, I saw most of the guys go back into the middle tents, which were round like the ones at a circus. They played checkers, cards, a gambling game called *petits chevaux;* others strolled around the camp and there were a few playing harmonicas and guitars which made me think of the Italians. Where were they now?

I played a game of dominoes with Ange, Jean, and my brother; at nine o'clock I was in bed. The fellow in charge of the tent — what we'd call a counselor nowadays — slept at the far end of the row of tents. He seemed nice, but strict enough to end all noisy talk after lights-out.

In the dark above me I heard the murmuring of the wind in the leaves of the trees surrounding the camp; there was also the buzzing of insects, but that wasn't what really bothered me. It was the thousand and one noises that spring from communal life: the whispering of two talkers, the creaking of the tent or the wooden bed, sniffling, coughing, sighs. Around me I felt the confused presence of reclining bodies, the breathing of sleepers intermingled, making a continuous, chaotic murmur. I had never experienced that and it wasn't until the small hours of the morning that I finally fell asleep.

A whistle blast pierced my eardrums and I sprang out of my bed in terror. The boys around me were already folding up their blankets and sleeping bags, trading the first clouts of the day, running to the washstands stripped to the waist.

Only Ange Testi seemed in no hurry to get out of bed.

"Joffo, Maurice and Joseph, report to the supply room — and fast!"

I acquired three shirts with name tags sewn over the

pocket and shoulder tabs, a pair of shorts, and three pairs of socks, all in the same blue.

I put on those clothes and felt down in the dumps: I couldn't stand regimentation.

"You two going to Vallauris? "

"Yes."

"Then move out to the main gate, on the double."

We amble slowly toward the gate. Nine or ten boys are waiting for us and the director is with them. He greets us with a smile that raises our spirits a few notches.

"Twelve," he said. "Okay, you can go ahead. Work hard and make us lots of good things. See you tonight."

The gardens were full of late roses. There was an odor of wilted petals in the cool air of the morning. Despite our group leader's urgings to march in step and to sing *Maréchal, nous voilà,* we went on walking in disorder.

Vallauris isn't too far from Golfe-Juan; it's the same *commune,* a village with a little square and, off to one side, a tall frame building the roof of which had collapsed. Within those ancient walls was the pottery workshop of the *Compagnons de France.*

The most recent models were lined up along one of the walls: vases of all shapes, all sizes, big round ones, thin graceful ones. They came with spouts, without spouts, with one handle, two handles, varnished, unvarnished. All of a sudden I found myself in front of a potter's wheel, a mass of clay, and a turning tool.

From that very first morning, one thing struck me with blinding clarity: you can love a trade and still learn to hate it if you ply it under the wrong conditions. I wanted to make my vases; I liked to see and feel the mass of clay turn; I felt that, with the slightest pressure of my fingers, the form would change, be more graceful, different. What I wanted more than anything was to create a model that was my own — in other words, produce a vase that would have been different from all those that I saw lined up against the wall.

But the master potter — who had taken me in his charge and his grip as soon as I arrived — didn't share this view. Perhaps he was right, perhaps you've got to be an imitator before being a creator, perhaps you've got to practice the scales before attempting a symphony. It seems fairly obvious, but somehow I'm still not really sure about it.

Whatever the case, every time I tried to give my work a personal touch I was shoved from my stool and, with two strokes of his thumb, my mentor re-established the right proportion, restored that swelling of the belly which I always tended to reduce. I took over again from him and, in spite of myself, reduced that portliness which seemed to me a glaring aesthetic error.

After two hours of this little game, the master potter stopped the wheel and looked at me perplexed.

"No sense of proportion," he murmured. "We're going to have trouble."

I took a chance.

"Could I make one without a model — just for fun?"

I had made the most serious mistake that could be made. It got me an angry lecture. Little by little his arguments destroyed me: the pottery workshop wasn't a place for fun; before working without a model, I had to learn to copy them; practice makes perfect; potters don't improvise, and so forth.

I thought he was having an apoplectic fit. When he seemed to recover, he flattened my mound of clay with the palm of his hand and said: "Start again. I'll come by in ten minutes."

I pedaled. He came back, blew his top, and stuck me behind one of his disciples who seemed to have been glued to his wheel for a thousand years. I got bored stiff watching him make a vase that I saw him produce over and over again. I went back to my own wheel after an hour, but then it was lunchtime.

Maurice didn't look any more delighted than I did. It looked as if the Joffos weren't born to work with clay.

After eating, I came back and so did the master potter. Two hours later, my head resounding with barked commands, in clay up to my armpits, sweat running down the small of my back, I said to myself that if I didn't want to give in to the temptation of smashing a healthy kilo of greasy earth in his face, I'd better give up pottery for good.

That's how people miss their vocations. That day was my one and only experience with an art which was to become famous on the very site where I began my career. Let it be known: I was once a potter in Picasso's Vallauris.

Anyhow, the first thing we did that evening when we got back to Golfe-Juan was go to Subinagui and dump our problem into his lap.

"I'm all through," I said. "Pottery-making isn't for me."

"Same goes for me," Maurice said. "We tried it and it didn't work."

He listened to us with a serenity that no catastrophe could shatter and asked us, "Could you tell me what it was that you didn't like?"

"But I do like it!" I exclaimed. "I really do like it. But I couldn't do work the way the . . ."

He motioned me to stop and when our eyes met, I could see clearly that he didn't blame me, that he didn't share the master's pedagogic notions, and almost approved of the fact that I couldn't go on working under his thumb.

That cheered me up, even more so when, after consulting a file, he added: "If it's all right with you, we're going to give the kitchen a try. I hope you'll like it better there. The work is less artistic, but you'll have a lot more freedom."

Maurice thanked him. I was happy; I would be back with Ange and everyone knows that the kitchen of any institution is always the scene of all kinds of deals that a smart fellow can capitalize on.

He walked us to the door and placed his hands on our shoulders.

"You did the right thing in coming here," he said. "If anything goes wrong, don't be afraid — the office is always open."

That was the start of three wonderful weeks.

The kitchen was a soft job. Maurice helped a professional butcher and spent his days cutting out steaks and playing a card game called *manille*, the second activity taking up considerably more time than the first. For myself, I remember stirring cauldrons of mashed potatoes, mixing great bowls full of salad, slicing cartloads of tomatoes, always in the company of Masso and of Ange, who gladly gave up his siestas and his hiding places to work with me. We were an inseparable trio.

Inside the camp there was a black market — mostly in powdered sugar and flour. I myself slipped a few extra bananas in my pockets or stashed a few chocolate bars under my shirt to eat with my pals, but I didn't take part in anything on a large scale. Not that I was such an honest boy, but I wouldn't have been able to stand it had Subinagui ever found out. I knew about the difficulties that he was encountering in supplying the camp with food; he often came to speak to the head cook and I could sense the strain he was under when the delivery truck that brought us provisions failed to show up.

There were happy evenings when we'd all sit around the fire and listen to guitar music. And I loved the smell of the pine trees and the sea when darkness fell; the night breeze sprang up, driving off the heat of the day, and with the exception of Gérard, who was still like an automaton, we would relax and chorus the melodies that the song leader threw at us. That did us good; it made us think of peace.

But the news circulated through the camp. It came to us from merchants making deliveries, from the boys who returned from leaves that the director readily granted. We knew that the war was still going on. Fighting raged in Italy; the Germans had captured whole regiments of their former allies and I wondered what had become of my pals from Tite's café . . . Was Marcello a prisoner or a civilian? What about the others? In any case, the Germans were still powerful and continued to fight back. Despite all their efforts, the British and Americans were failing to gain ground. They had been stopped south of Naples and it didn't seem that the city would ever fall into their hands.

The Germans were retreating in Russia, but less now than before, and I began to have doubts. Masso believed in the myth of an elastic defense: the Germans seemed to be getting ready for a great offensive that would engulf the whole planet.

We didn't talk much to others in the camp. Some of the boys had been sent by families that were staunch supporters of Pétain; others were even frankly pro-German. When they came near us, our conversations died out and Maurice told me not even to confide in my pals.

There were good reasons for that; in addition to the news about the war, we got other news. It was always the same: the hunt for Jews was being intensified. I overheard a few words on this subject between Subinagui and the head cook one day while I was clearing the tables of the refectory. Apparently all pretense had ended: any Jew — what's more, anybody suspected of being one — was being shipped off to German camps.

I spoke to my brother about it, but he was already far better informed than I was.

One morning toward ten o'clock, while I was cleaning the top of the kitchen stove, he came toward me with his big navy-blue apron, one corner of which was tucked up like the overcoats of French infantrymen in World War I.

"Jo, I've thought up a trick we can use if the Germans make a raid here and start questioning us. I think they'll know right away that we're Jewish."

My rag remained suspended in midair.

"Why? Up till now . . ."

He interrupted me and I listened to him. Later on I was very glad that I'd paid attention to his words.

"Listen, Subinagui talked to me about it. Nowadays, the Gestapo doesn't even bother making inquiries. They don't give a damn about records and files. If somebody says to them that we're named Joffo, that Papa owns a shop on the rue Clignancourt — in other words, right in the middle of the Jewish section of Paris — they won't look any further."

I must have turned pale because he made an effort to smile.

"So, if they make a raid, you've got to make up a story, a whole life history. And I think I've got something we can use. Come here."

I put down my scouring powder and followed him to the other end of the room, drying my hands on my already filthy shorts.

"Here's what we're going to do," said Maurice. "You know Ange's story?"

"Sure, he tells it often enough!"

"Good, because we're going to tell the same one."

He had me confused. I didn't see what he was driving at.

"You don't understand?"

He didn't have to take me for a bigger dummy than I was. "Yes, we came from North Africa to France on vacation and we stayed here because of the Allied landing."

"That's it. The big advantage is that they can't call up any friends or relatives, since they're still over there. It's impossible for them to check our story — they have to believe us."

I turned that over in my mind. It seemed impossible to

make up a new past from top to bottom without contra-
dicting yourself when you were interrogated.

"And where did we live? "

"In Algiers."

I looked at Maurice. I was fairly well convinced that
he had planned everything, but I had to be sure. To do
that, I had to ask the questions that they might ask us.

"What kind of work do our parents do?"

"Papa is a barber; Mama doesn't work."

"And where do you live?"

"Number ten, rue Jean-Jaurès."

He doesn't hesitate for a second, but that calls for an explanation.

"Why *rue Jean-Jaurès?*"

"Because there's always a rue Jean-Jaurès and number
ten because it's easy to remember."

"And if they ask you to describe the shop, the house,
the floor we live on, anything like that — what are we
going to say?"

"Just describe the house on the rue Clignancourt. That
way we won't make any mistakes."

I nod. It really seemed right to the point. He jumps to
his feet and grabs me by the shoulder. He shakes me,
shouting, "And vere ist your school, mein boy? *Mach
schnell!*"

"Rue Jean-Jaurès, on the same street, a little further
down. I don't remember the number."

He gives me an approving uppercut.

"That's good," he says. "Very good. You're not too
bright, but you've got good reflexes. Here, block this
one."

He throws a straight right to my solar plexus. I reel back, feint, and try to stay out of reach. He dances circles around me.

Masso sticks his head in and looks at us.

"I'll bet on the biggest and strongest," he says.

The same night, when we were already in bed, I raised myself up on one elbow and leaned across the aisle separating my bed from my brother's.

"Your plan won't work."

He raised his head. I saw his white undershirt against the brown blankets.

"Why not?"

"Because Subinagui has our identity cards. He knows where we come from and if the Krauts ask questions, he'll be forced to tell them."

"Don't worry," said Maurice. "I'm going to talk to him about it. That guy will help us."

Silence fell. Some boys were already sleeping or reading by flashlight under their sheets. Before finally going to sleep, Maurice added, "You know, I think some of the others are in the same boat as us."

In the shadows I saw the darker rectangle of the Marshal's photo that was hung on the middle pole of the tent. I felt a wave of gratitude for the *Compagnons de France* and I thought to myself that, for people hunted by the Germans, this kind of organization was highly useful.

"Hey, you Joffo brothers! Are you coming with me?"

The motor of the delivery truck is running and Ferdinand already has his foot on the running board.

The driver looks at us. He's the one who brings us the grub on Fridays, then has a bite to eat before going back to Nice.

It's Friday, just after the noon meal, so it's time to go. I've heard some rumors in the kitchen: there are problems over bills from the different stores that supply us. Apparently, two of the shops are tired of waiting for their money and, to even up the score, are delivering lighter and lighter sacks.

Ferdinand is twenty-four; a case of tuberculosis sent him to a sanatorium for four years and got him deferred from military service. He's the steward of the center, Subinagui's right-hand man. He's going to settle those problems.

Maurice and I just happened to be in front of the little truck. I was going to meet Ange and Maurice had a deck of cards in his hand, cards that he uses for his endless games of *manille*. That's when the proposition fell in our laps. The afternoon in Nice! A windfall.

"What about getting back?"

"We'll take the evening bus. What do you say — yes or no?"

Never hesitate.

"Yes."

It's too tempting. With our camp uniforms, there's no danger. And I want to know what's become of our parents. I have the feeling that just by seeing the front of the house, the way the shutters are ajar, I'll know that they're still there. And then, who knows? If everything's quiet, we jump in the elevator and we make sure.

The delivery truck turns, its wheels spinning on the gravel near the entrance. We go out the iron gate. I hold

onto the side rails so I won't fall. The tarpaulin isn't on
and the wind takes my breath away. I go over to Maurice
on the other side where the hump of the butane motor
makes a shelter. Ferdinand is sitting beside the driver
and turns to us.

". . . somebody in Nice?"

The motor makes an awful racket and the jolting doesn't
make things any easier. I cup my hands around my
mouth and scream.

"What?"

"Do you know somebody in Nice?"

Now it's Maurice's turn to try to make himself heard.

"No! We're just going to walk around."

This guy drives like a maniac. The truck bounces from
one side of the road to the other, throwing us across the
floor. I feel myself starting to get sick.

We stop abruptly. The driver curses at the top of his
lungs after noticing that he's done nine or ten miles on a
flat rear tire. The spare is wretched-looking, as patched
as a pair of old trousers, but it'll do the job. We start up
again. All in all, the pause has been beneficial for me:
I've got some blood back in my cheeks and my stomach
has righted itself.

Besides, we're almost in Nice. There's the bay suddenly broadening out at the bend in the road. It does
something to me to see that city again. In the jumble of
tiny houses swarming around the docks, where's Madame
Rosso's bar? Where's our house behind the church of La
Buffa?

Ferdinand argues with the driver and, at the red light,
turns to us.

"We're going down another three blocks. I want to see

a pal on the rue de Russie. I'll make it fast. Just wait for me a few minutes and then I'll show you where the bus station is so you don't miss the bus. Then you can go where you please."

"Fine."

The delivery truck stops and our feet touch the sidewalks of Nice.

"Let's go," says Ferdinand.

I have trouble keeping up with him. He's as tall as he is skinny. His nose and Adam's apple are big and sharp.

"There, that's the bus depot. Wait a couple of minutes. I'll be right back."

He has already disappeared into the main entrance of an old building.

I had forgotten how hot those streets were. Buildings separate us from the sea and that's enough of an obstacle to keep any cool air from reaching us. The streets are deserted. There is now a signpost in German planted at the fork in the road. I don't remember having seen any like it in Paris before leaving.

"What's he up to?" murmurs Maurice.

Without a watch I find it hard to judge how much time has gone by.

"He's been gone two minutes, if that much."

Maurice gives a start.

"You're out of your mind. He's been gone at least ten minutes."

Now this is the kind of argument that always gets me angry.

"How can you say that he's been gone exactly ten minutes? What are you using to tell time?"

Maurice puts on that superior air that infuriates me.

"I'm not using anything. My intuition tells me. If your intuition doesn't tell you when you've been waiting two minutes or three quarters of an hour, you might as well jump off the nearest dock."

I shrug my shoulders.

"I'm telling you there's no way of knowing. We haven't been here for more than two minutes."

"Moron," murmurs Maurice.

I let the insult slide. It's just too hot to fight. I sit down on the sidewalk in the shade of the wall.

Maurice stamps his foot with impatience; he paces back and forth. He makes up his mind abruptly.

"I'm going to see. We can always find our way back to the bus depot, and I don't want to spend the whole afternoon cooling my heels here."

He pushes open the door and goes inside.

It's true; he's right. Time is passing and we're just wasting it stupidly, standing on a stifling street. Or maybe I've become accustomed to fresh air and can't take the city heat anymore, heat that seems to emanate more from the buildings than the sun.

And now it's Maurice who isn't coming back. That's the last straw.

At least if I had something to play with — but there's nothing. My pockets are empty and there aren't even any pebbles to take the place of a set of jacks.

I walk to the corner and back, counting my steps.

Thirty-five going, thirty-six coming.

That's odd. I take longer strides when I go someplace than when I come back. Or else the sidewalk is expanding with the heat. Or maybe I counted wrong. In any case, I'm terribly bored.

What the hell are those bastards up to? I was so happy to go away a while ago and now look what happens: first I almost puke in the truck and then I die of boredom waiting in front of that door, while . . . I'm going inside. They're not going to push me around just because I'm the youngest.

It's pleasant in the courtyard. There's ivy on one of the walls and an arbor in the back. The toys of children lie near a little pile of sand. No *concierge*. Just the stairs over there and that's it.

I cross the courtyard and put my foot on the first step.

The wall hits me; my palms smack against the bricks as I throw out my hands to keep from splitting my skull open.

Pain radiates through my back. I turn around.

A soldier stands there. He has sent me flying with the barrel of the submachine gun. The gray-green of his uniform captures all the light in the hallway.

Maybe he's going to kill me. The black circle of the muzzle is a few inches from my nose. Where is Maurice?

He bends over me. He reeks of cigarettes. His hand squeezes my arm and my eyes fill with tears. He squeezes hard, very hard.

The mouth opens.

"Kike," he says. "Kike."

He catapults me headlong against a side door that shudders under the impact.

The soldier rushes at me and I raise my arm to protect my face, but he doesn't hit me. He unlocks the door and I go reeling into a room, as the door closes behind me.

Maurice is there; so are Ferdinand and two women, one

of whom is crying. She's got blood trickling down her forehead.

I sit down, still in a daze. I don't understand. It's all a dream. Just a few minutes ago I was out on a street; it was hot; it was summer and I was free. Then there was that courtyard, a brutal shove, and now here I am.

"What's going on?"

I have trouble forming words. I'm afraid that I've spoken in a trembling voice, a tiny, piping voice, a ridiculous one.

Ferdinand's eyes look watery and strange. And my brother doesn't have quite the same face as a little while ago. Maybe we'll never again have the faces we used to have.

"It's my fault," whispers Ferdinand. "We walked into a trap. There was a *Résistance* center here where they made fake identity cards. They had an underground railway to get people into Spain."

Maurice looks at Ferdinand.

"But why did you come here? Did you need to go there?"

Ferdinand nods.

"With all the rumors going around the camp lately, I got panicky. I had this address and I wanted to get away before the Boches land in Golfe-Juan."

I stare at him stupidly.

"But why do you want to run away?"

Ferdinand glances at the door and his lips twitch:

"Because I'm Jewish."

He looks at us and I see his Adam's apple go up and down.

"Don't worry, nothing's going to happen to you. When they find out you aren't Jews, they'll let you go."

"Well, we'll see," murmurs Maurice.

He looks at me. Don't be afraid, my brother, I say to myself. I know the lesson. I've got it all up here in my head. There isn't going to be any mistake.

"What are you going to do, Ferdinand? Do you know what you're going to tell them?"

His peaked shoulders are shaken by a sob.

"I don't know . . . I don't understand. I'd had it all worked out to get a new identity card and just when it looked like I was going to be all right . . ."

The women in front of us watch him cry. They're young — twenty, twenty-five years old maybe. They don't seem to know one another. They sit on their chairs, motionless.

The room has been painted with shiny enamel. There are a few chairs and a mirrored wardrobe and that's all. No window. The electric light is burning; without the bulb in the ceiling we would see nothing.

There's something else about this room . . . suddenly, I understand: there is a window that should open onto the courtyard, but the wardrobe has been pushed in front of it to eliminate an exit and to discourage any attempt at escape. We've only met up with a single soldier, but perhaps there are more of them.

As I was being thrown into the room, I didn't get the feeling that the German had locked the door behind me; but trying the door or attempting to escape is a sure way to get a bullet in the head.

"What's going to happen now?"

Maurice has closed his eyes. He looks like he's sleeping.

"We're going to be questioned and when they realize the mistake, they'll let us go."

He's a little too optimistic for me. It's useless to try to talk to Ferdinand; he's huddled in a chair, rocking, nursing an unbearable grief. The women are still silent, and it's better that way: it may be a good thing for them not to talk to us. Now the heat is intense. The temperature in the street was moderate compared to this.

I look at my companions, their faces running with sweat. I have the feeling that the room would be cooler if I switched off the light. The heat seems to be coming from that tiny sun — the bulb overhead. I make an association between darkness and coolness.

"What if we switched off the light?"

Everyone gives a start. We've been there for what seems like hours, sweating in silence.

One of the women, the one with blood on her forehead, smiles at me.

"I don't think we should. They might get the idea that we're planning something or trying to escape . . ."

I see that she's right. The guy who showed me in looks as if he doesn't mind clubbing people with the butt of his submachine gun.

"What time is it, please?"

Maurice has asked the young woman this question. She is wearing a very delicate watch-bracelet, almost a chain; the watch is small and rectangular.

"Five-fifteen."

"Thanks."

We've been there for three hours.

Nobody has come yet; nobody has been caught but us.

Weariness slips stealthily over me. My buttocks ache from sitting for so long. Maybe they've forgotten about us. They don't give a damn about us anyway. They must be after the heads of the underground railway, the big shots, men who have been wanted for a long time. Us! What are we worth to them? Absolutely nothing. Talk about hunters' bags: two frightened women, two kids and a skinny beanpole of a guy — that's really a great haul! Now that they've gotten their hands on us, they're sure to win the war; that's no longer a problem for them.

Pictures flash through my mind, appearing under my eyelids which are filled with a painful yellow from the harsh light.

What I least understand is the soldier's brutality. The way his machine gun was aimed at me, his angry blows, and most of all his eyes. I had the feeling that his life-time dream was to drive me through the wall. I keep wondering: Why?

Am I his enemy?

We've never seen each other before; I've never done anything to him and he wants to kill me. It is only now that I begin to understand Mama and the people who used to come to the barbershop in Paris, the ones I heard arguing; they said that war was stupid, absurd, and that didn't seem right to me. It appeared to me that warfare had a reason for being, one that I couldn't quite put my finger on, but one that existed in the minds of important people. In the newsreels, regiments paraded in orderly ranks; long lines of tanks passed in review; men with grave faces, severe ties, or chestfuls of decorations discussed, signed, spoke with vigor and conviction. How could people say that it was all absurd? The ones who said that didn't understand; they spoke out of ignorance. But to the child that I was, war in no way resembled chaos, disorder, or the police. Even in my history book — aside from the fine illustrations that made war picturesque and exciting — war had been depicted in an aura of agreements, treaties, decisions . . . How could anybody get the idea that Philippe Auguste, Napoléon, Clémenceau, and all the ministers and councilors, all these people full of wisdom holding the highest offices, had been crazy? No, war wasn't absurd; people who said that didn't understand anything.

Then along comes this war, one that was wanted, planned by grownups whose neckties are still very severe and who wear even more glorious medals, and they end up throwing me, a kid, into a locked room, depriving me of the light of day, of freedom — I who had done nothing, who didn't know a single German. That's what Mama had meant; it turned out that she was right. And what's more, it was possible that . . .

The door opens.

They laugh and now there are two of them, with weapons slung across their bellies.

"Outside. Hurry up."

There's a rush for the door. Right away, I have Maurice's hand in mine. Whatever happens, we mustn't separate.

There's a truck outside.

"Come on, hurry up."

My head is spinning. I run behind the two women, one

of whom twists an ankle in her high-heeled shoes. Ferdinand pants and puffs just behind me.

There's a truck waiting on the corner with two officers.

At one bound we surge into the back of the truck. There are no benches, so we have to stand.

One of the two soldiers climbs in after us; the other raises the heavy iron tailgate sealing the rear halfway up. Then I see him jump, hoist himself aboard, and fall among us with a clatter. His submachine gun gets in his way and he swears.

We hang onto one another. I see the street turn sharply and disappear.

We are silent, spreading our feet apart to keep from falling. Through the rear of the truck I can see only the streets disappearing in the distance.

The truck stops abruptly. The soldiers let down the tailgate and jump out first.

"Come on, hurry up!"

I'm out in the bright sun and I don't have any trouble figuring out where I am.

In front of me stands the Hôtel Excelsior, headquarters of the Gestapo in Nice.

IX

THE LOBBY IS JAMMED with people, children, suitcases. Men with lists and dossiers go dashing past soldiers.

The noise is infernal. Near me stands an old couple — people in their mid-sixties. He's bald; he's wearing his Sunday best. She's short, and must have just had a permanent wave. She's trying to be stylish. In her hands she rolls up a handkerchief that's the same color as her scarf. Both man and woman are calm, leaning against a column. They're looking at a little girl of three or four who's asleep on her mother's lap. From time to time they look at each other, and I'm afraid.

I was young, very young, but I think that even if I'd been younger than I was, I would have understood that those two old folks were looking at each other like people who have lived together all their lives and who know that they are about to be separated; they know that they will each go the rest of the way alone.

Maurice leans toward a man who is seated on a suitcase, staring into space.

"Where are you going?"

The man's unseeing expression doesn't change.

"Drancy." *

He says it as casually as he would say "thank you" or "goodbye" — without attaching the slightest importance to it.

Suddenly there's a great stir. At the head of the stairs, two SS men have just appeared with a civilian who's holding a list clipped to a rectangle of cardboard. As he reads off a name, he looks to see if someone stands up; then he crosses off the name on the sheet with his pen.

The roll call takes a long time. Little by little the crowd in the lobby thins out. As soon as their names are called, the people go out through a side door. A truck must be taking them to the train station.

"Meyer, Richard. Seven-two-nine."

The old gentleman standing with his wife doesn't flinch. Slowly he bends down, picks up the little suitcase at his feet, and walks forward unhurriedly.

I admire him for his easy tread, for his confidence; in that second, I know he isn't afraid.

"Meyer, Marthe. Seven-three-o."

The little lady with the waved hair has picked up a suit-case even smaller than her husband's. I get a lump in my throat — I have just seen her smile.

They are together again at the door. I'm glad that they haven't been separated.

Our two guards are still there. The one who hit me is smoking. I steal a furtive glance at him. It's crazy how

* Internment camp set up by the Germans. From 1941 to 1944 almost 10,000 persons — mostly Jews — were held there before deportation to Germany. *Translator.*

his face looks just like any other face; he hasn't got a brutal mug at all — so then *why?*

Slowly the lobby empties out. SS men go back and forth, always carrying papers in their hands. They seem to have some important, worrisome job to do. Soon we'll be all alone — just the five of us with our two guards, leaning against the rear wall.

An officer snaps his fingers, calling one of the soldiers guarding us. Instantly he springs forward. The SS man calls the second guard.

Now we're almost alone; the lobby is deserted. I notice that I am still holding my brother's hand.

What time can it be?

A man in civilian clothes comes down the stairs and looks us over while knotting his tie. Maybe he's going to tell us to go. In German, he speaks to someone I can't see, someone on the floor above; he points to us.

He motions to us, and we go upstairs.

I want to pee — it's been a long time and I'm afraid. There are officers on the next floor and Frenchmen acting as interpreters. We come to a corridor; we pass many doors.

"Give us your identity cards."

The two women hand over theirs; so does Ferdinand.

The interpreter enters the office and comes right back out.

"Go in, you two," he says, motioning to the women.

The three of us go on standing in the corridor; no one is guarding us. A muffled clacking of typewriters and the drone of voices comes from the floor above, but I can't hear what they're saying in the room that the women entered.

Maurice looks at me. He speaks through teeth that he can hardly unclench.

"You going to be all right, Joseph?"

"I'll be all right."

The door in front of us opens. The two women come out. Both of them are crying. I know they haven't been beaten — that makes me feel better.

The women go back downstairs and we go on waiting. It reminds me of the dentist's office on the rue Ramey, when Mama used to take me there after school.

The interpreter appears. This time it's our turn. All three of us go in.

It used to be a hotel room but the bed isn't there anymore; instead there's a table with an SS man behind it. He's in his forties, with glasses; he seems tired and yawns several times.

He's holding Ferdinand's identity card and looking at it. He says nothing and motions to the interpreter.

"You're Jewish?"

"No."

The interpreter has a childish voice and a Provençal accent. He's certainly from Nice.

"If you aren't a Jew, why do you have a forged identity card?"

I don't look at Ferdinand; I know that if I look at him, I won't be brave when my time comes.

"But . . . that is my identity card."

There's a brief exchange in German. The SS man speaks and the interpreter translates.

"We can easily find out if you're a Jew or not, so start talking and don't give us any trouble — otherwise you're going to annoy people around here and get yourself a beating. That would be stupid, so let's have the truth right away and we'll forget the whole thing."

He gives the impression that we need only talk and everything will be all right — we'll be set free.

"No," says Ferdinand. "I am not Jewish."

There's no need for translation. The SS man gets to his feet, removes his horn-rimmed glasses, goes around to the front of his desk, and plants himself squarely before Ferdinand.

A ringing slap on Ferdinand's sickly cheek sets his head wobbling; a second crack sends him reeling back a couple of steps. Tears stream down his face.

"Stop," says Ferdinand.

The SS man waits. The interpreter encourages Ferdinand.

"Go ahead, talk. Where are you from?"

In a voice that can scarcely be heard, Ferdinand speaks.

"I left Poland in 1940. My parents were arrested. I went through Switzerland and . . ."

"Fine. We'll see about all that later. But you do admit that you're a Jew?"

"Yes."

The interpreter goes up to him and gives him a friendly pat on the shoulder.

"There, you see? Don't you think you should have talked sooner? All right, you can go downstairs. Show that to the clerk at the foot of the stairs."

He holds out a green ticket, which Ferdinand takes. I'm soon going to learn what the green ticket means.

"It's your turn now, you two. Are you brothers?"

"Yes, he's Joseph and I'm Maurice."

"Joseph and Maurice what?"

"Joffo."

"And you're Jews."

This is no question; this guy is stating a fact. I want to help Maurice.

"Oh no, you've got it all wrong."

He's surprised by my vehemence. Maurice doesn't give him a chance to get a word in edgewise.

"No, we aren't Jewish. We're from Algiers. If you want, I can tell you all about it."

He knits up his brows and speaks to the SS man, who now has his glasses on and is looking us over. The German asks us a question. I understand him better and better; it's really very close to Yiddish, but I musn't show him that I understand.

"What were you doing on the rue de Russie?"

"We came from New Harvest, the camp of the *Compagnons de France.* We went along with Ferdinand and were waiting for him — that's all. He told us that he was going in to see a pal."

The SS man rolls a pencil between his fingers.

Maurice gains confidence. I can sense that he's in perfect control of himself. He begins to give him our story right away: Papa, a barber in Algiers; the school; the vacation; and then the landing in North Africa that kept us from going back. It all goes like clockwork until — the only thing we hadn't planned.

"And you're Catholic?"

"That's right."

"Then you've been baptized?"

"Yes, we've also made our communion."

"What church?"

Rotten luck! But Maurice's voice is loud and clear, even clearer than before.

"La Buffa. In Nice."

The interpreter strokes his belly.

"Why not in Algiers?"

"Mama wanted us to make our communion in France; she had a cousin in this part of the country."

He looks at us, writes a few lines in a notebook and closes it.

"All right, we're going to check and see if everything you've said is true. First, you go for physicals. We're going to see if you've been circumcised."

Maurice doesn't flinch. I try to remain absolutely calm.

The interpreter looks at us.

"You understand?"

"No. What does that mean — *circumcised?*"

Both men look at us. Maybe you've gone a little too far, Maurice, a little too far. In a few minutes they may make us pay for that confidence. In any case, our pretty house of cards is about to go tumbling down.

A soldier pushes us up the stairs. They'll find out everything. I don't give a damn — I'll jump from the train while it's moving. They won't take me to Germany.

Then I'm in another room; this one is empty. There isn't any desk — just three men in white smocks.

The oldest one stares when we come in.

"Oh, no, we're not staying here all night. I went off duty half an hour ago."

The other two grumble and slip out of their smocks. One of them is German.

"What are these two?"

The soldier accompanying us hands him a slip of paper.
Meanwhile the two others put on their jackets. The old
one reads. He has very black eyebrows that contrast with
his iron-gray hair.

"Take off your shorts and drop your underpants."

The two other men are still gabbing; I hear words,
street names, the first names of women. They shake
hands with the doctor who's going to examine us, and
they leave.

The doctor sits on a chair and motions us to come
closer. The German who led us in is behind us, near the
door. Our backs are to him.

With his right hand, the doctor lifts the shirt-tail covering Maurice's penis. He says nothing.

Then it's my turn. He looks.

"So you aren't Jewish, eh?"

I pull up my underpants.

"No, we aren't Jewish."

He sighs and, without looking at the soldier who's still
waiting, he says: "Don't pay attention to him. He doesn't
understand French. We're alone here — you can tell me
the truth and it won't go out of this office. You're Jewish."

"No," says Maurice. "Our parents had us operated on
when we were little . . . because we had adhesions;
that's all."

He nods.

"A phimosis, that's called. Do you know that every guy
who comes in here says he had a phimosis in his childhood?"

"It wasn't a . . . what you said . . . it was an adhe-
sion."

"Where was the operation performed?"

"In Algiers, in a hospital."

"What hospital?"

"I don't know — we were very small."

He turns to me.

"Yes, Mama came to see me. She brought me candy and a book."

"What book?"

"Robin Hood — it had pictures."

Silence. He leans back in his chair and studies each of us in turn. I don't know what he sees in our eyes, but there's something that makes him try a new tack. With a wave, he has the soldier leave the room.

He walks to the window, looks at the street that's all yellow from the setting sun. His hands toy with the curtains. Slowly he begins to speak.

"My name is Rosen," he says. "Do you know what it means when your name is Rosen?"

We look at each other.

"No."

I add politely, "No, doctor."

He comes near and places both his hands on my shoulders.

"Well, it just means that I'm Jewish."

He gives us a chance to take in this fact and, after glancing at the door, adds, "It also means that you can talk with me."

I am still silent but Maurice reacts quickly.

"All right," he says. "You're Jewish — but *we aren't!*"

The doctor doesn't answer. He walks to the coatrack, fishes around in his jacket pocket, takes out a cigarette, and lights it. He goes on studying us through the smoke.

It's impossible to guess what's going through the man's mind.

All of a sudden, as if he were talking to himself, he murmurs, "Well done!"

The door opens and there in the doorway stands the SS man with the glasses who interrogated us.

He asks one brief question. I catch only a single word of the doctor's reply, but it's the one that counts; it has saved our lives: *"Das ist chirurgisch gemacht worden."* *

We have been led into one of the rooms where the hotel staff used to sleep; I can't fall asleep. At six o'clock, there's another interrogation. This time we're separated.

The SS man who interrogates me is very different from the first. He stops the questions now and then to put drops in his nose. There's also a new interpreter. The moment I come into the office I can feel that there's unspoken agreement between us; I know that he's going to back me up. The interpreter is everything during an interrogation — just one word, a tone of voice, and it all changes.

"Describe the room that you lived in on the rue Jean-Jaurès."

I know that they're going to compare my statement with Maurice's, but it's unlikely that they can trip us up on this point.

"I slept with my brother. He had the bed near the door; mine was near the window. There was a parquet floor with a rug next to each bed, a little red rug — one for each of us. We each had a night table with a lamp on it,

* "This has been performed for surgical reasons." *Translator.*

but the lamps were different. Mine had a green shade
and . . ."

"Don't talk so fast — I've got to translate."

The interpreter launches into a long sentence. The SS
man snorts and adds something. The interpreter looks
worried.

"Your brother said that your lampshade was pink."

"No, he's wrong. It was green."

"Are you sure?"

"Yes, I'm sure."

An exchange in German. The interpreter quickly
comes to my aid.

"You're right — he said green. What about your two
elder brothers — what did they do?"

"They worked in the barbershop."

"Did they get mixed up in politics?"

I screw up my face in doubt.

"I don't know. I never heard them talk about it."

"Did your father read the newspaper?"

"Yes, every evening after supper."

"The *Alger Républicain* or some other paper?"

Watch it. That's a hint, but it could backfire on me.
The interpreter seems to be helping me, but I mustn't
trust anything or anybody.

"I don't know the names of the newspapers."

"All right, you can go."

More corridors and then I'm in a former chambermaid's
room where Maurice is waiting for me.

The door closes. The soldiers never lock us in, but it
would be crazy to try to leave.

There's one window; we're way up high, on the top
story. We lean our elbows on the windowsill. If some-

body looks at us through the keyhole or through any opening in the walls, he won't even see us talking.

"Another thing," says Maurice. "On Sunday we used to go to the seashore. We used to swim at a beach, but we don't remember the name."

I think to myself that there are an awful lot of things we don't know the names of anymore.

"One thing you can throw in," whispers Maurice. "There was a mosque not far away, overlooking a square."

I memorize everything. I'm trying to come up with a touch that will make our story perfect. Suddenly it dawns on me.

"What if we had an Arab pal?"

Maurice sneers.

"And his name was Mohammed. No, don't make up anything. Later on we'll get all mixed up. Did you know any Arabs in Paris?"

"No."

"Well, you didn't know any in Algiers, either."

I think it over.

"But you're more likely to meet Arabs in Algiers than in Paris."

"No. We lived in the European quarter and didn't have anything to do with the Arabs."

That strikes me as a little farfetched, but I keep still. I subsequently learned that people could actually live in Algeria and not know the Arabs; that Maurice had certainly put his finger on the future colonial problems of France.

Soon it'll be noon and I'm hungry. We haven't eaten anything in twenty-four hours. Footsteps in the corridor; it's the interpreter.

"Joseph Joffo, interrogation."

It's the third since last night: there's no end to it.

It's the same SS man with a cold. This time he's suck-ing on a cough drop.

"What games did you play in school?"

That's an easy question; I could talk to him about that for two days.

"We played tag, hide-and-seek, cross-tag, handball, marbles. Oh, we had loads of games with marbles: ringer, potsies, knucks, chasies, and we played jacks, too."

The interpreter breaks my momentum and translates. I see that he can't find the word for "jacks." Maybe Ger-man children don't play that game.

"I can show him with coins."

He begins to laugh, fishes in his pocket and hands me some change. I take five small coins, place them in the hollow of my palm, throw them up in the air and catch three of them on the back of my hand.

The officer watches the performance carefully. I go on with my demonstration. The interpreter laughs and I sense that the ice has been broken a little, but the Ger-man catches himself.

"Describe the city for us."

"It's very big; there's the ocean — Papa took us there on Sundays when the weather was nice. And there was a square — right near the rue Jean-Jaurès — with a white mosque that always had Arabs around it. And there was a big street and . . ."

I began to describe it, using the Canebière for a model: the cafés, the moving-picture houses, the department stores.

". . . The harbor is very big; it was always full of ships."

"What kind of ships?"

I had seen some in Marseille. If they were in Marseille, they must also come to Algiers from time to time.

"Most of them had red and black hulls with smokestacks — one or two. Mostly they had two."

"Talk about your friends and your brother's too."

"We had the same friends because we were both in the same class. My best friend was Zérati. One day . . ."

In two hours I'm going to learn that Maurice also spoke about Zérati. The name strikes them as Algerian enough to leave us alone for the rest of the day.

Around seven o'clock a soldier leads us to the kitchen, where we eat a bowl of soup as we stand before rows of blackened pots.

The second night begins. I wonder if they've arrested Papa and Mama. If they do it and my parents are carrying forged identity cards, we'd have to pretend not to know them. No, that would be awful; I mustn't think about that.

Sleep is slow in coming and the soup doesn't go down. I mustn't vomit though, for I've got to keep my strength. Tomorrow they'll go on interrogating us and I mustn't weaken. God of Jews, Arabs, and Catholics, please don't let me weaken.

In the dark I can make out the lighter-colored square of the window. Maurice breathes regularly beside me. Maybe we'll be free tomorrow. Maybe.

Six days.
Six days they hold us and don't let us go.

There was another interrogation on the morning of the third day and again on the afternoon of the fourth. For two days now there's been nothing. Maurice asked an interpreter whom he passed in a corridor of the hotel. It seems that our case is still pending, that the Germans are waiting for a more telling piece of evidence before disposing of the case — in other words, before either releasing us or sending us away for deportation.

The different departments are swamped with work. In the lobby, in the two drawing rooms and in the corridors on every floor, there's a continuous swarm of people. The stairs are choked with civilians, SS men, soldiers. There is an identity department, one for verification, another that issues the *Ausweis;* finally, one department for the registration of residence. Day after day we see the same people in the corridors, the same pallid faces lined with weariness and fear. There's a man who's been standing on the third-floor landing for three days — just waiting there. He comes first thing in the morning and goes away at the end of the day. Who is he? What does he want? What paper is he vainly seeking? It's all so incomprehensible. Mainly, it's that contrast: first there are the barked commands of the SS corporals driving their herds down the stairs (their expressions and voices tell me that they would like to beat and kill) and then there's this painstaking investigation, those rubber stamps so stingily wielded, the fingerprints, the signatures — all this incredible detail which fascinates me. How can they be killers and such fussy, diligent clerks all at the same time?

Anyway, since yesterday the duty sergeant at the Excelsior has come up with a scheme. He's got two less soldiers on K.P. — he's using us to replace them. The first

morning I was glad to get out of our room, but that soon
wore off: after peeling the potatoes, there's the lettuce
and tomatoes, the endless washing of dishes. In the afternoon it's cleaning the kitchen. More than sixty SS men
and office workers eat in what used to be the hotel's dining room. Last night, I was so tired that I couldn't fall
asleep; I heard a tower clock strike two. Perhaps it was
the steeple in the church of La Buffa.

At seven o'clock this morning they came to wake us up.
We had to go downstairs to the kitchen. I have the feeling that when they've gotten enough work out of us,
they'll kill us. I can also sense my morale snapping; it's
some kind of illness that's getting me down. I've had
headaches almost constantly since the last interrogation.

As I was going back upstairs yesterday, I passed the
doctor on his way out. He wasn't wearing his white
smock and I barely recognized him. But he saw us all
right. He looked surprised and went by very quickly,
disappearing through the revolving door.

Why did he do that? Why did he save our lives when
he must condemn hundreds of others every day? Because he felt sorry for two kids? That's very unlikely; just
yesterday there was a whole contingent of Jewish women
in the drawing room with green tickets and some of them
were carrying kids in their arms, kids a lot smaller, a lot
cuter, a lot more endearing than the two of us.

Maybe it's because we wouldn't talk — he liked our ob-
stinacy; he must have said to himself: "Look at these two
kids, the way they're hanging onto their lives; they deserve to stay alive — I'll give them a break."

It's possible. But does he know it himself? Maybe he
surprised himself by saving our necks. Maybe he still

hasn't realized . . . I don't know. And it's too hard for me to think with this headache. Maurice asked for aspirin, but there isn't any.

"Look."

While we're going down to the lobby, Maurice's hand squeezes my arm brutally. He has stopped. The main drawing room is packed with people; it looks as if they're stepping up the number of arrests, and then I remember that it's Friday, the day when they load the trains. Who is that he sees?

"To the right," whispers Maurice, "near the column."

Then I see them, all three in short pants. Jean Masso is there and so are two others from the camp. The tallest one was beside me that day in Vallauris when I worked on pottery.

Jean sees me. He raises his arms, his face lights up. I suddenly feel like crying and I run to him with Maurice at my heels.

We shake hands in the midst of the hubbub. Masso embraces me, laughing.

"At the camp we all thought you'd gone away for good. What . . . what are you doing here?"

That would be hard to explain. I prefer asking, "What about you? What are *you* doing here?"

He looks quite all right; his hair is tousled. He quickly brings me up to date.

"Last night the SS surrounded the camp and came in. We had to get out of bed and take off our pajamas. They looked at our pricks with flashlights and they took all the kids who were circumcised. They took me because I'd had an operation when I was six. I still haven't been able to explain it to them . . ."

Rising up on the tips of his toes, Maurice looks all around.

"There's just you three? Weren't there any others?"

The guy from the pottery shop winks.

"When he heard that Ferdinand and you two had been arrested, Subinagui started to watch out."

Maurice motions eloquently: we mustn't speak so loud; Gestapo agents in civilian clothes mingle in with the suspects and they're listening. If they hear something, they have the talkative ones taken down to the basement and nobody knows what happens there.

The boy understands and lowers his voice; now he whispers.

"You know, there were quite a few Jews hiding in the camp. Subinagui gave them addresses and made them leave in the middle of the night. The two of us got picked up on the road, near Grasse. We didn't have papers."

I look at Masso. He wears a broad smile and smacks me on the back.

"Let me tell you this, Joffo. We don't give a damn about all this stuff. They're not going to ship us anywhere, because we aren't Jewish."

Maurice pulls me by the arm.

"Come on. We've got to get back to the kitchen, because we're going to get bawled out if they don't see us."

We shake hands quickly. Before going down the office stairs, I turn around: I see the face of Jean, still smiling at me. I still don't know that I will never see him again, that no one ever saw Jean Masso again.

When Friday morning came, the Germans didn't have time to study his case. The Gestapo of Nice had to supply a contingent of 1200 for each train. At ten o'clock he listened with stupefaction as his name was called out, and he went aboard the death train. He made up the quota. Thanks to him, the statistics on arrested Jews were correct that week.

In the days that followed, my headaches grew worse. Now, even at night, the hotel was full of noise, footsteps, cries, and I used to wake up with a start, bathed in sweat. I was sure that they were beating people in the basement.

They had stopped interrogating us now and I didn't know what to make of that oblivion into which we were gradually sinking. Had they forgotten us completely? Had the file folder been mislaid? Or were they really carrying out a thorough investigation? The one thing certain, the one thing that comforted us, was the fact that they couldn't go to Algiers. But maybe they had other ways of finding out who we really were.

Every lunchtime and every evening, it was the same story: I couldn't eat and Maurice had to force me. Then we would yell at each other, and one evening, when I was forced to swallow a plate of mashed potatoes with a few pieces of blood-sausage, I vomited on the staircase going back up to our room. I was terrified, for if a German had seen me he would have beaten me — maybe even knocked me out. Someone was climbing up the stairs behind us and my brother dragged me along as fast as we could go. I collapsed on my bed, my heart pounding, my stomach still gripped by spasms. Before falling asleep I felt Maurice removing my shoes and mopping my brow with his shirt-tail. I fell asleep.

During the night I had the curious impression that someone was scratching at our door. I woke up and felt no fear at all. My fingers groped under the bed and came across the cold steel of a submachine gun. I felt the cold floor on the soles of my bare feet and I went to open the door. There I found myself face to face with the SS man who had interrogated me the second time. His face was up against mine — enormous, distorted by the proximity; I could distinguish every pore of his skin with perfect clarity. His eyes grew wide, like two monstrous pools in which I was going to be swallowed up and drowned — just at the second when I pressed the trigger. He crumpled up against the wall, covered with blood.

I felt marvelously well and went out into the corridor. Germans in uniforms and Gestapo agents suddenly appeared around a corner. They rushed at me, screaming, and I let them have a burst. I saw them reeling; the walls turned red and I started down the stairs. Panic-stricken, they were all running wildly now; I began to fire without stopping, marveling at the fact that my gun was perfectly silent. It was a real slaughter; I could see holes in their bellies, in their chests; I saw their heads shatter. Delighted, Jean Masso was applauding, shouting: "Nice going, Joffo! Kill them all!" Other men came up from the basement and I aimed the barrel at them, spraying them, too. They fell down like miserable puppets and the blood kept running, reaching my boots. I splashed through it, splattering myself up to the knees. I was choking with horror and began to vomit again before falling on a heap of corpses. Then I saw my father coming toward me at the end of a tunnel and I wanted to run to him, but I couldn't manage to get free of the arms and legs that crushed me in their grip. I was going to suffocate in that pile of corpses, and I made a tremendous effort to reach the surface, an effort so great that — I managed to open my eyes.

I was in a room that I had never seen before, and there was complete silence. The ceiling was glossy, as if it had been varnished, and I could see my own reflection. I looked ridiculously small; only my head emerged from the covers, resting on a pillow.

I closed my eyes again and a few seconds later I felt a hand on my forehead; once more I managed to spread my eyelids apart. There was a young woman, smiling at me. She seemed very beautiful; her smile was sweet and her teeth gleamed.

She understood that I didn't have the strength to open my mouth and she answered all the questions as if she had seen them in my eyes.

I had been found lying unconscious in the corridor early in the morning. I had been moved into another room and the doctor who came said that it was serious — the early stages of meningitis.

I listened to her. I would have listened to her for days on end. I knew that I was still in the hotel.

She left me for a few seconds and came back with some stewed fruit which she fed to me with a teaspoon. Once I tried to bring my arms out from under the covers and take the spoon but my hand was trembling too much. I was afraid of vomiting but that didn't happen again; I was glad of it, for I didn't want to stain the covers and make trouble for that nice young woman.

After she left I closed my eyes again, but one picture kept appearing beneath my eyelids, a picture that I couldn't drive away: I saw a door.

I knew that the door was the one in the basement of the

Hôtel Excelsior; there was nothing special about it, but I was in mortal terror that it would open, that beings would emerge, the form and color of which I had no idea, but I knew that they would be terrifying. The moment I saw it come ajar, I let out a shriek that brought my nurse running back. Once again I was bathed in sweat and she sponged my face and neck. I was able to say a few words to her and that seemed to make her happy. She told me that it was a good sign; it was proof that I was on the road to recovery.

She stayed with me for a good part of the night. Every time I awoke I could make out her outline in the armchair and that calmed me.

At dawn I realized that I was alone in the room. And then a strange thing occurred: I rose and went to the window. Though it was still quite dark, I could make out a form lying on the sidewalk below. It was a boy lying in a pool of his own blood. I looked at the face more carefully; it was turned toward me and suddenly I recognized it: it was the face of Joseph Joffo.

It was odd. All at the same time, I could be dead on the sidewalk and alive in a hospital room. The important thing was to find out which of us was real. My brain cells must have been working properly, for I arrived at this conclusion: I was going to go out and I would certainly meet someone. If this someone spoke to me, it would mean that I was the real Joseph; if nobody spoke to me, then the real Joseph would be that dead boy lying there near the gutter.

I went out and found myself standing in a corridor. It didn't take long. A voice gave me a start.

"What the hell are you up to, there?"

I turned around and smiled. The real Jo was alive.

Tranquilly I returned to my room. The doctor immediately diagnosed me as a sleepwalker and from that moment on I never again saw the basement door.

Now the passing days were calm, almost happy. I was recuperating rapidly and my nurse — whose name was Mademoiselle Hauser — congratulated me on looking better from one day to the next.

One morning after I had been there for almost a week, I asked her why she didn't wear a white smock like the doctors and nurses. She smiled and said, "This isn't a hospital and I'm not a nurse."

I was speechless for a moment; then I asked, "Well, then why are you taking care of me?"

She turned aside and began to plump up my pillows. Before I could ask another question, she said simply, "I'm Jewish."

I never had more trouble resisting the overwhelming urge to tell her, "Me too," but I couldn't do it; that was out of the question. At that very moment, there might be men listening behind the door. I didn't answer but I caught her neck as she went by and kissed her. She kissed me in return, stroked my cheek with her fingers and went out.

With all my will, I wished that the Germans would go on needing her for a long time, a very long time, right till the end of the war; that they wouldn't put her aboard one of those Friday trains . . .

That evening, she came back with a book and handed it to me.

"You should read a little, Jo. You haven't been to school in a long time and it will do you good."

So I began to read. I managed to plow through two or three books a day. Now I could be up and around as I pleased. I often asked Mademoiselle Hauser for permission to write to my brother, but the rules were strict — all letters to the outside world were forbidden.

Around nine o'clock one morning, while I was devouring a Jack London novel, the door opened and the doctor stepped in, the one who had been caring for me here.

He read the fever chart at the foot of the bed, told me to stick out my tongue, and then didn't look at it. He came closer, raised one of my eyelids, and said simply: "Get dressed."

I couldn't believe my ears.

"Your clothes are in the closet."

I decided to try anything to stay longer.

"But I can't get out of bed — as soon as I set foot on the floor, I get dizzy and fall."

He didn't even bother to reply. He looked at his watch.

"In five minutes you've got to be downstairs. Hurry up."

I got dressed. My clothes had been washed and ironed. I was sure my nurse had done that. When I went out, I didn't see her in the little glass-enclosed office close to my room, where we had chatted so often. I was about to write "I never saw her again," but I see that I've already used that phrase a good many times. Unfortunately, the "never again" phrase applies in this case too. Where did they send you from there, Mademoiselle Hauser? Which camp did you reach on one of those cold and foggy mornings in Poland or Eastern Germany? So many years have gone by and yet I can still see her tender face bent over me; I feel her sweet hands on my brow, I hear her voice.

"You should read a little, Jo. You haven't been to
school in a long time. . ."

There was Maurice again. He had lost weight and
grown pale.

"Things aren't going too well right now. There's a new
officer in command. It seems everything was all disorga-
nized before, so they put in this new guy. He's a mean
bastard. We're going to have to watch our step."

He didn't know how right he was: less than two hours
after my return, a French civilian came to get us in the
kitchen.

"Maurice and Joseph Joffo, interrogation room."

Our file folder lay open on the desk; there were more
papers now and some letters too.

In other words, they hadn't dropped our case at all, and
it knocked me for a loop. They had a world war on their
hands; they were retreating before the Russians and
Americans; they were fighting at the four corners of the
globe; and yet they could still use men and time to find
out whether two kids were Jewish or not — and spend
three weeks doing it!

The German in civilian clothes who reigned behind the
desk must have been the mean bastard Maurice had
warned me about. He was wearing a rough tweed jacket.
Even though he was seated, you could tell that he was
quite short. The interpreter had changed too.

Maurice and I stand there waiting, our bellies even
with the edge of the desk.

The little man looks at us, shuffles some papers, and

murmurs a sentence. The translation follows automatically.

"The director of the New Harvest camp backed you on every point of your story."

He stops and a sensation of warmth comes over me; in five minutes we may be on the outside.

Still murmuring, the German speaks again. He's going too fast for me to understand it all, but the interpreter performs his function, and he comes right to the point. His voice isn't a human voice with intonation, warmth, accent; it's a recording machine that must announce births and deaths in the same tone. Without moving his body, he jerks his chin in Maurice's direction.

"Your case has been lying around too long; we can't keep you here anymore."

That's the way I feel, too. He continues, "You, the biggest one, get out of here. You've got forty-eight hours to bring back proof that you aren't Jewish. We've got to see certificates of communion. Find the priest in Nice. You figure it out."

The German adds something. The interpreter steps in again.

"If you're not back in forty-eight hours, we'll make mincemeat out of your brother."

Maurice clicks his heels. I imitate him without knowing why; my brother must have learned that they like it.

"Thank you, messieurs," he says. "I'll be back."

The Gestapo man dismisses us the way you'd brush off a speck of dust with your hand.

There's no time to lose. Maurice gives his shoes a polishing with a corner of his blanket. I sit on my bed.

"Maurice, if you see you can get me released, come back. If not, stay away and hide someplace. It's better that one of us gets through than neither."

He combs his hair rapidly, looking at his reflection in the windowpane.

"Don't worry. I'll be seeing you in two days."

The door is already closed. I hear his hurried steps on the carpeted floor. He has neither kissed my cheeks nor shaken my hand. Should we hug and kiss when we part for two days?

The strange thing is that those two days didn't seem longer than any others. I didn't spend any more time than usual watching the clock. I knew — or let's say, I hoped — that they weren't going to make mincemeat out of me; I would simply get a green ticket for Friday and, as I planned to escape from the train, it really wasn't all that serious.

I felt considerably better than I had before my illness; I worked in the kitchen and people were getting to know me. Sometimes as I was walking along a corridor or going down a flight of stairs, I would meet one of the Germans or an interpreter who would smile at me or stop to shake my hand. I had the feeling that I was gradually becoming one of the regular faces at the Hôtel Excelsior.

That day they took particularly good care of me: after peeling the artichokes, shelling the beans, and sorting out the lentils, I was handed a big can of metal polish and two different kinds of rags and set to work shining up the doors on each landing.

I was just starting on the first door when I got a kick in the behind; it wasn't a hard one, but it was enough to make me drop the can of polish.

It was Maurice, all smiles.

I gave him a right to the body; he countered with a pair of hooks, danced around me, and wound up singing, "I got the certificates."

I left my door-polishing materials and we went into a little room at the end of the corridor, a room where they kept the brooms and all the cleaning supplies. It was a spot where we could be sure that no one would hear us. He told me what had happened.

Gambling everything, he had gone home: our parents were still there. They no longer went outside and hardly ever opened the shutters. Both of them had lost weight — a neighbor had to do all their shopping. When he'd explained the situation to them, Mama had cried. Then Maurice had left and gone to the church nearby.

"You see," he told me, "I remembered the priest in Dax. If a priest had been willing to save our lives once, maybe another one would do the same thing again."

Nobody was in the church — just an old man straightening the rows of chairs. Maurice asked him where he could find the priest. The old man answered that *he* was the priest. The sexton was working in a factory in Germany and he had to do everything himself.

He ushered Maurice into his residence, put on a soutane, and listened to him. Maurice told him everything. The priest didn't even let him finish the story.

"Don't worry. I'm going to make out the communion certificates and I'll give them to you right away. I'm also going to explain your case and your brother's to Archbishop Rémond, who will almost certainly come to your assistance. Go back and tell Joseph not to worry. I'll come to see you at the Excelsior."

When Maurice left the church he was beaming; he had the certificates in his pocket.

Instead of going home directly, he went out of his way to Golfe-Juan to see Subinagui and began explaining the situation once more.

"Just relax," said the camp director. "I'm going to phone the Archbishop myself — two people pushing for you are better than one and I can assure you he'll do everything possible."

He said nothing more, but Maurice knew that Archbishop Rémond had tried to keep as many people from going to Drancy as he could.

This time things were going to turn out all right. We were hardly out of the storage closet when the "interpreting machine" pounced on us.

"Well, did you get the proof?"

"Sure, I've got the communion certificates."

We couldn't tell if he was pleased or disappointed by the news.

"Wait outside the office. I'm going to tell the officer in charge."

I have trouble restraining myself, but we can't make a big show of joy; we've got to look casual. We made our communion at the church of La Buffa, we've brought in the proof — and that's all. There couldn't be anything more natural.

We go in. The German is wearing the same tweed jacket. Maurice hands him our papers. He looks at them, turns them over.

"*Das ist falsch!*"

I can never admire my brother's reflexes enough.

"Great! Then you're going to let us go?"

The interpreter lets the words filter through his lips.

"No, these papers are faked."

Maurice has had the time to prepare himself.

"Tell him he's making a mistake. Anyway, the priest is coming to see us and he said he's going to take us away."

"We'll see about that. Get out of here."

Our two certificates are safely tucked away in the file folder. But they haven't been enough to get us released.

Outside, Maurice swears softly.

"Damn it, damn it, damn . . ."

A voice roars from the floor below.

"Hey, you Joffo boys. Get to the kitchen — they're looking for you."

We go back downstairs. One of the staff hands us a flat wicker basket, a large one that's almost circular.

"Go get tomatoes and make it snappy. Bring in the ripest ones."

I knew where the tomatoes were. There was a little staircase adjoining the landing of another building and these stairs, which were only nine or ten steps, ended up on a covered terrace that was shady and cool. There, piled up on wicker trays, were the fruits and vegetables not yet ripe enough for the kitchen. The tomatoes lay in the last row.

I knew my tomatoes, having lugged my share of them from the marketplace to Tite's bar. These were scarcely yellow and the green veins on their tops were like emerald stars.

Maurice looked around. It was a quiet back-yard scene; surrounding us were high walls yellow with sunlight.

I picked up a tomato and put it in the basket, but I

didn't have the will power to take a second one: I was staring at the low wall which separated the landing we were on from the building across the way.

It wasn't even fifty centimeters high. Freedom was half a meter away.

I looked at Maurice. He was breathing faster too. We had to choose quickly; there were only a few minutes in which to decide.

Over there on the other landing we could run down the stairs and be outside on the street away from the hotel. We could end all that anxious waiting, the forged papers, the interrogations, the cold sweat. A wall half a meter high and we were away from death forever.

I didn't dare speak; I knew that Maurice was as taut as a bowstring. I placed a second tomato beside the first. Then it was Maurice's turn to take one, but he held it in his hand.

"Let's go," he murmurs.

I straighten up. A shiver runs through me. Four steps to take.

The shadow of the wall projects a precise line on the ground, an ink blot drawn out with a ruler. Maybe the sun has changed position but there's a protuberance at the far end of the shadow line, something that moves and then disappears.

I stoop and pretend to be catching an imaginary insect. Chances are the sentry doesn't speak French, but it's better to be cautious.

"I missed it! It got away!"

Maurice has already filled half the basket.

"You're out of your mind if you expect to catch butterflies with your bare hands."

I help him and we start working again.

Before going back downstairs, I leap up like a coiled spring, turn in midair, and drop back down.

"Damn it, missed again!"

The sentry disappears. I catch a fleeting glimpse of him ducking away; I see the black shape of the submachine gun barrel.

One of the army cooks turns around as we enter and watches us set the basket on the table.

"What the hell have you got there?"

"We're just bringing you the tomatoes."

He stands there gaping for an instant; abruptly, he turns away.

"Okay, just leave it there. We won't be needing you anymore."

His surprise hasn't escaped my notice. I'm going to understand it even better when I see that on the next three menus — supper of that evening and the two main meals on the following day — not a single tomato dish appears.

Maurice certainly knew what he was talking about: the Gestapo chief at the Excelsior is a man to watch out for. This trap may not be his last.

The priest from the church of La Buffa came three days later. He sat on a chair that an SS man brought him. It was a sign of respect rarely seen at the Excelsior, but it was the only one. He remained seated, motionless, for three hours without being asked to speak a word. At the end of that time, somebody came to inform him that he would not be received.

He rose and beckoned to an interpreter who was going by in the corridor. In a gentle voice, he explained that he knew quite well that the Gestapo offices were very busy, in fact swamped with work, and that he would return the next morning at seven and stay till closing time. He added that he would keep on doing so until the victory of the Third Reich if need be, so as not to allow the Nazi administration departments to commit a grave error involving the lives of two children. He went on to say that the Archbishop, who had been informed of the steps he had taken, was ready to intervene at the highest level — in Berlin, if necessary. As the good priest spoke, a knot of SS men gathered around him.

We had stumbled upon the most stubborn, the most witty priest in the whole Alpes-Maritimes province; above all, he was the priest most bent on snatching Jews from the clutches of the Germans.

The next morning, before the door had opened, when the sentinels on night duty were still waiting to be relieved by their daytime counterparts, the sentry posted at the lobby entrance saw the priest of La Buffa arrive. Giving him a friendly little wave, the priest trotted to the staircase, took hold of a chair, murmured "Don't go to any trouble for me . . ." to the SS men playing cards at a table nearby, and settled himself opposite the office. This time he had come equipped with his breviary, and you had only to see him to know that it would have been easier to move Mont Blanc than to even imagine this man being swayed so much as a millimeter from the task that he had assigned himself.

Every time an interpreter, clerk, or anybody at all went by in the corridor, they made a slight detour.

At noon he still had not been received.

At five minutes after twelve the priest plunged his hand

into a deep pocket of his cassock and came up with a packet wrapped neatly in white paper. It contained two chunks of whole-wheat bread around a slice of mortadella.

The priest ate his sandwich with gusto, carefully folded the paper up again, and put it back into his pocket. An SS guard was watching him in anger a few yards away and the priest rose and asked him in careful German, "Soldier, would you kindly bring me a glass of water?"

After this performance he quickly became the hotel's main attraction and the senior officers soon realized that this could present a certain danger; accordingly, at two o'clock, he was the first one admitted. The interview was brief, cool, but courteous.

He returned the next morning but this time he didn't need to take a seat; he was shown into the office immediately. He brought the papers demanded and even more: there were our two baptismal certificates and a handwritten letter from the Archbishop explaining that the two certificates had been issued at the cathedral of Algiers, the city in which we had been born. The letter went on to say that these documents had been in his possession since they had been required for our communion ceremony which had been held at the church of La Buffa on the date mentioned. He therefore asked that we be released immediately and said that if this proof was not deemed sufficient he was ready to come to Gestapo headquarters in person.

Apparently the Gestapo would have been very displeased to see the Bishopric take an official stand against them. To this very day, their reasons are still obscure; nevertheless, one of them is clear enough. Even in those years when France was drained of her manpower, food, supplies, even at a time when workers were going off to German factories, the policy of European cooperation had still not been abandoned. Thus, they couldn't afford to lock horns with the Catholic Church of France — with its millions of followers — over the question of whether or not two kids should go to the gas chamber. So, to keep up its policy of neutrality with regard to the Catholic Church, the Gestapo decided to release Maurice and Joseph Joffo — after more than a month's detention.

More often than not, one's life hangs by a thread; but that year, for us, there wasn't even a thread — only the fact that we had been arrested on a Friday, that we had come to the Hôtel Excelsior when the quota for the weekly train had already been filled, and there was time for the Germans, with their administrative obsession, to set up a file folder headed *RE:* Joffo, Maurice and Joseph. Few were as lucky as we were.

It was the priest who led us away, holding each of us by the hand. When the man in the tweed coat signed the release papers, our priest stuffed them in his pocket and didn't say thank you. There was even a hint of irritation in his manner which seemed to be saying: "It took you long enough to make up your minds." Before leaving the office, he nodded to the German and told us, "Maurice, Joseph, say goodbye to the gentleman."

We obeyed in chorus.

"Goodbye, m'sieur."

The German watched us go without a word; the interpreter had no need to translate.

Outside, I was dazzled by the sunlight and the wind that was coming from the sea. I gave a start. Standing before the hotel was the delivery truck that had brought

us down from the camp. Subinagui was sitting behind
the wheel. He kissed our cheeks joyfully.

"Fine, let's go. We're going back to New Harvest.
You've been hanging around this town long enough."

The truck starts up. I turn around. The sentries in
front of the hotel grow smaller and smaller; they disappear when we turn a corner. It's all over. We made it.

We're riding along the beachfront road. There's the
water with its shining sequins. The sun will sink into the
sea before long.

The little truck comes to a stop.

"I'm going to try to get my cigarette rations," says Subinagui. "The tobacco shop in Golfe-Juan is all out.
Maybe I'll be luckier here."

We get out.

It's the spot where the beach is the most primitive.
The flattish stones are bigger, rounder than elsewhere. I
twist my ankles in my wood-soled shoes, but the closer
we get to the edge of the sea the smaller and flatter the
stones become, until finally they turn into a wet and slip-
pery gravel lapped by the fringes of the little waves.

My laces are hard to untie. Maurice already has his
stockings off.

There, that does it. I'm barefoot and the water runs between my toes.

We wade out together. It's cold at first, but pleasant.
The sea is flat and motionless, an immense pool turned
red by the sun. Gulls are standing on the beach and suddenly they all take wing, skimming over our heads; they
rise, gliding out to sea.

Now the water is up to our knees and we stop. The sky
is at its bluest. We go on standing there, without a word.

I'm not thinking about anything; my mind is a blank. I only know that I'm going to live, that I'm free like the gulls.

Behind us, leaning his elbows on the top of the seawall, Subinagui looks down at us.

Gérard appears at the kitchen door. He's still as starched as ever; each night he puts his short pants under the mattress so they won't lose their crease.

"Jo, report to the phone."

I drop my string beans. You could circle the world twice with all the beans I've sliced.

I run across the camp to the office.

Subinagui is talking and hands me the receiver as soon as he sees me.

"It's your father."

My voice must have changed for he doesn't know that it's me.

"Is that you, Joseph?"

"Yes, how are you?"

"Fine. Just fine. Mama is, too. I'm glad you're both up there."

"Me too."

I sense that he's choked up, trembling a little. He adds, "It's wonderful, the way you stuck it out. I can tell you, we got a scare when we saw Maurice, but I knew that everything was going to turn out all right."

To hear the relief in his voice, he couldn't have been very sure of that.

"Were you afraid?" he asks.

"No . . . well, not really. I was sick for a while but I'm all better. I'm fine now. What about Henri and Albert?"

"They're all right too. I hear from them. They're going to be just fine."

"I hope so."

"Well, listen, I can't stay on too long. Your mother's going to be worried — you know how she is . . . Kiss Maurice and I'm giving you a big kiss, too. We're going to see you pretty soon now."

"Yes, Papa."

"Goodbye, Jo, and . . . be good . . ."

When he says "be good" to me, it's because he doesn't know what to say anymore and I'm afraid I'll burst into tears over the phone.

"Goodbye, Papa. See you soon."

There's a click. He has hung up.

It was stupid that Maurice wasn't there; he was working on a farm a mile or two away.

I go back to my string beans. Life at the camp isn't what it used to be. Testi is gone; his aunt came for him and I won't see my pal again. And then, since the raid the Gestapo made in the middle of the night, people here aren't as friendly as they used to be. And there are fewer of us now; some boys have gone away. They say that one of the big boys has joined the *Milice*.* We don't stay around the fire as long these evenings; everyone's become distrustful. Still, even the way it is, the camp is paradise for me. It's good to be able to come and go as you please and especially to be out in the air. The days are growing shorter; we're getting on toward winter. One more winter of war.

* An organization set up by the Vichy government in January 1943. This militia collaborated with the Germans in the fighting against the French *Résistance*. *Translator*.

"Is the war going to end soon, Monsieur Subinagui?"

He laughs and draws a line under the last figure in the column. He closes the ledger book and declares: "Three months. I bet it won't last three months."

I think he's a little too optimistic. It seems as though we have been in the war forever, that it has become a permanent state. War and existence have been confused. There's no need to run away from the war anymore; it's everywhere. Words are whispered, evoking strange settings: Guadalcanal, Manila, Monte Cassino, Benghazi. They stir up images of palm trees, minarets, snow, pagodas, monasteries at the top of mountains; the war is at the bottom of the sea, in the sky — it's everywhere, triumphant. And the days go by . . . Soon it will be two weeks since we came back from the Excelsior.

I'm on the boat that's heading for the Château d'If. The captain is shaking me harder and harder. I see the gold-braided anchor shining on his visored cap and what astonishes me is the way he knows my name.

"Jo, Jo."

This guy is getting on my nerves. I've got to run away from him. I've got to burrow deeper into the warmth, I've got to . . .

"Jo!"

This time I wake up. The circle of the flashlight blinds me. It's pitch dark.

"Quick, get dressed. Don't make any noise . . ."

What's going on? The others are asleep in the tent; in the other row, someone rolls over and the snores that were stilled for a moment have now resumed — louder than before. In the darkness I pull on my shirt. Damn it,

I've got it on inside out. I sense Maurice close to me, scraping his soles on the floor.

This can't be a Gestapo raid; there would be cries, everyone would be up. Subinagui is the one holding the flashlight.

"Come on. I'll meet you in the office."

Outside, the night is cool; there are millions of stars. The wall of the tent is already wet with the moisture rising from the ground.

Everyone in the camp is asleep. Everyone except us.

The office is open. Subinagui reaches the building just behind us. His darker shadow scarcely stands out against the sky. He's carrying two bundles. When he comes into the little room that smells of rough-hewn lumber and old paper, he lights a small lamp and I see that he's carrying our two knapsacks.

So I know that we'll have to go on our way again. Maybe I've known it all the time.

X

"YOU'RE LEAVING right now. I've put everything you'll need in your knapsacks — two shirts, underwear, stockings, and a bite to eat — and I'm going to give you some money. You'll cut across the fields till you reach Cannes. Then you take a train for Montluçon and from there you'll go to the village where your sister is waiting. The name of it is Ainay-le-Vieil and . . ."

Maurice interrupts him.

"What's going on?"

Subinagui lowers his eyes.

"I'd rather you hadn't asked me that question, but it had to come."

He ponders for a moment, then announces bluntly: "Your father was arrested in an SS roundup yesterday and taken to the Hôtel Excelsior."

Everything is starting to spin. The Gestapo was stronger than the Czar's army; it had finally managed to get my father.

"That's not all — your father was carrying his identity papers, made out in his own name. It won't be long before the Germans link you with him and they'll be up here looking for you. There isn't a minute to lose. Get going."

Maurice already has his knapsack slung over his shoulders.

"What about my mother?"

"They warned her in time. She has already left. I can't tell you where, but you can rest assured that your parents had a hiding place picked out. But go now. And don't write, don't give us any word — they may be watching the mail that we get."

I've taken up my knapsack too, and the weight of it presses against my back.

Subinagui has switched off the lights. All three of us stand in the doorway.

"Go along the trail in back and stay off the roads. You ought to have a train toward seven o'clock. Goodbye, boys."

We start out. Everything has happened so fast that it still hasn't registered with me. I only know my father is in Nazi hands and the Germans may already be on our heels. What a triumph for the one in the tweed jacket if they get us in their clutches! But what about the priest of La Buffa? Priests have been deported for less than that. Anyone caught helping a Jew must share his fate. No, we'd better not get caught.

The earth is hard and dry, but as we brush past weeds and vine leaves the dew wets our short pants and our shirt-sleeves.

The camp already lies far behind us. The night is so

light that the crest of the hills casts its shadow on the plains and on the terraced farmland.

Where is the town of Montluçon? I have no idea. I certainly didn't work hard enough on geography in school. Maurice doesn't know any more than I, so it's pointless to ask him. But then, with the train, there's really nothing to worry about. It will get us there.

I have the idea that the town is far from the sea, a long way inland; it's the only thing I'm sure about. It makes me sad to leave the Mediterranean. I'll come back to it when I'm bigger and when there's peace.

The path goes uphill. We've got to stay away from farmhouses so that the watchdogs won't bark. The trouble is that we have to make wide detours which take us out of the way.

Maurice stops. We can clearly see a road ahead of us.

"We're going to cross it," whispers Maurice. "Straight ahead is Vence; we've got to go around the other side."

There's no one coming, so we dash across the road. After we scramble up a grassy bank, the sea reappears at our feet, broad, gray, shimmering. Cannes, bordering the sea, is still invisible. Now we've got to work our way down through vegetable gardens to the train station.

We squat at the foot of a tree. It's pointless to hurry; walking through the streets at this hour would be too dangerous. We'd better wait until daybreak.

Dawn smells good, a strong, dry odor — a little like the pepper plants of Menton. Little by little the shapes around us grow distinct and the colors emerge one after another; the reds, blues, greens settle into their places. There are rooftops about us that blend into the rocky hillside.

Drowsily I watch for the first rays of sunshine, which burst to the surface of the sea like a trumpet blast announcing the clash of the brass. It's time for us to make our entrance.

We set out again and, after passing villas that are boarded up, reach the center of town. People ride past us on bicycles; shopkeepers are beginning to raise the corrugated metal shutters.

There's the station. It's already crowded, though not like Marseille.

"Two one-way tickets for Montluçon."

The clerk operates a machine, consults books and timetables. I get the feeling he'll never figure out our fare. There, finally; he's got it.

"One hundred and fourteen francs, twenty centimes."

Maurice scoops up the change while I ask, "Where do we have to change trains?"

"It's complicated. Go to Marseille; you'll get the express in three quarters of an hour. After that you head for Lyon. If there's no delay, you'll only have to wait two or three hours. At Lyon, take the motor train for Moulins, and in Moulins you've got to change again for Montluçon. Or you can go another way: via Roanne, Saint-Germain-des-Fosses, and Gannat to Montluçon, or else, Saint-Etienne, Clermont-Ferrand, and the Bourges track. But, one way or the other, you're bound to get there. Only — I can't rightly say *when*. Besides, where you're headed, I can't tell you when you'll get there or even *if* you'll get there, because . . ."

Spreading his arms to represent an airplane, he imitates the sound of a motor and exploding bombs.

"Understand what I mean?"

We've stumbled over a talkative one. Winking, he adds, "And there's more than just the bombings; there's also the . . ." Joining his two fists, he pushes down the handle of an imaginary detonator; he puffs up his cheeks till he turns crimson. "Ba-a-b-oom! See what I mean?"

We nod with fascination.

"And there's more than just the sabotage! There are slowdowns, stops, derailments, tracks torn up, and besides that there's . . ." Cupping his hands around his mouth, he produces an ominous whine. "See what I mean?"

"Air raids," says Maurice.

He looks delighted.

"Yes, exactly — air raids. So what it all means is that I can't tell you when you'll get there — maybe in two days, maybe in three weeks. In any case, you'll see for yourselves."

"That's right," says Maurice, "we'll see. And thanks for the information."

"Don't mention it. The train for Marseille is standing on track C."

We try to keep straight faces as we walk away from the ticket window. I'm about to burst out laughing when I see him five meters away — the interpreter from the Excelsior.

My brother has seen him too. It's too late for us to hide and/or run away.

We go on moving toward him. I have the feeling that he must be able to see my heart pounding right through my shirt. He stops. He has recognized us.

"Good morning, m'sieur."

If he tries anything, if he pulls out a gun, a whistle, or jumps us, I know what I'm going to give him: a swift soccer kick with the iron tip of my shoes. That ought to fix him.

"Good morning."

He's still got that mechanical, expressionless voice, but for the first time I see the beginnings of a smile on his face.

"Making a trip?"

"Yes, we're going to another *Compagnons de France* camp."

"That's good. Where is it?"

We were lucky to have stumbled across a particularly informative ticket agent; I launch into one of those improvisations that I'm so fond of.

"It's in Roanne. But that's far from here. We've got to change in Marseille, Clermont-Ferrand, Saint-Etienne, and Moulins."

"I see. Very good."

Maurice perks up. If we haven't been arrested, it's because the interpreter still hasn't heard about my father's arrest.

"And you, m'sieur, still working in Nice?"

He nods. "I had a few days off. I'm going back now."

We go on standing there, shifting our weight from one foot to the other.

"Well, goodbye, young gentlemen. I wish you a pleasant stay in Roanne."

"Thank you, m'sieur. Goodbye, m'sieur."

Whew!

"If this keeps up," Maurice says, "we're going to die of heart failure before the Germans catch us."

The train pulled in. Contrary to what the ticket agent had told us in Cannes, there was a connecting train for Lyon almost immediately. Up to Avignon, the journey was almost pleasant; but once we'd gone through that town, an unexpected enemy confronted us: the cold.

The trains were of course unheated, and we were making our way to the north, moving further and further from the balmy Mediterranean. In the town of Montélimar, I sought refuge in the public toilet, put on three pairs of underpants one on top of the other, three undershirts, and then pulled on two pairs of stockings. In Valence, I put on both my short-sleeved shirts, two pairs of short pants, and my third and final pair of stockings. I just managed to squeeze into my shoes.

Despite these many layers, my arms and knees were still bare. In Lyon, on the platform of the train station which was swept by a damp, chill wind, we held a contest to see whose teeth could chatter the loudest. I won hands down, though Maurice claimed just the opposite. This provided the excuse for a boxing match that warmed us up a little. But when the train pulled in after an hour and a half wait and then made its way still further to the northwest, the situation became serious. In the compartments the passengers were already wearing their winter clothing — overcoats, gloves, mufflers. We were still dressed for a summer vacation. I would never have believed that there could be such different climates in one country. Back in my school in Paris, I had learned that France had a temperate climate; now I could prove that this was untrue. France is a cold country and of all the towns in France, Montluçon is by far the coldest.

Blue and trembling with cold, we got off the train onto

a gray platform, under gray skies; a gray ticket inspector took our tickets, and then we were out in a town stripped of the slightest color, a town swept by a glacial wind. It was only the beginning of October but never was there a winter so early as the one in 1943. The people tramped up and down the sidewalks trying to keep warm, but the wind seemed to blow from everywhere at once. The town was one big icy draft where, despite a triple layer of stockings, my toes seemed to become hard as marble. The wind flew up my shirt-sleeves and slid under my armpits. I had had gooseflesh since the town of Valence.

Between the chatterings of his teeth, a frozen Maurice managed to say, "We've got to do something before we die of pneumonia."

That was just how I felt about it, and we began running along the dreary streets.

The well-known axiom, "Run a little — that'll warm you up," is undoubtedly one of the biggest absurdities that adults can utter to children. After my experience that day I can safely state that, when you're really cold, running doesn't help in the slightest. Running leaves you breathless, tires you out, but doesn't warm you up at all. After half an hour of frantic galloping and hand-rubbing, I was puffing like a walrus but shivering even harder than before.

"Listen, Jo. We've got to buy coats."

"You have ration stamps for clothing?"

"No, but we've got to try."

On a street that wound around a bleak square, I saw a tiny shop. It had a dusty show window, a faded façade with lettering that was almost invisible: *Clothing for Men, Women, and Children.*

"Let's go."

I experienced one of the pleasantest sensations of my life when that door swung shut behind us: the shop was heated.

The warmth entered through each of my pores at once; I could have happily sprawled out on the floor in relief. Without so much as a glance at the good lady who looked at us from behind the counter, we glued ourselves against the pot-bellied stove.

The proprietress looked at us with round eyes. We must have been a sight to behold. How many times had Montluçon seen two boys arrive in summer shirts, their arms bare in bitter cold weather, hugging their knapsacks against their chests?

I felt my rear end getting done to a turn and was in ecstasy when the lady asked us, "What would you like, children?"

Maurice ripped himself away from the delights of the stove.

"We'd like coats or heavy jackets. We don't have any ration stamps, but maybe if we paid a little extra . . ."

She shook her head ruefully.

"Even if you paid millions, I couldn't sell you anything. We haven't had any goods come in for quite a long time; the wholesalers just don't deliver anymore."

"You see, madame," said Maurice, "we're cold."

She looked at us with compassion.

"You didn't need to tell me that," she said. "A body can see it plain as day."

I joined the conversation.

"Don't you have any sweaters, something that would give a little protection?"

She laughed as if I had just told her a particularly funny story.

"We haven't seen a sweater in so long that we don't know what they are," she said. "The only thing I can show you is this."

She stooped, reaching under the counter for two mufflers. They were *ersatz*, imitation wool, but better than nothing.

"We'll take them. How much are they?"

Maurice paid and I took my courage in both hands.

"Excuse me, madame, but would it bother you if we stayed here a few more minutes?"

The very idea of plunging back outside made me shiver again and my voice must have had just the right plaintive note, for she said no. She even seemed happy to have someone to talk to. When she learned that we had just come from Nice, she got all excited. She used to spend her vacations there, and she had us tell her about all the goings-on, about the changes that the town had undergone.

I was still glued to the stove and was thinking of removing one of my two shirts when I noticed that it was growing dark outside. It was too late to take the bus for the village where my sister lived; we had to find a hotel for the night.

I was explaining my fears to Maurice when the good woman spoke up.

"Listen," she said. "You won't find a hotel in Montluçon. Two of them have been requisitioned by the Germans and the third for the *Milice*. If you did manage to get a room, it wouldn't have any heat. But I can offer you my son's room; the bed will be a little narrow for the two of you, but at least the room is warm."

That good woman of Montluçon! I could have jumped for joy. That evening she made the best *gratin dauphinois* that I've ever had the pleasure to eat. She went on talking while we ate, and made us a cup of herb tea after the meal. I fell asleep instantly, buried under a red comforter stuffed with feathers. There was an alert during the night but the sirens didn't even wake me up.

She kissed us when we left and wouldn't let us pay.

It wasn't quite so cold outside and now we had our warm mufflers.

The asthmatic bus was the same color as Montluçon; it was gray, and the only cheerful notes were the patches of red lead that had been slapped on its body over the rust spots.

It jolted its way across a countryside that seemed terribly grim compared to the one we had just left. Already there wasn't a single leaf on the trees, and through the windowpanes we saw that it was beginning to drizzle.

In less than an hour, the bus left us in front of the church in Ainay-le-Vieil.

It was more a hamlet than a village: a few houses leaning one against the other, one narrow street, a butcher shop–bakery, and a grocery–hardware store–tobacconist's–bar. The fields began right at the end of the village. I noticed at once that, although the houses were inhabited, the barns were empty. The huge haylofts on the edge of the road housed no more than half a haystack each.

Our sister Rosette lived with her husband in one of the houses that leaned against the church. She kissed us and cried when we told her that Papa had been arrested by the Gestapo.

In the enormous tiled kitchen, she served us real milk in great earthenware bowls and made us put on pullovers made of real wool. They were too big for us, but with the sleeves rolled up and the hems tucked into our short pants they were all right. We were ready for winter.

From the first moment we were there I sensed that, despite her obvious happiness at being together again with her little brothers, Rosette was uneasy, afraid of something. Maurice was aware of it too, for after a while he said, "You look like there's something bothering you."

She gave us huge slices of buttered bread, poured milk in our bowls, and sat down next to us.

"Listen," she said, "I don't think you can stay here. It wouldn't be wise."

We looked at her in silence.

"I'm going to explain," she said. "There's an informer in the village."

She rumpled her apron nervously.

"A little less than two months ago, two women came here; one of them had a baby. They moved in with a farmer who lives at the other end of the village. They hadn't been there a week when the Gestapo came. They were taken away with the child, and the farmer was arrested along with them. He came back three days later and . . . they'd broken his arm. He told us that if anyone else tried to hide Jewish people, he would be shot."

"But who was the informer?"

"That's just it," Rosette said. "Nobody knows."

I sat there taking in the story and then said, "But at least you must have an idea."

She shook her head.

"It's impossible to say. There are about one hundred and fifty people in this village. If you subtract the kids, that makes eighty to ninety adults. We all know one another. Everybody suspects somebody else. That's all we talk about here . . . When I bump into the schoolmaster, he says it's the old woman from the hollow who spies on everything from her window. According to our neighbors, it's the schoolmaster himself. They say he has a photo of Pétain in his dining room. Other people claim it's old Viaque who was a member of the *Croix-de-feu* * and fought the Germans in the First War. It's getting terrible; each one suspects the other. I was at the grocer's yesterday and nobody spoke to anyone; people were giving each other sly looks. Apparently the Gestapo gives the informers money, so nobody dares to buy anything anymore for fear of looking as if they have too much money to spend, but then people get just as suspicious of the ones who stop buying . . . It's a vicious circle."

"What about you — aren't you afraid that the informer will . . ."

Rosette shrugs in resignation.

"No, I don't think so. I've been here a fairly long time now and I hope that my identity card will get me through. Just the same, I've got a hiding place ready that Paul found — in case they come searching."

I sigh. I would have liked to live here in this village a while. We could have found jobs, roamed around, played. But it's clear that we can't; we've got to keep moving — and fast.

* A veterans' organization founded in 1927. This influential rightist group was dissolved by the Popular Front Government in February 1936. *Translator.*

Maurice is thinking aloud.

"I don't think anyone saw us come in . . ."

Rosette smiles, wistfully.

"At the beginning, I didn't think the people were paying any attention to me either. Then, very soon, I realized that even when the street is empty, when the shutters are closed, they don't miss a single move you make; they know everything around here. You wouldn't believe it."

She stops and looks at us. When she has that thoughtful look, it's amazing how much she resembles my father.

"Do you know what you're going to do? You're going to Henri and Albert in Aix-les-Bains."

"Where's Aix-les-Bains?"

"In the Alps, right up in the mountains. I'll give you the money for . . ."

Maurice refuses with a princely gesture.

"No need to. We're still getting along on the money we put away in Nice and . . ."

There's a knock at the door.

Rosette freezes. I sit there, not daring to swallow my mouthful of milk-soaked bread.

Should we hide? That would be stupid, the worst mistake possible; they've seen us come in. Rosette understands this perfectly and motions us to stay seated.

She goes to the door.

We hear her exclaim, "Oh, it's you, Madame Vouillard! Have you come to get your eggs? Come in, please . . ."

"I don't want to disturb you; I see that you have company . . ."

It's an old woman's voice. And in fact it's an old

woman who comes in; she's slightly built, wearing a black shawl, a black coat, gray stockings, fur-lined shoes. And she's got wrinkles going every which way — a real country grandmother like the ones you read about in Alphonse Daudet.

We get to our feet.

"Bonjour, madame."

"Oh, how big they are! And healthy-looking! That one must be the younger. I'll bet you're brothers. You certainly look alike . . ."

She goes on gabbing while my anger mounts: if there's one thing I can't stand, it's being told that I look like my brother. I don't know why; he's no worse-looking than the next guy, but it just drives me insane. It makes me less *me*. Hearing that remark is enough to make my suspicions fall on her. I'll bet that she's the informer; her nosy face can't fool an espionage expert like Joseph Joffo. She saw us come in. She's just made sure who we are. In two hours' time she'll be making her report to the Gestapo.

"I suppose you've come to see your big sister?"

It's looking more and more suspicious: now she's asking questions. There can't be any doubt.

Rosette returns with four eggs.

"Here you are, Madame Vouillard."

The old woman says thank you, fishes around under her apron, and struggles to pull out a wallet bound with a rubber band. I don't take my eyes off her. Obviously, she's rolling in the stuff; there are loads of bills in her wallet, money from the Nazis.

"You boys are going to stay around here for a while?"

Now that's pushing things a little too far, granny.

"No, we just came to say hello to Rosette and then we're going straight back to Roanne."

She ties up the eggs in a big handkerchief.

"Well then, goodbye, children. See you soon, Rosette."

She even walks like a stool-pigeon, dragging out her steps to put off leaving until the very last moment — that way, she picks up one or two extra details as she goes. But I've seen through her all right.

Rosette shows her out and comes back. She sits down again and throws a weary glance at the door.

"She's awfully lonely, the poor soul. She comes by all the time, for one thing or another. Actually, she just wants to chat a little."

I sneer.

"Yeah, I'll *bet!*"

"Besides, her name isn't Vouillard; that isn't her real name."

I'm more and more certain that the shoe fits; every spy has an alias — sometimes they even use code numbers.

"As a matter of fact," Rosette continues, "her name is Marthe Rosenberg."

The dreams I've had for the last three minutes about becoming a private detective have just vanished for good.

The denunciation of the two Jewish women and their baby had deeply shaken Marthe Rosenberg, who has been living in the village since 1941. Poor grandmother. Silently I apologize to her and go back to the conversation.

So it's been decided: the wisest move is to leave for Aix-les-Bains. Actually, I like the idea; after the sea, the mountains. While we're at it, we might just as well get to see the country. And then, I'll be glad to see Henri and Albert.

"You've got to have lunch with us at least; you haven't even seen your brother-in-law . . ."

Maurice shakes his head. If Rosette had ever been arrested she would know that when you're in danger of any kind, you've got to run away; there isn't a second to lose. A tenth of a second may spell the difference between life and death, between prison walls and freedom.

She swiftly packs our knapsacks, stuffing them full of warm stockings and sandwiches. There isn't any bus; once again, we'll set off on foot. Now I can walk for hours without getting blisters. The soles of my feet, the skin of my heels have hardened. I no longer feel those pains I used to get in my calves and thighs. I can tell by my shirt sleeves and the hem of my short pants that I've grown.

Grown, hardened, changed . . . Perhaps my heart has also accustomed itself, has inured itself to catastrophes; perhaps it has become incapable of feeling real sorrow . . . The child that I was eighteen months ago, that child lost in the Métro, in the train carrying him to Dax — I know he isn't the same today. I know he's been lost forever in some country thicket, on some back road in Provence, in the corridors of the hotel in Nice; each day that we were fleeing, he crumbled away a little more . . . Looking at Rosette boiling eggs, saying words that I don't hear, I wonder if I still am a child . . . I doubt if playing jacks or marbles would appeal to me now; perhaps a soccer match or maybe . . . But these things do belong to my age; after all, I'm not quite twelve years old. They should excite me . . . but they don't. Perhaps I've had the idea up to now that I was going to come through this war unscathed; but that may be my mistake. They haven't taken my life; they've done something worse — they've robbed me of my childhood. They've killed the child that I might have been . . . Perhaps I'm already too hard, too mean; when they arrested Papa, I didn't even cry. A year ago, the very thought of it would have been unbearable.

Tomorrow I'll be in Aix-les-Bains. If that doesn't work out, if some obstacle crops up, we'll go elsewhere, further away, east, west, north, south, anywhere. It's all the same to me. I don't give a damn.

Actually, I may not even care if I go on living . . . But the machine has been started up; the game must go on according to the rules. The hunted always run from the hunter, and while I still have my wind I'll do everything I can to rob them of the pleasure of getting me. Through the window, the sad fields, already gray with winter, have disappeared; the flat, dreary prairies have faded away. It seems as if I can already see the snow-covered peaks, the deep blue lake, the russet leaves of autumn. I close my eyes and at once the flowers and fragrance of the mountains come over me.

XI

THE HARDEST PART is making sure that you don't tear the paper and, most important of all, that you don't spoil the color under the number. You've got to do a precision job, work to within a quarter of a millimeter. The ideal thing would be a very bright lamp and a jeweler's eyepiece, one of those little black cylinders that you screw over your eye and keep from falling out by wrinkling up your brow.

I stick out my tongue, bend my head down even with the tabletop, and continue my precision work. The razor blade scratches gently; little by little, the black bar of the 4 disappears. And what's left when you remove the crossbar of the figure 4? You simply get the figure 1.

At first sight, that may not seem terribly interesting, but at the close of 1943 the advantage gained is incalculable; Number 4 ration stamps entitle you to buy starches; Number 1 stamps are good for a kilo of sugar apiece. So, if you've got a flat surface, a steady hand, and an old razor blade, you can ask all the people you know for their Number 4 stamps and convert them into Number 1 stamps. That way, even in this year of intense privation, you can die of diabetes.

I've begun to get a reputation in the village. Those who know about my talents stop me in the street and entrust their precious stamps to me. I return them "converted." In exchange for this work I receive a little money, and if things keep going the way they are, I'll be making profits almost equaling those I used to make in Nice.

I blow on my fingers. It's impossible to do this work with mittens on; that would be like a surgeon working with his eyes closed. But I sure would like to have those mittens right now, for in the room it's freezing. I don't even have the nerve to look at the thermometer, which hangs over the head of my bed like a crucifix with the horizontal part missing. In any case, the ice I broke in the earthenware vase this morning hardened back into a more delicate film, trapping a sliver of soap like a dead fish.

Seated before the little folding table that takes up half of the tiny room, only my head and arms can be seen. The rest of me is bundled up in the bedspread. If I add to that my jacket, two sweaters, one shirt, two undershirts, it's clear that I'm still fond of swathing myself in as many layers as possible. In the faded yellow of the spread's heavy fabric, I look like a huge, shivering caterpillar.

It's dark. I'm sleepy and I should really go to bed now, because tomorrow morning at four old Mancelier is going to be banging the tip of his cane against my door and I can already feel the enormous difficulty I'm going to have trying to rip myself from the tepid warmth of the blankets and plunge into clothes that are cold even after a night under the mattress; then, the icy water in the porcelain pitcher and the nocturnal morning that I'm going to be pedaling through in silence so complete that it seems to come out of the very snow. Ahead of me, the bicycle light casts a pale yellow stain; the anemic wavering gleam doesn't even light the way for me.

That doesn't matter; I know the village blindfolded. And it's a big village that's fast growing to the size of a town, with Mancelier's bookshop–stationery store at its hub. It's right in the heart of town. The building is located on the nicest side of the square, where you can see the whole mountain range, a vast amphitheater which serves the town as a backdrop. Even in summer, the sun soon disappears behind the line of the summit. I live in a region of shadow, whiteness, and cold.

New people have come into my life in the two months that I've been living in the village of R——. The most important of these are the Manceliers, my employers. Here's the family portrait.

That's the father in the middle. He's got a mustache and the eyes of a man who isn't easy to live with; he's somewhere in his fifties, with a knee that won't bend any more and a hip that bends too much. This double misfortune explains the cane that he uses to get around with. You'll see two ribbons in the buttonhole of his lapel — the Military Medal and *Croix de Guerre* (with bronze *palme*, he's quick to point out). He received both wounds and decorations in the First World War. He went through the battles of the Marne, Craonne, Les Eparges, and Verdun in particular, under the command of Pétain who still ranks as his number one idol. He keeps photos of Pétain in the parlor. One, in black and white, sitting on the pedestal table, shows the Marshal on horseback; the other, in color, hangs over the door and shows him standing. Leave the parlor and you find Pétain again in the hallway, in profile and bare-headed; if you enter the bedroom, you'll meet him full-face, wearing a visored cap, but this time he's a little figurine standing on a lace doily covering the marble-topped night-table.

Ambroise Mancelier reveres the Marshal; he thinks that collaboration with Hitler is the only hope for the survival of a France rotted by years of meddling parliamentary government. He explains the reverses that Germany is presently suffering as "a temporary crisis within the German General Staff."

One important detail: my venerable employer has particular enemies — the Jews. He says that he can't stomach any of them.

Personally, I have the feeling that he's begun to make friends with me these last two months. Of course, I don't have anything to do with the "accursed race," as we all know. But to continue with the gallery.

Beside him stands his wife, Marcelle Mancelier. Just looking at her makes you not want to describe her. There isn't a distinguishing feature about this gray-haired lady, who wears a smock in the store, an apron in her apartment, and a black shawl to church. A hard worker, she handles the administrative end of the business.

Standing behind her is Raoul Mancelier, the son. He rarely comes into the bookshop. He lives in a rather distant part of town where he plies the noble trade of notary's clerk. He's a notorious supporter of Pétain and makes no bones about it; he displays his pro-German sentiments quite openly.

And then, standing beside them, is Françoise.

Françoise Mancelier.

When I think back to those years, perhaps nothing comes to mind faster than that young girl's face — much faster than the faces of the SS men at the Excelsior, even faster than Papa's face. If I hadn't had my love story during that period of flight, something would be missing from the picture. And I'm stretching things a lot to call it a love story; nothing happened, nothing took place — no kiss, no promise, nothing . . . How could it have been otherwise? Françoise Mancelier was a little over fourteen and I hadn't quite turned twelve.

How do you tell about something that has no story? It's just that I felt her blond, smiling presence constantly — whether I was in the shop, in my room, or out on the road. It's incredible when I think of it — how little she said to me: "Good morning, Joseph," "Good-bye, Joseph," "Joseph, would you go to the grocer's, to the baker's, to the farm . . ." In the winter she wore a thick cap knit of unbleached wool, with a pompom that hung down and bobbled against her cheek. It was a pink cheek, a very pink one — like the cheeks of children in advertisements for ski resorts. And there I was, a prisoner because I hadn't even reached the age of twelve. I became more and more monosyllabic when I answered Françoise Mancelier. I felt that she could never love me, that a difference of two years was too great, that she was a young woman and I was a little boy.

And then, I had gotten off to a bad start in that family and could never hope to marry her. I came to R—— one Saturday after spending two days in Aix-les-Bains. Albert, Henri, and Mama (who had gone to live with them) were delighted to see us, but it was too dangerous for all five of us to be together. So Maurice left for R—— where one of Albert's friends, who ran the Hôtel du Commerce, had hired him. A few days later Maurice heard that Mancelier's shop was looking for a delivery boy, and that's when I landed there. I had concluded the agreement right away, but the very morning after I got there — on Sunday — Ambroise Mancelier came to me dressed in the dark suit that he wore only at the Armistice Day parade and at Sunday mass; he placed a firm hand on my shoulder.

"My boy," he said, "you sleep under my roof, eat at my table, and work in my shop. You're part of the family, so to speak. Do we see eye to eye on that score?"

"Yes, M'sieur Mancelier."

I didn't see at all what he was driving at and I saw those words as nothing more than an excuse for one of those speeches with which he barraged his entourage and which were variations on the theme "Work-Family-Country." Inevitably they wound up glorifying the Vichy government and its undisputed leader, Philippe Pétain.

But that wasn't what he was talking about on the day in question.

"And if you're one of the family, you must take part in all its customs and you'll see that the custom we hold most sacred is that of going to church every Sunday at a quarter past eleven to attend mass. So hurry and get dressed."

I no sooner heard his cane against the floor than I saw the comedy of the situation. But three things prompted me to obey: first, you just didn't contradict a man like

Ambroise Mancelier; then, I was curious about seeing a Catholic service; and finally, I would spend almost an hour in the intoxicating company of the beautiful Françoise with her rosy cheeks.

I pulled on the coat I had bought in Aix-les-Bains and very quickly found myself kneeling on a prayer stool next to Ambroise, who didn't kneel (because of his infirmity), and his devoted spouse. My beloved was kneeling just in front of me, which enabled me to admire the nape of her blond neck and her well-turned calves. I conscientiously imitated the worshippers as they knelt and made the sign of the cross; I was being lulled into a downy, drowsy state when all at once the organ burst forth and everyone rose.

I'd rather tell the rest in the present tense. That may make the incident seem more everyday and perhaps take away the hallowed aspect given to a story by "was" and "were." The present tense has no surprises; it is a straightforward kind of tense, where we see things as they happen, still new and living; it's the tense of childhood, the one that suited me at the time.

The stained-glass windows are red; the morning light splashes the stone underfoot with the scarlet shadows of saints, who seem to lie bleeding on the floor.

I follow the slow steps of the flock that shuffles outside to the town again. Already their whispering is growing less subdued.

Little by little the pews empty out. As if they were in a restaurant, the choirboys clear the altar table, while the organ rumbles. I love the organ. It sounds like a gigantic troop of cavalry. Billions of wagons with spokeless wheels roll over our heads; the thunder resounds and dies, like a storm fading away.

We're among the last ones. It looks as though the crowd is having trouble getting through. There must be a bottleneck near the door. Françoise is behind me. Even in the constant hubbub, I can sense her footsteps — lighter than the others, almost gliding.

Suddenly, in front of me, a very stout lady dressed in black dips her hand in a kind of clam shell set on a pedestal. She turns around, staring me right in the face, and extends two pudgy fingers toward me. I'm surprised because I don't even know her. She must have seen me going by on the bike one morning; maybe she's one of the three hundred subscribers on my newspaper delivery route. Anyhow, she seems to know me all right.

I give her a hearty handshake.

"Good morning, madame."

Why has Françoise burst out laughing? Why is old Mancelier turning around and raising his eyebrows like that? There's even a tall beanpole of a guy who must be the stout lady's husband and he's laughing out loud.

I sense that I haven't done quite the right thing — but, worst of all, there's Françoise: she'll never again take me seriously. What girl would marry a fellow who shakes hands with a lady who's offering him holy water? To make up for it, I'll have to perform some brilliant feat of arms, something incredibly difficult. I'll have to win the war singlehandedly or save her from a fire or shipwreck . . . But how do you save somebody from a shipwreck in the province of Haute-Savoie? Maybe I could save her from an avalanche! But the snow covering the mountains never comes down as low as our village. Well, I'd better resign myself to it: Françoise will never become my bride, I'm unworthy of her. It's terrible.

Another Sunday, the meal after mass. Madame Mancelier is wearing her apron again; she has put on her slippers with the pompoms and is bustling around the kitchen stove. Françoise has opened the door of the sideboard and the porcelain bowls clink as she takes them out. They have blue flowers drawn all the way round and red flowers at the bottom. When the soup is clear enough, I always think that the flowers are going to float to the surface and I'll be able to fish them out with my spoon; that would be geranium soup.

Mancelier is seated in the armchair. He reads thick books on whose sturdy bindings the title and author's name stand out in gold letters. They're books by generals and colonels. From time to time, he neighs with satisfaction. I get the idea that the author and the reader must be as alike as two peas in a pod. For quite some time now I've imagined that all high-ranking officers have faces like Mancelier's.

The meal starts off with radishes from the garden; they're all hollow. This is something that keeps my employer permanently baffled. He's the only one in the region to own a plot of land that produces only hollow radishes. Nevertheless, he watches them grow; he waters them, adds fertilizer to the earth, sprinkling it with lots of whitish chemicals that he measures in the privacy of his toolshed — but no good ever comes of it all. Once through that thin red film, your teeth encounter empty space. Maybe next year old Mancelier's radishes will just float up into the sky like tiny balloons.

What surprises me is the fact that he still hasn't blamed his hollow radishes on the Jews. True, he's too busy with something else right now — Europe.

"You see, Joseph, they don't teach you about that in the public schools, for the schools have become *public* — like a girl that turns . . ."

After a rather uneasy glance in his wife's direction, he resumes, now he's sure that she hasn't heard anything.

"That's why the schools will never teach you that what characterizes a great man is having an ideal. And an ideal isn't an *idea* — it's something different."

He doesn't say what it is and helps himself to a generous serving of kidney beans; his fork scrapes the bowl, trying to find as much pickled pork as possible.

"It's something entirely different. But you've also got to know what ideal you're talking about. Now, when it comes to politics, there's only one way to think — that is provided you aren't a Turk or a Negro or a Communist, and provided you've been born in a nation between the Atlantic Ocean and the Ural Mountains. The way to think is — Europe."

It's clear-cut enough; there's nothing to argue about. Besides, I don't have any inclination to argue about it; I'm too busy stealing furtive looks at Françoise . . . She isn't hungry. I see her fiddling with her fork on the fine Sunday tablecloth.

"Now, who wanted to unite Europe? To create bright, clean Europe, a Europe capable of fighting its adversaries from the west, east, or south? History doesn't record

many of them. There are only . . . How many of them
are there, Joseph?"

I give a start and look at him. He's extending his thick
hand toward me with thumb, index finger, and middle
finger raised.

"Well, how many are there?"

"There are three, Monsieur Mancelier."

"Very good, Joseph. That's right. There are three."

He lowers his thumb.

"Louis the Fourteenth."

The index finger disappears.

"Napoléon."

The middle finger joins the others.

"Philippe Pétain."

He drains his glass of red wine, rewarding himself for
this splendid demonstration, and resumes with even
greater zeal.

"And the strangest part is that not one of those three
men was understood during his own lifetime. The
masses, that pack of bastards and morons . . ."

Looking up at the chandelier, Madame Mancelier sighs.

"Please, Ambroise, do watch your language."

Ambroise beats a retreat. I have never seen an ardent
militarist who could beat a hastier retreat.

" . . . So the masses have always opposed those great
minds. They guillotined the first one's grandson; they
threw the second one into prison; and I know that the
third has enemies. But he's a tough customer, that one.
He's been through Verdun and you've got to bear one
thing in mind, my boy — when you've been through Verdun, you can get through anything."

I wasn't listening anymore. I had finished my beans

and was waiting for dessert. Ambroise aimed his discourse mainly at me; he was glad to have me as a new listener, for neither Françoise nor her mother hid the fact that they were bored to tears. They didn't say it, but their expressions were perfectly eloquent. When coffee was served, Raoul and his wife showed up. Then it started in again, worse than ever. Raoul was more lucid than his father. The son was no longer very sure of a German victory; he foresaw difficulties, serious obstacles — in particular, "the juggernaut of American technology." For a long time afterward, I imagined that the Americans had invented some kind of fabulous weapon, an enormous sledge hammer that was smashing whole divisions of the German army.

"If they'd listened to me," said Raoul, "we'd have become allies with Hitler and Mussolini back in '36. Nothing could have stopped the three of us. And Franco was with us. We'd have invaded England easy as could be. Then we'd have taken care of Russia. We'd be the rulers of the world. What's more, France would have avoided defeat that way."

Then Raoul's wife, long-limbed and insipidly fair with protruding eyes that gave her the appearance of a sheep, asked: "And why didn't we do that?"

Ambroise Mancelier, holding a demitasse, burst out with a laugh that spilled his coffee into the saucer.

"Because," he said, "instead of being governed by Frenchmen defending their own soil and their rights, the government was rotten with Jews."

Raoul held a pedantic finger aloft.

"Now wait," he said magnanimously. "They weren't the only ones."

Words resounded that I didn't understand, words that sill come to mind: foreigners, Freemasons, Socialists, Popular Front.

Françoise had long since left to do her homework in her room, so I stood up, asked permission to leave, and rushed out into the street.

Then I sprinted toward the Hôtel du Commerce. Usually Maurice would wait for me, pacing up and down on the sidewalk, his pockets bulging with everything he had been able to swipe from the kitchen. He did quite nicely for himself, having gotten into a very complicated deal with a butcher, a deal that brought him in plenty of money. Then, what with my ration-stamp deal, our pooled resources took on interesting proportions.

As we walked, he told me the latest news. He was working under the head chef, who belonged to the *Résistance* and listened to Radio London. The news was good: the Germans were still falling back.

At the edge of town, he pointed to a far-off mountain shrouded in fog, hidden among the peaks.

"That's where the *Maquis* hide out. They say there are plenty of them; they're knocking off trucks and trains."

I jumped with excitement.

"What if we went up there?"

That was the chance I had dreamt of, my chance to win Françoise. I would come back a colonel, with a rifle in my hand, covered with roses, and she'd ride behind me on my horse and we'd go galloping away. Then too, it would be fun to get revenge, to be the hunter instead of the hunted.

"No," said Maurice, "they won't take us — we're too young. I asked my pal."

A bit disappointed, I walked out onto the soccer field and we kicked a ball around until six o'clock.

At first, we'd had trouble being accepted by the local kids. They all went to school and we didn't. That made us jealous and created animosity. Then they saw me on my bike with my canvas bag slung across my chest as I delivered papers along my route, and finally the Joffo brothers were accepted.

The soccer field was in miserable condition; tufts of grass sprouted here and there. We booted the ball into dandelions. There were no nets in the goals anymore. The crossbar was missing from one of them, so that there was nothing left but the goal posts. This gave rise to countless fights: Maurice claimed that the ball had gone too high, I argued that it had gone in.

And then the snow came on the first Sunday of winter — as if it were keeping an appointment. A foot of snow fell overnight and there we were — a dozen of us kids — knocking our heels one against the other to keep warm. We couldn't play: the ball went up in the air and buried itself in the whiteness, unable to bounce anymore. That was really an unlucky break.

The snow gave me trouble on the paper route, too. It became almost impossible to ride the bike and my bag of papers was heavy. I remember racking my brain for hours, trying to think up a sled with a wooden box for those damned papers, but I never got around to making it.

Christmas 1943.

I puff ahead of me and my breath goes out into the cold air in white spirals. Maurice has gotten a postcard for both of us from Henri. Everyone is all right; they all send us their regards and wish us well. My brother worked late last night. A group of Germans and *collabos* were throwing a Christmas Eve party. So today Maurice can't keep awake; he didn't get to bed until four in the morning. He slips me a shoe box full of liver pâté sandwiches, some shrimp in a paper bag, a breast of chicken, and three-quarters of a cake that's shaped like a yule log. I walk through the streets, my provisions under my arm. Behind the windowpanes, the people are still eating; you can hear the clicking of knives, the clinking of glasses, laughter. The streets are sad and I'm alone there.

My feet have brought me to the soccer field; I've come there like a robot. At the edge of the playing field, the roof of the grandstand is ready to collapse under the weight of the snow; still, it shelters part of the bleachers.

When I cross the field, my feet disappear up to the ankles and, as they pull free again, there's a little squeak, the only sound that breaks the total silence.

I find a dry seat in the bleachers; the wooden wall keeps me out of the wind. I'm almost comfortable there.

So, alone in the grandstand, before an empty, snow-covered soccer field, surrounded by the Alps, Joseph Joffo stuffs himself with liver pâté and mocha cream cake, wishing himself a merry Christmas. He knows that it's a Catholic holiday, but he's never stopped a Christian from observing Yom Kippur.

My belly full, I go back to the bookshop, remove my shoes at the doorstep, and sneak up the stairs: I don't want to let the veteran of Verdun get me. He's solemnly listening to Philippe Henriot's* news commentary on the

---

* Catholic rightist militant who, in January 1944, became secretary of state under Laval. *Translator.*

radio. He's never missed one since the start of the Vichy government.

He nods his head gravely nine or ten times during the broadcast and, when Henriot is done, he turns the set off and without fail murmurs: "If they published those commentaries in a book, I'd be the first one around here to buy it."

I've reached my room, where it feels colder than outside. I lift up my mattress and grab the book I swiped from the shop: *Le voyage en ballon.*

Inside the book there are about fifteen Number 4 stamps. That gives me plenty of crossbars to take off. I wrap myself in the bedspread and start to work, slowly, ever so slowly — so as not to tear the paper.

Hey, that's the third person who's guffawed behind my back. What do I have — a hole in my pants?

On my bicycle, I slide a discreet hand behind me and my fingertips touch the long paper fish that's hanging down from the middle of my back.

True, I had forgotten the date: April 1, 1944.

It's funny, the way kids love April Fool's pranks. The war is still there, making itself felt more and more now, but that doesn't stop them from ringing doorbells or tying pots to the tails of the few remaining cats that still haven't been made into stew.

Nevertheless, things are bad — well, good and bad at the same time. For the Germans, it's defeat; tomorrow, it'll be a rout. That's certainly true around the village of R——. The *maquisards* are striking all over the place. Two days ago the roundhouse of the train station blew up.

In a fury, old Mancelier rushed into the hallway, slicing the air with his cane and wishing that he could give a few good thrashings to all those young bastards that won't be happy until they bring the English back to France and completely destroy the work of Joan of Arc.

Old Mancelier is very restless just now. I catch him looking at Pétain's portrait; his gaze still isn't critical, but it's not an entirely admiring one anymore, either. That's how I can tell that the Allies are advancing; Ambroise's gaze is more revealing to me than Radio London.

In any case, the weather is nice and the morale of the people of R—— has clearly risen. The baker slipped me a *brioche* in exchange for my newspaper and tips have been skyrocketing.

I feel happy and I pedal like a fiend. Just four more papers for the Hôtel du Commerce and my morning's work is done. I'm way ahead of schedule.

The hotel door slams behind me and I greet the customers drinking at the tables along each wall. The proprietor is there, chatting with someone. He speaks in the local dialect and it's hard to understand him.

"Hi, Jo. You want to see your brother?"

"Yes, I'd like to, please."

"Go ahead downstairs; he's in the wine cellar."

The squealing of brakes makes me turn around; despite the door being closed, the sound pierces my ears.

Through the curtains I see the two trucks blocking the street.

"Look!"

There's no need for me to tell them: all the drinkers grow silent and watch the soldiers jumping down. Their uniforms are black; they wear berets sloping down over one ear. They're the most hated ones. They're the hunters of *Résistance* fighters. They're *miliciens.**

His submachine gun athwart his belly, one of them runs towards the ruelle Saint-Jean. They must know this part of the country. They must know that you can get away by going down that alley and then crossing the fields.

One of them in the middle makes big sweeping motions with his arm and I see four of them head straight toward us.

"They're coming in," says the proprietor.

"Hey, boy . . ."

I turn around and look at the man who has spoken: he's one of the customers, but I've never seen him before. A little man, fairly old, all dressed in dark corduroy, he smiles at me calmly and comes toward me.

They can't see us out on the street.

A crumpled envelope falls into my delivery bag. He has taken it from his pocket. He throws the newspapers he was holding into the bag, on top of the envelope.

The *miliciens* push the doors open.

The little man's lips don't move, yet he's speaking. His eyes aren't on me anymore, but I'm the one he's talking to.

"Monsieur Jean," he says, "at the Cheval-Blanc."

His hand pushes me toward the door. I go out and bump into two black torsos crisscrossed with belts. Their faces are tanned; the shadow of their berets hides their eyes.

"Hands up. Fast."

The skinny one springs like a cat. With a push of his

* Members of the *Milice. Translator.*

hip, he sends a glass pitcher flying to the floor and the barrel of his submachine gun zigzags through the air. The proprietor opens his mouth and a tanned hand seizes him by the shirt-front and shoves him up against the bar. The second *milicien* looks at me and motions me to the door.

"Get out, boy."

I go past the two soldiers, my newspaper bag under my arm. That bag is real dynamite, but dynamite doesn't always explode.

I'm outside. The square is swarming with men in black. I go for my bicycle on the sidewalk and set out. Who's going to pay attention to a little newspaper boy? I think it over as I pedal. Who was that little man in corduroy?

At the corner of the square I turn around.

There he is, between the two *miliciens*. He's got both his hands on his head. He's pretty far away; maybe it's just a face he's making because the sun is in his eyes, but I get the idea that he's smiling and that the smile is for me.

Now to the Cheval-Blanc — and fast. I know the café; I slip the paper under their door every morning.

There are only a few customers at this time of day. When I come in, Maryse, the waitress, looks surprised to see me; she stops wiping a marble-topped table.

"What are you doing here?"

"I'm looking for Monsieur Jean."

I see her give a start. Besides, she looks uneasy; they must have seen the trucks full of *Milice* go by and that's never a good sign.

Maryse runs her tongue over her lips.

"What do you want with him?"

"I want to see him — I've got a message for him."

She hesitates. The three farmers sitting at the back of the room shuffle their cards on a green mat covering their table.

"Come with me."

I follow her. We cross through the kitchen, the courtyard, and she knocks at the garage door. She knocks in an odd way, a group of raps that sound like the hoofbeats of a galloping horse, and then another one after that, with an interval between . . .

The door opens out on its hinges. There's a man inside, a man with hunting boots. He looks a little like my brother Henri. He doesn't speak.

Maryse points to me.

"It's the paper boy. He'd like to talk to Monsieur Jean."

"What do you have to say to him?"

There's something stern about his voice. I get the idea that it's better to be this man's friend than his enemy.

"A customer at the Hôtel du Commerce gave me a message for him."

The man moves into the light. Abruptly, he looks interested.

"What did he look like?"

"A short gentleman, all in corduroy. The *miliciens* have just arrested him."

Both of his hands are resting on my shoulders, two hands — strong, but tender.

"Give me the message," he says.

"I can't do that; the little man told me to give it to Monsieur Jean . . ."

Maryse gives me a dig with her elbow.

"Go ahead," she says. "That's Monsieur Jean."

He looks at me and I hand him the envelope.

He tears it open, takes out a slip of paper that I don't try to read; I sense that you've got to mind your own business in this game.

Monsieur Jean reads, then puts the letter in his pocket and runs his fingers through his hair.

"Well done, my boy. Maryse will be our go-between. When I need you, she'll let you know. Go straight home now."

And that's how I joined the *Résistance*.

Actually, that was my one very modest contribution to the cause of Free France. I waited impatiently for Maryse to contact me and I would often go past the Cheval-Blanc, but the waitress just dried her wine glasses and turned up her nose at me. In retrospect, I think that they must have considered me too young. Perhaps, most of all, the presence of Ambroise Mancelier made them distrustful. As to that gentleman, he no longer left the house; he rarely even listened to the radio anymore.

The sixth of June, the day of the Normandy landings, was indeed the longest day of the year and the most tragic for the old Pétainist. The hereditary enemy was infecting the Normandy beaches. An armada of helmeted Negroes, New York Jews, English Communist workers was assaulting *la douce France*, the cradle of the Christian Occident. His cane hammered the hallways and his wife wouldn't come downstairs to the shop anymore. There had been a few affronts by the customers which indicated clearly that the climate had changed.

One afternoon, as I'd been unpacking a crate of books that had just been delivered, the baker's son came in, bought a newspaper and, while handing over the coins to Madame Mancelier, pointed to the show window where a book illustrated with color photos glorifying the Marshal stood on prominent display.

"How much?"

I thought I would choke, for I knew him a little: he was Maurice's pal and they said that he was helping the guerrillas, supplying them with flour and bringing them bread. Madame Mancelier made a pretense of rummaging through invoices.

"Forty francs."

"I'll buy it. But I'm not taking it with me. Just leave it in the window. That won't bother you, will it?"

The proprietress turned red. She mumbled that she couldn't see any reason why it should bother her, but that she couldn't understand why he wanted to buy it since he wasn't planning to read it.

She understood soon enough.

Young Mouron picked up a price tag that happened to be lying on the cash register and, with a red pencil, wrote in neat block letters: SOLD.

Then he took the tag and stuck it right on the book's cover, smack on the tie of old Pétain, Savior of France.

She turned pale and said, "I'd rather put it aside for you; I can't keep a book that's been paid for in the window."

Her tone was cold and Mouron stared at her.

"Then I won't buy it. No sense me plunking down my forty francs when I'll be getting it for free in a few weeks."

He opened the door and, before slamming it with all his might, said, "See you *very* soon, Madame Mancelier."

From that time on I did practically everything in the bookshop. Fortunately the customers were few and far between; in 1944 there weren't many readers in R——. Aside from the newspapers and the comic books for kids, which I consumed avidly and carried to my brother by the armload, I didn't sell more than three books a week.

I also did the shopping, and at Mouron's bakery the father or son would wait on me and repeat each time: "Has that old idiot Ambroise started to wet his pants yet?" Everyone in the shop began to laugh — including me. But it embarrassed me just the same: they were making fun of Françoise's father. Françoise had gone away at the end of June to an aunt's house near Roubaix. And I was left there, sad at heart, with those two old people who didn't dare go out of their house anymore. One evening there was a clatter of glass. I ran downstairs: a windowpane had been broken in the kitchen. Mouron was right; it wasn't going to be long before the old man wet his pants.

I'd go out each evening after adding up the day's meager receipts; I used to meet Maurice and we'd go up to the church steeple, a squat tower with enormous beams. From up there we could see the road, the highway that zigzagged in the distance where the plains were, and we saw trucks full of soldiers speeding along, on their way up from the south. Sometimes, there were long convoys of ambulances. We didn't hear from Aix-les-Bains anymore, as the mail no longer came through. Trains were being blown up; nobody traveled.

Maurice saw *maquisards* one night at the Hôtel du Commerce. They got out of a car; they had leather jackets, pistols, submachine guns, and hobnailed boots. They were well-armed and very optimistic. It was rough at times, they said, but there wouldn't be more than a few weeks' effort.

One evening I carried an enormous package of books to the Hôtel du Commerce on the rack of my bike. I had stolen them from the bookshelves; they were intended for the *maquisards*. I was a bit surprised that they had the time to read, but Maurice explained that the books were mainly for the wounded who were being treated in grottoes and needed something to help them pass the time.

Since the time the little man was arrested, the *miliciens* haven't come back. Maurice told me a few weeks later that they shot him against the wall of a farmyard. That made me sick for a whole day; my mind went blank, the way it did in Nice. I had a feeling that nothing made any sense and that bad people would always win.

The Germans have hardly been moving from their camp anymore, but one day there's suddenly traffic to and from the front. The baker spends the day up on his roof watching them through field glasses. He says he's seen tanks, Panzers, come in.

By evening, everybody has heard the news and there's a panic. Mouron is convinced that the Germans are going to use R—— as a stronghold to stop the Allied advance. After a few minutes' discussion, our little area becomes the last bastion before Berlin; if we are liberated, the Third Reich will collapse.

"We're going to have to live in the cellars," says one farmer. "Maybe for a long time. The Yanks don't give a damn — they smash everything. They don't look where they're going when they start attacking. They're not going to stop on our account."

I know that country bumpkin. Every other morning he yells at me because his paper isn't on time; he's a real pest.

Old Flandrin bawls him out and then announces that they've made American flags at the town hall with the help of the schoolmistress. It won't be long now; they say they're no more than fifty kilometers away.

God, it's true; it's going to be all over. All of them wear serious looks when they say that; I wonder if they really believe it, if they realize what that means. "It's going to be all over." I still don't dare say it. I scarcely dare think about it, out of a kind of stupid superstition, as if words were sparrows and when you say them too loud, you make them fly away to never-never land for good.

I'm doing the bookkeeping all alone in the empty shop. The Manceliers have shut themselves up in their rooms over head. Ambroise paces back and forth; three quarters of the time he doesn't even come out of his bedroom. He no longer listens to the radio; it's been a long time now since I've heard Philippe Henriot.

On the other side of the metal shutters it's a summer night. There's a group of young people talking on the square, despite the curfew. There's a dull roar in the distance; it seems to come from beyond the mountains. Maybe it's the war coming to us. Or maybe it's the avalanche that I wished for so that I could save Françoise; now that avalanche is going to engulf us all.

I'm sleepy. It's already late and I've been up since five this morning. Besides, I'll have to start all over again tomorrow — pedaling along those roads . . . I'm doing the hills faster and faster these days; a few more months of this training and I'll be a champion bicycle racer.

There, I've finished the addition. At the beginning of the ledger, the figures were neatly aligned in Madame Mancelier's fine calligraphy — lines drawn with a ruler, the sums to be brought forward marked in red ink at the top of the pages. For some time now my scrawled handwriting has been replacing that perfect order. I erase a spot and, after the horizontal line separating one day from another, I write in tomorrow's date.

July 8, 1944.

"Jo!"

It seems like Maurice's voice calling me, but that can't be; at this hour, he should still be sleeping. And when Maurice sleeps, I sleep too. So it must be a dream . . .

"Jo! Damn it, wake up!"

This time I open my eyes. There's a distant thunder, a rumbling, as if the mountains were closing in on us.

I push the shutters ajar. The square is still deserted. It's light out, but the sun hasn't yet come up. It's just before dawn, the time when things and people are shaking off the last mists of the night.

My eyes blink. Down below, Maurice raises up his face toward me. He's all alone; there isn't another soul on the little square.

"What's the matter?"

Maurice looks at me and smiles.

"They're gone."

It was as simple as that, so simple that I felt almost disappointed. I was expecting more of a spectacle, more uproar. I thought that wars and chases had to end dramatically with lots of arm-waving and people striking poses. But it wasn't like that at all.

I was leaning out my window one fine summer morning and it was all over. I was free. Nobody was trying to kill me anymore. I could go back home, take trains, walk in the street, laugh, ring doorbells, play at marbles in the schoolyard on the rue Ferdinand-Flocon. But no, that wouldn't be fun anymore.

For a few months I had been the one running the bookshop and I had to admit that it was a lot more fun than any of that.

I went downstairs and the two of us walked to the village. There was a crowd in front of the baker's shop: young fellows on bikes with F.F.I.* armbands and small pistols stuck in their belts. I knew some of them; they weren't the real members of the underground. No, these guys had just blossomed out all of a sudden on the very morning that the Krauts had packed up to go further north.

And then the streets grew crowded. The windows were decorated with flags: French, British, American. There weren't too many American flags — sewing forty-eight stars, that's a lot of work, but there were some anyway. Everybody was hugging and kissing at the Cheval-Blanc and the Commerce and I was deliriously happy because I'd made it all right and there weren't any papers to deliver that morning. They didn't come until the next day and then they weren't the same ones anymore: *Les Allobroges, Le Dauphiné Libéré,* and some others . . . I

* *Forces Françaises de l'Intérieur* (French Forces of the Interior), the official name of the *Maquis. Translator.*

sold hundreds of copies; people came running up to me, threw down money, and didn't even wait for their change; I was really raking it in.

As I look back now, it's hard for me to bring to mind any images from that whirlwind. Perhaps clearest of all I see the pallid face of Ambroise Mancelier backed up against the flowered wallpaper in the parlor and everybody around him; the crowd was headed by young Mouron, who stuck an angry fist under Mancelier's chin. The time to settle old scores had come. In the afternoon, three girls were paraded through the streets lined on both sides with F.F.I. men; the girls' heads had been shaved and swastikas painted on their faces. People were saying that a neighbor's son had been shot in the woods; they'd caught him in the act of burying his *Milice* uniform. Now it was the old Pétainist's turn.

The first slap rang out like a pistol shot. I had just come in and I saw old Mancelier's head strike the wall, and when I saw those old lips which I had heard speak so much drivel begin to tremble, I squeezed past the others and went up to Mouron.

"Let him go. He kept me hidden here for a long time and it could have cost him his neck to hide a Jew."

I had certainly done a good job of bringing silence to the crowded room. But Mouron still managed to recover.

"Fine, maybe you're a Jew — but did that old fool know about it?"

I turn to Mancelier, who is wild-eyed with horror. I know what you think, old man. I can still hear your words: "Those kike bastards," "Jewish scum," "A good clean sweep is what they need," "When you wipe out half of them, that'll make the other half stop and think."

Well, do you understand now? You had a kike living in your house — a real live kike and, what's more, it's the kike that's going to save your skin.

"Of course he knew!"

Mouron is dumbfounded. "That doesn't stop him from being a *collabo*. We had to take all that shit from him and . . ."

Somebody interrupts him. "Yes, but maybe he was just putting all that on to hide Joseph . . ."

I get out of there. It's a good sign if they're arguing that way: they won't kill him. They didn't kill him, in fact; they took him to the prison in Annecy with his wife. When he climbed into the back of the truck, all his limbs were shaking, but I was the only one who could know the true cause of his trembling. To owe his neck to a Jew after applauding Henriot every evening for four years — that wasn't the kind of thing he could stomach.

Perhaps the strangest twist of all is that I'm now the proprietor of the bookshop; I feel like taking a paintbrush and blacking out the name "Librairie Mancelier" and putting my name up there. That would be only fair. Now that they're printing newspapers, new ones are appearing every day — all the little underground papers have come out in the open. The people want to know what's going on, so I've become more important than the mayor or the baker: I'm the big dispenser of world news. A key role! Sometimes I put in more than fifteen hours a day. The till is overflowing; the money will go to old Mancelier's successors, but for the moment I'm running things and I've got to stay on my toes.

And suddenly one day, on all my papers, in enormous letters that cover the whole front page — letters that I never even thought they had in printing plants:

PARIS LIBÉRÉ

It is early morning and I can still see the truck fading into the distance. Nobody is awake yet in the village. I've got these big bundles tied with twine, stacks of papers all saying the same thing, and I sit down on the curb in front of what has become my store.

Water is running past under my legs in the gutter . . . it's the Seine. The little heap of earth, that clod near my left heel — that's Montmartre; near the twig — that's the rue Clignancourt; and there, right at the spot where the moss starts — that's my house. The sign JUDISCHES GESCHAEFT is gone and will not reappear.

The shutters are going to be opening over the shop; the first bikes will be appearing. In the street, there must be a clamor that's already rising, that's climbing over the rooftops.

I'm already on my feet and I'm running up the stairs to my room. Under the bed lies my knapsack, and I know that it's the last time I'll be needing it.

No doubt I'll have trouble finding a train and even more trouble getting aboard. But nothing can stop me.

Nothing can stop me. Now that's the kind of sentence you mustn't ever say or even think.

It isn't far from the bookshop to the train station — it can't be more than half a mile. The street, lined with shade trees, is straight and there are massive benches which nobody ever sits on and which are covered with dead leaves in autumn.

I whistled as I trotted up the street. It seemed to me that when I reached the end of it I would be seeing the entrance to the Marcadet-Poissonnier station of the Métro.

That wasn't what I saw.

There were three of them coming, F.F.I. armbands on their biceps, their belts kind of slack as if they'd just seen the latest Western; one of them had a scarf knotted around his neck like a Foreign Legionnaire and wore hunting boots. They had rifles slung over their shoulders — three ugly German Mausers.

"Hey, come here, you."

Stupefied, I stop.

"About-face, my little friend."

I didn't know them. I'd never seen them in the village. They must come from some other *Maquis* unit; in any case, they don't seem to be fooling around.

"What's wrong?"

The man with the scarf cinches up the sling of his rifle and points to the square where I've just come from. They're going to march me back.

This takes the prize. Arrested by the Gestapo, chased throughout the whole war, I get myself picked up by French *Résistance* fighters on the day Paris is liberated.

"You must be crazy or something! What do you think I am — an SS man in disguise?"

They don't answer. They're stubborn as mules, the F.F.I. men in this area. But I'm not going to stand for it. They're going to listen to me and . . .

But here I am, back at the village square. There's a crowd gathered around the shop now — mostly guys in leather jackets, all of them armed. There's a real young one, very skinny, that everybody calls *mon capitaine,* and a group further on, with maps spread out on the hood of a delivery truck.

One of my bodyguards clicks his heels in front of the skinny guy.

"We got him, *mon capitaine.*"

That takes my breath away. Now I'm being hunted just like the Krauts.

The skinny one looks at me, one eyebrow higher than the other.

"Where were you headed?"

"Me? Well . . . Paris."

"Why Paris?"

"Because that's where I live."

"And you were going to leave all this here?"

His open hand sweeps over the pile of newspapers and the bookstore.

"You bet I was going to leave all this!"

He stares at me and both his eyebrows come back to the same level.

"I don't think you understand the situation very well."

Motioning with his hand, he leads me inside the shop. The other men follow him and fall into a single rank. Whether they're doing this to throw a scare into me or if it's just their custom nowadays, I don't know; but they line up behind the big table, with the captain in the middle.

I'm on the other side, like the accused before the judges.

"You don't understand the situation," the captain resumes. "You are in charge of circulating news in the village. You must stay at your post, for we're still at war and your job is like that of a soldier who . . ."

"You don't want me to go back to Paris?"

He stops, somewhat taken aback, but recovers very quickly. He says, simply, "No."

I don't waver. Listen, *mon capitaine*, the Gestapo couldn't kill me, so don't think a guy like you can scare me.

"Fine, then shoot me."

The big man at the end of the rank drops his cigarette.

This time the captain can't come up with an answer.

"I left home three years ago. My family is scattered all over. Today I can go back, so I'm going. And you can't stop me."

The captain spreads his hands out on the table.

"What's your name?"

"Joseph Joffo. I'm a Jew."

He takes a slight breath, as if he is afraid of injuring his lungs by taking in too much air.

"Have you heard from your family?"

"No, I'm going to Paris now to find out where they are."

They all look at one another.

The big one taps on the table with his index finger.

"Listen, couldn't you just stay for . . ."

"No."

The door opens. I know this one — it's Monsieur Jean of the Cheval-Blanc.

He smiles. I was right in thinking that it's better to be his friend; he's going to prove it now.

"I know this boy. He's worked for us. What's wrong?"

The captain looks up. Actually, he seems nice. It's

only those eyebrows that make him look a bit like the Devil.

"He wants to go back home and that's creating problems for the bookshop."

Monsieur Jean places both his hands on my shoulders the way he did the first time we met.

"You want to go?"

I look at him.

"Yes."

I already know that it's won. My judges aren't wearing the faces of judges anymore. A feeling of relief makes me break into tears, which come treacherously, as if trying to make me ridiculous.

It's hard to make them stop running.

I'm on my way again. Fifteen of them came along to see me off — among them the one with the scarf who'd looked so mean at the beginning. He even carried my knapsack for me. My back hurt from all the backslapping I got.

"Want a sandwich for the train?"

"You think you'll get a seat?"

"Give the Eiffel Tower a kiss for us."

They left me a little bit before we got there, because a truck came with other *maquisards* and took them away. I waved goodbye to them and walked on to the station.

And what about Maurice?

I saw him quickly before I first left for the station. As with me and the F.F.I., his boss didn't want to let him go. No getting away from it, these people have some kind of obsession. No sense worrying about it; he'll manage to get away — and fast, if I know him.

*

At the station I went through a turnstile that led to the platform. Standing on that platform were ten million people.

In the books I've read since then, writers often say that a place is "swarming" with people. Well, the platform at R—— wasn't swarming — there wasn't that much room. It was jammed to capacity. Where had all these people come from?

From every corner of the province, maybe other places too . . . maybe they'd all had to go in hiding. Now they were on their way back up to the capital with bundles and crates. There must be next to nothing to eat in Paris: people in the crowd have sacks of flour, baskets piled with meat, hens with their feet tied — it's an exodus in reverse.

"We won't all be able to get aboard."

I turn around.

The lady behind me has a chin that trembles when she speaks. The two long hairs sprouting from her cheek also tremble a little. She's breathing hard. She's got a bag under her arm and an enormous suitcase held together with twine; it's splitting at the seams, a potential disaster.

"Let me through, damn it!" Standing on tiptoe I can just manage to see the stationmaster climbing over mountains of bundles like an alpinist.

The crowd eddies back and forth; the ones right at the edge of the platform hump their backs to keep from being pushed down onto the tracks.

I hear what they're saying around me. There's been a delay — an hour already. That isn't all: many lines still haven't been repaired.

The main thing is to get right up close before the train

pulls in. I've got an advantage over all these people: I'm the smallest.

I crush a foot; its owner yelps and grabs me by my knapsack, opening a mouth as big as a tunnel. I'm faster.

"Excuse me. I've got to get my little brother over there; he's going to be run over."

The guy mutters something and actually succeeds in moving himself over to let me wriggle through. Before me there's a wall formed by two trunks, one on top of the other.

I heave my knapsack on top and scramble up like a climber. I'm at the summit; I'm looking down over all the heads. I look as if I want to make a speech.

"Get right down off there, you whelp!"

"But my little brother's over there ..."

I've slipped back into my little boy voice, a grammar-school voice. That gets me down the other side of the obstacle. I adapt to my element, crawling between two rear ends. The one on the right doesn't seem to have suffered from food rationing. I lean to the left. A miracle: there's a space between two legs. I squeeze through, crawling sideways, and who do you think is standing in the first row? Jo Joffo.

There's no chance of sitting down; either I'd never get back up or I'd die of suffocation. I'm scared just thinking about the stampede there'll be when the train pulls in. There's a lady standing next to me — to be exact, against me. High wooden heels, a huge handbag, hair piled high on her head, she's all dressed up and I hear her moaning softly. She smiles at me weakly.

"I hope this isn't going to last much longer."

We stand there two and a half hours.

It's the knees that get you. It feels like there are two boards stuck to your kneecap, one in front, one behind. And they're squeezing you, gently at first — then hard as can be. So you raise one leg in the air, but the one still on the ground gets a cramp within ten seconds, so you switch. You do a slow, primitive dance like a heavily laden, waddling bear that . . .

"Here it comes!"

A murmur goes through the crowd; there's a kind of wave as fingers tighten over the handles of suitcases and on the straps of knapsacks. Heaps of objects are being gathered around their owners' feet.

I lean forward a little, but not much; I don't want to end up on the tracks.

Yes, I can see it. The locomotive is moving ahead very slowly; there's no smoke in the morning sky. Funny, I hadn't even noticed that it was a fine day.

I jump back. I slip under the sling of the knapsack and I wait, tense, my muscles aching. Jo, I tell myself, you'll have to be quick on the trigger if you want to see Paris again.

The train.

Jammed.

Clusters of bodies seem on the verge of falling through the compartment doors. It's going to be terrible. I feel the surge building up behind me. Imperceptibly I move forward despite my resistance. The footboards of the moving train brush past my belly.

"Watch out, over there . . ."

There are shouts. Bundles must have fallen under wheels. I don't even glance that way; if I take my eyes off this thing for one second, I won't make it.

The brakes squeal as if they're going to split the rails and the train halts.

All by themselves, the doors open and a vacuum seems to suck me aboard. I've got two guys ahead of me; I cannonball past them. I give somebody a bump with my back and then I've got half a shoe on the first step of the footboard. Grit your teeth, Jojo. I push with everything I've got; they're all pushing behind me, hard enough to snap my rib cage.

I've got my chest in a vise and there's no more air. I force my way out and — I'm up against a wall. I've gotten myself into a fix: there's a big bruiser — he's got shoulder muscles that bulge under his shirt; he's the biggest bozo I've ever seen. He goes up one step, two; he gives another shove, heaves himself aboard, and doesn't move — that big ox has blocked the door with his body.

Women are crying and screaming behind me.

I see the big bozo's hand groping — trying to slam the door behind him. I'm on the second step and that skunk won't give me the few centimeters that I need to get in. I see his hand, a mass of muscles about to clamp down. Then he gives me a brutal bump with his backside. He sends me flying onto the platform; the same blow pushes back the crowd that's crushing me.

Furious, I bounce back, head first. Chomp. With every tooth in my jawbone, I tear into the flesh of his hand.

He lets out a bellow, turns halfway around, and I plunge into the gap like a rugby player. I'm perfectly horizontal. I hear the door close behind me. My head is on somebody's forearm; the rest of my body is stretched over a mound of suitcases and my feet are sticking out the compartment window.

It's going to be a good thirty kilometers before I regain a vertical position.

The big bruiser that I bit glares at me but doesn't say a word. He knows that he's better off keeping his mouth shut. The bump he gave me with his backside wasn't exactly fair play, he knows that very well. And then, really, I don't give a damn anymore. The train is moving — slowly, but it's moving, and every time the wheels go around, I'm closer. I know that I'll get there: tonight, tomorrow, in a week — I'll be home.

While I was driving myself into the compartment like a nail into a board, my brother Maurice wasn't exactly standing still. He'd preferred to make the trip by car rather than by rail. That boy has always had very definite tastes.

The deal was handled swiftly. A friend of his boss has a car but no gas. Maurice goes straight to the fellow's house: if there's a seat for him, he'll supply the gas (of which he hasn't a drop). He goes flying down into the wine cellar, finds a bottle of old cognac, and then fills nineteen others with weak tea to get the right color. He runs out and gets some sergeant to sample the good bottle in exchange for five jerry cans of gasoline; that's enough for the trip from R—— to Paris.

Maurice packs his things and goes up to his boss with an outstretched hand, with the double purpose of bidding him farewell and collecting his wages. Nothing doing. That's where the *reblochon* cheese deal comes in.

Paris is on the verge of famine and a *reblochon* there is like an ingot of gold. Maurice grumbles about not being paid; the boss talks about sending him a postal money order. But Maurice comes up with a better idea.

"If you want, I'll take some *reblochons* up to Paris," says Maurice. "I'll sell them there and send you back the money."

There's no need to say another word — the boss understands. He's a bit leery of the plan, but it's a tempting offer. Anyway, why not? This boy isn't a cheat. The boss evidently reminds himself that he's always managed to avoid paying Maurice by slipping him a nice sandwich now and then at teatime, or by giving him a friendly pat on the shoulder. But he can't quite make up his mind.

"You like it here with us, right, Maurice? You can't complain about the way you're treated here, and it's wartime, you know: times are hard for everyone and at least you eat your fill here. Of course, I can't pay you what I pay Léon — he's seventeen and twice as big as you . . ."

Finally, he decides.

"All right. Take the *reblochons* up there."

Then comes lots of advice about prices, time-limits for spoilage, and other precautions to take.

And that's how, via nineteen empty wine-bottles, a can of tea, and a bottle of cognac, Maurice Joffo returned to the capital, luxuriously seated in the back of an old roadster with his head resting on a cushion of *reblochons* which he sold within a week, the proceeds of which were never to be seen by the legitimate owner — and which was only justice.

*

MARCADET — POISSONNIERS

That's what it says over the entrance to the Métro.

One fine evening three years ago, I took the Métro to the Gare d'Austerlitz. Today, I'm coming back.

The street is the same. There's still that metallic sky between the rain-gutters of the rooftops; there's a smell floating in the air, the smell of Paris in the morning when the wind stirs the leaves on the few trees that there are.

I still have my knapsack. I carry it more easily than I used to; I've grown.

Granny Epstein isn't there anymore. The straw-bottomed chair in the recess of the doorway has also disappeared. Goldenberg's restaurant is closed. How many of us have made it back?

Joffo — Coiffeur. The same neat lettering, the same upstrokes and downstrokes.

Despite the reflections on the shop window I can see Albert cutting a customer's hair. Behind him Henri is handling the broom.

I see Mama already.

I also see that Papa isn't there; I understand that he will never be there anymore . . . The wonderful stories told in the evening in the gleam of the green lampshade are all over.

In the end, Hitler turned out to be crueler than the Czar.

Henri looks at me; I see his lips moving. Albert and Mama turn toward the street. They're speaking words that I can't hear through the pane of glass.

I see myself in the shop window with my knapsack.

It's true, I've grown.

EPILOGUE

And that's that.

I'm forty-two years old now and I've got three kids.

I look at my boy the way my father looked at me thirty years ago and a question pops into my mind; maybe it's a senseless one as so many questions are.

Why did I write this book?

I should have asked myself that before I started; it would have been the logical thing to do, but things don't often happen logically. The book came out of me like something natural; maybe I needed to write it. I say to myself that maybe my son will read it later on, and that satisfies me. He could toss the book aside, consider it just a lot of boring reminiscences. But it could, on the other hand, make him stop and think. It's up to him to make of it what he will. In any case, I imagine having to tell him this evening, at the time when he goes into his bedroom next to mine: "My son, take your knapsack. Here's some money you'll need. You must go now." It happened to me, it happened to my father, and a feeling of boundless joy comes over me when I think that it won't happen to my son.

There's an old gentleman that I really admire: Albert Einstein. He wrote very learned things about the relativity of time; he once said that when a man sits with a pretty girl for an hour, it seems like a minute. But let him sit on a hot stove for a minute — and it's longer than any hour. As I look at my sleeping son, I can only wish one thing: that he may never experience the kind of hours that I knew in those years.

But what do I have to fear? Those things won't happen ever again. The knapsacks are up in the attic; they'll stay there forever.

Perhaps . . .

AFTERWORD

Conversations with My Readers
Translated from the French by Jennifer Terni

Since *A Bag of Marbles* was published in 1973, I have maintained an unbroken dialogue with my readers.

Over the years a large number of letters have come my way and I have tried to answer them as best I could. I was not always able to respond as promptly as I would have liked and for that I am sorry. Trying to keep up with this kind of correspondence is a monumental task, and the questions that my story has provoked have sometimes surprised me and, at other times, disturbed and disconcerted me. I have made many school visits over the years and I have found them every bit as engaging as the correspondence with my readers. Meeting so many children the same age that I was during the war has been a tremendously moving—and fascinating—experience. Their spontaneity, their kindness, and the pertinence of their questions have often touched me and sometimes they have overwhelmed me. I owe a huge debt of gratitude to the teachers who invited me to their schools and made these precious moments possible. I am always delighted when they tell me my story opened up special educational opportunities for their students.

Despite the obvious rewards of these exchanges, there have nonetheless been some very good questions raised over the years that I feel I have never adequately explored in the on-the-spot atmosphere generated by young audiences. The pace is so quick during these meetings that it is not always easy to figure out exactly what you want to say when faced with so many raised hands. Each time I invoke my childhood years, I experience the same terrible anxiety I felt when, day after day, hour after hour, I had to hide or outsmart those interrogating me. In this context, I have found that only time and careful reflection have allowed me to formulate the kind of objective answers that these questions really deserve—especially because I do not want to distort or forget anything that happened.

This, then, is what has propelled me to write this afterword. Given the interest and curiosity that my story has continued to elicit, especially amongst young people, it seemed like a good idea to set out the questions that have been asked most often and answer them as fully and clearly as I could. Many touch upon the human and psychological aspects of my adventure. Others concretely address the history of the period which many young readers do not know. In any case, I wanted to help them to better grasp the historical context of my story which now, over a half century later, is sometimes difficult to understand.

Questions often arise about the very beginning of my adventure, that is to say, about my departure toward Free France with only my brother as a companion. And in particular, there are always questions about the decision my parents made once they had carefully evaluated the dangers posed by the Nazi occupation and come to the conclusion that it was vital that we go underground. How many times have I heard people passionately proclaim: "My mother would never have let me go off alone with only fifty francs in my pocket, even if I had been accompanied by an older sibling!"

This comment, natural coming from children today, reflects the real difficulty they have imagining such extraordinary, and to them, distant circumstances (thank God).

Beyond the obvious fact that fifty francs then were worth a lot more than fifty francs today (which barely buys you lunch), the answer to this question lies elsewhere. In another book, *Anna and Her Orchestra*, I tell my mother's life story. I feel that one must know her story to really understand how she was able to make the decision she finally made—to let us go off on our own. And most of all, that far from being an irresponsible decision, what she did was in the spirit of the very best mothers; it was brave and full of love. Allow me to give a summary of her story.

My mother was born in a small village before the 1917 Revolution when czars still ruled Russia. While she was still a very young child, she experienced the pogroms first-hand. These explosions of anti-Semitic hatred were characterized by the pillaging and burning of homes and businesses, and the systematic harassment and murder of Jews. In 1905, Odessa witnessed the violent repression of an anti-czarist rebellion, one episode of which was the famous sailor's rebellion on the *Potemkin*. During this unrest, my mother was able to flee Russia aboard the ship *Constanza*. She disembarked in Turkey where she hoped to meet up with several family members. She managed to find them and they ended up creating a gypsy orchestra. They toured the great cities of turn-of-the-century Europe, Constantinople, Vienna, Warsaw, Budapest and Berlin, after which they finally stopped in Paris. One must keep all of this in mind to understand her reaction, when later, in an occupied Paris, it became more and more obvious that Jews would be persecuted once again. She had already survived the dangers I faced—or something close to them. She knew that at ten or twelve years of age, if you had to do it and there was no other way out, you could survive alone. The adventures that she experienced had taught her all about adversity. Of course she did not let us go without anxiety and sadness, even terrible suffering. But that was what the fight to survive was all about.

I would add—and I have often been asked this very question—that if a similar situation reoccurred, I would not hesitate to do exactly what my parents did. We have all seen adventure movies in which heroes, when pursued, split up to increase their chances of escape. This was the same game. It was better for one of us to be taken than the entire group.

Another person who has attracted a lot of attention is the priest on the train. Guessing that my brother and I did not have papers, he declared categorically that we were with him when questioned by the Germans. Many people have asked: "Did he know you were Jewish?"

I don't know. I think basically that he never thought about it. All he saw were two kids who would certainly have had problems with the German police without his help. So he didn't hesitate. A gesture of the hand, a phrase: "These children are with me!" It was clear, quick, irrevocable. I think that he was basically a saintly man—the only thing missing was the halo. I never think about him without experiencing deep emotion.

I will come back to the unexpected help we were given at various times which saved our lives more than once. But since I'm on the subject of that priest, I'd like to clarify that he was nothing like the one portrayed in the film that Jacques Doillon directed based on my book. In the film, Maurice and Jo were obliged to beg for the priest's help. The priest is portrayed sipping red wine while he considers what to do. Pressed, he finally asks: "Well, where are your parents? And why should I say that you are with me?" He only reluctantly consents to help the boys. Perhaps Mr. Doillon wanted to make this scene more suspenseful, but his priest had nothing to do with the man that we actually met on the train.

The same problem arose with respect to my father. Mr. Doillon portrayed him on the verge of a nervous breakdown, desperately torn about what he should do with his children. This portrait bears no resemblance to my father, who always showed extraordinary resolve and who, from the very beginning of the war, faced events unflinchingly.

I have often aired my reservations about the film publicly—and each time I have been asked why I let it proceed the way it was. I can only respond that I had no experience with film adaptations, and that I did not collaborate in writing the screenplay. And when, after many requests, I was finally allowed to see the "rushes," it was already too late—the film was nearly completed.

But these are secondary issues. A much more fundamental issue, I think—especially with my younger readers—is the question of fear. "Weren't you scared?" they ask. And sometimes even: "Do you consider yourself a hero?"

Fear is not a simple matter. I should point out that at the beginning of my journey, I mostly felt that I was part of a gigantic game. Nothing seemed very serious. I was simply going off with my brother, the long-time accomplice of all my adventures. I had the impression that we were playing a grander version of cops and robbers, actually living an episode of one of the cartoons that we used to read at the time. This episode would have been entitled *Bibi Fricotin at the SS!* With the carelessness typical of that age, I could never have imagined what kind of situations we would face nor could I have foreseen their gravity. Imagine going off with your best friend, money in pocket . . . with your parent's blessing to boot! This was adventure, the World was ours to discover, and a zest of danger had even been thrown in to spice it up. It was all pretty exciting to me.

When fear—real fear—finally caught up with me, it came at the very moment when I least expected it, when, in fact, I had forgotten all about being afraid. It was in Nice when in the Rue de Russie, I was caught in an ambush organized by the SS. Once I had a machine gun actually trained on me, I understood that the game was over and that this was no movie. When you actually experience it yourself, this kind of situation is nothing like any scene you've ever watched on television, no matter how violent the portrayal. Everything goes through your head so fast. In a second you understand that the person with his finger on the trigger need only increase the pressure on that finger to dispatch you, in no uncertain terms, to the so-called "world beyond" which, some claim, is a "better" one. To be honest, I don't think I'll ever forget that kind of fear.

At the same time, it is a remarkable fact that people actually adapt to constant fear. I think human beings have an ability to adapt to and overcome seemingly impossible situations. After a few days of incarceration at the infamous Excelsior Hotel, I became used to seeing men from the SS and the Gestapo lounging about the corridors. In the end, and this may seem strange, I was far less afraid of my would-be executioners than I was of seeing my friends cry. The daily routine, the SS and the Gestapo, these were all my enemies: I had to fight, to resist, no matter what the cost. In contrast, witnessing the suffering and the tears of the persecuted only increased my distress and my despair. I have to admit that their suffering weighed heavily upon me and became an important part of the suffering I had to bear. I understood their need to express their pain, but I had a hard time dealing with it nonetheless.

I have known other fears in my life: the fear of dentists, the fear of being hit (I boxed a little), the fear of car accidents, the fear of traffic police, the fear of the dark as a child, and even the fear of illness. I was once seriously ill and was not sure I'd survive. But I can tell you none of these fears has anything in common with the kind of fear I described earlier.

In the end, the four years of the Occupation left me with a strong personal philosophy. After it was all over, I felt more than strong enough to cope with the challenges of living and with life's disillusions, disappointments, and failures. To put things in perspective, I only have to think back to that time. And I remember Nietzsche's aphorism: "What doesn't kill you makes you stronger."

There is another kind of fear, and this is one we feel when we are confronted by the unknown. Recently I was taking a train in the suburbs. A lady accompanied by a seven- or eight-year-old child sat down next to me. At the next station, a black man got on the train. The child drew back and let out an exclamation of fear and dismay. The woman, embarrassed, explained: "Sir, please excuse my child. It's the first time he's ever seen anyone of color." And the man answered: "Oh, that's OK. . . . I had the same reaction the first time I saw a white man."

Not long ago, I received a letter from an eleven-year-old boy. "Opposite my school, there is a wall on which someone wrote: 'If history has given us a Hitler, why should we listen to fear?' I don't understand what this graffiti means. Can you explain it?"

I must admit that I was troubled by this problem. Finally I answered the question this way: I honestly believe that it is better to listen to fear. At least it teaches us caution. A soldier charging into enemy lines without fear is unconscious of himself. Fear helps us to defend ourselves. If the major democracies had been less sure of themselves when Hitler took power—when he revealed ever more explicitly the true nature of his aggressive and militaristic policies based on hate and racism—we might have avoided World War II, with its millions of victims from all countries, all religions, and all walks of life.

The other part of the question still remains: were we heroes? Well, if we ever were, it was not on purpose. We never looked for and certainly never wished for the situations we faced. They happened to us. In order to keep alive, we had to overcome many obstacles, we had to learn to react, to plan, to keep on our guard, to improvise, to survive ... I don't believe, however, that we should confuse our survival instinct with heroism. Heroism consists of deliberately choosing to risk your life because you are fighting for a cause which you believe is just and good. This is courage in its purest form. Heroes, for instance, are like the Bourgeois of Calais, six men from the fifteenth century who gave themselves up as hostages in order to save their city. Or another example would be Dr. Korczak, who went singing into the gas chambers in cheerful solidarity with children about to die. Or yet again, Guynemer and Mermoz, the pioneers of aviation. We, on the other hand, found ourselves with our backs to the wall and no choice but to defend ourselves. And to tell the truth, I just thought it would be too idiotic to die without ever having fallen in love.

At this point, I would like to return to our priest on the train and to the other unexpected "saviors" we met along our voyage. I'm thinking of the doctor from the Excelsior. He knew perfectly well that we were Jewish, and yet he said nothing when it was his job to do precisely that. I'm also thinking about the priest and then the bishop of Nice, and about the director of the Youth Camp, an institution that was especially set up by the Vichy government! And even about Ambroise Mancelier, a staunch *pétainiste* and collaborator, who discovered, after the fact, that he had hidden two Jews at the end of the war. If you remember, Mancelier's justification for collaborating was that it was important to support a Unified Europe. A lot of people believed that Germany had definitively won the war and that, therefore, the smartest thing to do was to "collaborate" in the unification of all Europe ... even if it was a Europe under the German boot. We have a pretty different conception of what a unified Europe means these days.

All this is to say that you never knew who you might come across in the chaos that was France during the Occupation. A doctor saves two young Jews, God knows why, when he must surely have sent others to their deaths in the concentration camps. There were also the "mules" who risked their lives to help people reach the free zone . . . and those others who robbed their charges of everything they had before abandoning them to their fates in the forest.

It is important to me to take this opportunity to honor certain compatriots from this period. First, Mgr. Jules-Gérard Saliège, bishop of Toulouse, for his courageous message to the French and for his rebellious spirit. He wrote: "Jews are men, Jews are women. We cannot just declare open season on these men, these women, these people, who are also mothers and fathers with families. They are part of the human race. They are our brothers like anyone else. A Christian can never forget this." This plea was circulated throughout France in September of 1942. In a similar vein, we must not forget the police officers who took it upon themselves to alert Jews who were about to be picked up in round-ups organized by the authorities. These raids would certainly have been far deadlier had these men not intervened to sabotage Nazi efforts. I would like to quote the police commissioner who lives in Montpellier to this day: "There are circumstances in which people are called upon to have the courage to disobey. The French had gone to war against the Germans and they had lost. Seeing members of the French Resistance being arrested broke my heart, but it was a legitimate consequence of war. On the other hand, the arrests of Jewish men, women and children simply because they were Jewish had nothing to do with war. It was pure racism." This officer personally visited those targeted for arrest in order to warn them in advance. Certain people did not believe him, and the next day, he was faced with the unenviable task of arresting them in the company of his colleagues.

I would like to add that despite the Vichy regime's anti-Semitic laws, despite the exclusion of Jews from specific professions, despite their humiliation and their persecution, French Jewry maintained an extraordinary sense of identity throughout this period thanks to a rebellious spirit which inspired them to fight for their survival with the help of a large number of French citizens and Jewish organizations. When, following the round-ups of 1942, it became obvious that admitting that one was Jewish was tantamount to a death sentence, many Jews decided to hide, to fight or to flea the country. The Vichy government carries a huge burden of guilt for the deportations; but without the aid of the French clergy and a large portion of the French populace, the "final solution" as envisioned by the Nazis would have been achieved.

This brings me back to yet another of the questions that I have been asked most often: why didn't I identify the village—Rumilly in Haute-Savoie—where the last part of my wartime odyssey unfolded?

The answer is very simple. This entire story is true, the things I described actually happened. Without returning to the places where I had sojourned, I knew that certain protagonists in my story would still be alive. This whole period, with its bitter conflicts between *pétainistes,* "collaborators" and the Resistance, followed by the Liberation and the retributions rightly visited upon the guilty (but with inevitable excesses), left a deep scar in people's memories. I did not want to reopen old wounds by giving the impression that I was singling out this village—especially as people there were neither better nor worse than anywhere else during the war.

Then why name it now? Simply because the situation changed after the book was first published. And I think it is important to tell the story of how this happened.

Two or three years after the publication of the novel, I received a phone call:

"Is this Monsieur Joffo, author of *A Bag of Marbles*?"

"This is he," I answered.

"My name is Henry Tracol and I am the Deputy Mayor of Rumilly."

Henry Tracol! All of a sudden I could see myself in short pants, playing marbles in the Place d'Armes with another ruffian of my own age, the station-master's son: Henry Tracol.

"You know, Jo," he explained, "Here everyone recognized himself, from Father John at the White Horse, to Lechat at the dairy and the story of the cheeses . . ."

And then Henry explained the reason for his call. I had been invited to Rumilly. And more precisely, I was being invited for a book signing at the Mancelier bookstore! The very same bookstore where I had worked for old man Mancelier under the stern gaze of Maréchal Pétain, who stared down at me from the many portraits and busts that adorned the store.

I must say that I was very moved . . . The phone call completely overwhelmed me, taking me thirty years back into the past. I also have to admit that I did not have a particularly warm place in my heart for Rumilly. I had never returned there. Despite this, I immediately accepted Henry's invitation. We set a date, and on a May morning, after a night spent on the train, my brother Albert and I pulled into the train station at Rumilly.

It was about nine in the morning. Because we were pretty tired, we did not immediately grasp what was going on: a fanfare, majorettes in uniforms, Henry Tracol, the municipal council, everybody was there! I couldn't believe my eyes. Albert, who had gotten off the train ahead of me, turned around and said:

"Look! There must be some celebrity coming in after us!"

Obviously. All of this could not be for us. I turned around to see: there was no one behind us. We were the only passengers getting off the train at Rumilly that morning.

What a welcome! After a speech given by Henry Tracol on the

quay, we proceeded to City Hall surrounded by a group of twirling majorettes. Mayor Louis Dagand was standing there waiting for us, accompanied by the regional deputy to the National Assembly, the rabbi from Annecy, and a television crew that had come especially from Grenoble. Each gave a lengthy speech flattering us extravagantly.

Without doubt, the greatest moment for me in this extraordinary day was provided by Louis Dagand. He announced that henceforth I would be known as an "honorary citizen" of Rumilly. This title is more precious to me than any more formal decorations could ever be—and for a pretty simple reason: those who have been decorated with the Legion of Honor and the Military Cross number in the thousands. To my knowledge, I am still the only honorary citizen of the village of Rumilly.

That day, I also received a congratulatory telegram from Françoise Mancelier. I learned that she had moved to Montauban, where she had married a rugby player and had had three children.

The best picture of the day was taken by my friend Henry when the "Alpine Mistress of the Cheese" portioned out my weight in Beaufort cheese. The book signing at the Mancelier bookstore was also a high point. I would like to thank my friend "Pounet," the new owner of the bookstore on Montpezat road, to which I return often. I would also like to thank the people of Rumilly who welcomed me with such open arms. Their kindness and spontaneity helped me to forget all of my painful memories.

This is one of the most disturbing questions that has ever been asked of me. It was asked by a student who put it this way: "Sir, I am Jewish. My grandfather, who is a rabbi, told me after having read your book that, in your place, he never would have exchanged his Star of David for a bag of marbles. He later wrote an article dedicated to you, which argued that never admitting your Judaism during the war could be construed as a kind of religious conversion in itself, and that in other circumstances, you and your family would certainly have become *marranos*. I was wondering if you agree with him."

I should specify that *marranos* was a term used to describe Spanish Jews who converted to Christianity under the Inquisition, to avoid either exile or death. This has always been controversial . . . I must say, that when all is said and done, I cannot agree with this boy's grandfather. I will put myself in the hands of the great Jewish philosopher and theologian Maimonides. His *Guide to the Perplexed* contains one answer to this problem. He wrote the guide in response to a community in Yemen that had written for his opinion on whether it was legitimate to renounce one's faith when threatened with death. Maimonides answered that the first duty of men and Jews was to stay alive—provided that they remained true to their faith in their heart of hearts. God alone should hold the power over life and death. I must add, that if the Nazis had given any choice to those who died in the gas chambers, there never would have been a holocaust. Death denies the possibility of choice.

This is basically what I told the boy that day. With hindsight, I would like to add the following: I prefer a living *marrano* to a dead Jew. A *marrano* can always come back to his faith. A corpse can only be mourned by his or her loved ones. This said, each of us has a different relationship to death. Refusing to renounce one's faith can be considered suicidal, or it can also be seen as the ultimate act of courage and heroism. Personally, I tend to agree with Maimonides.

Many youngsters have expressed dismay that so many Jews allowed themselves to be taken peacefully and then deported without resistance. They have asked me whether I would not have preferred to fight, weapon in hand.

I think that in order to understand, you have to place yourself within this specific historical context.

One first has to recognize that the Nazis were meticulously organized in the planning and execution of their crime. The fact that they were going to die was hidden from the Jews until the very last moments of their deportation. Survivors of the gas chambers have described again and again how, right up until very last moment, an elaborate charade was contrived to convince the victims that they were merely going to take showers. Besides, how do unarmed families with women and children defend themselves against trained soldiers with machine guns? Fathers in this situation faced a terrible moral choice: could they in all conscience risk their families' lives? Mothers did everything in their power not to be separated from their children. The Nazis were so elaborate in their cruelty that they deliberately maintained the illusion of hope by making their victims believe that they were merely being deported to work camps where they would live and work in peace.

And then there were many of us, it must be acknowledged, who just refused to face reality. The crime was so inconceivable, so colossal, that when the camps were liberated, the entire world was simultaneously shocked, disgusted and ashamed. Another thing that should be noted is that when Jews realized that they were in fact being shipped to their deaths, they tended to rebel—witness the heroic revolt at Warsaw. Fifty thousand starving Jews from the Warsaw ghetto repelled an entire division of the SS for a month without heavy arms. This revolt is one of the greatest heroic resistances in the annals of Jewish history. All in all, the revolt of the Warsaw ghetto lasted longer than the entire French campaign of 1940.

Personally, I believe that I would have preferred fighting actively during the war. Even though I am a dedicated pacifist, I nonetheless believe that there are times when war is inevitable. The world should have reacted to Hitler and his regime of conquests far earlier. The temporizing that often characterizes democratic governments has a tendency to be interpreted by dictators as a lack of courage and resolve.

I still occasionally think of my experiences during the war. It is a story that inhabits me, that is an integral part of who I am: a Jew to the bottom of my soul, and one who paid dearly for being precisely that! If I ever found myself in an analogous situation, I would do everything necessary to fight back, weapon in hand. Or better yet, I would try to flee to safer ground. One should not let oneself be caught in the same trap more than once.

And if it ever happened that I somehow forgot that I was a Jew, I have no doubt that life would intervene to bring me back to myself quickly. A recent incident illustrates this. I was cutting one of my regular client's hair in the salon, when she said to me: "Monsieur Joffo, I have just returned from a trip to your fabulous country!" I understood perfectly well what she was suggesting, but I decided to play it coy: "You mean the region around Tours? The people of the Touraine are certainly fabulous!" All of the salon regulars know that I have owned a property in the Touraine for a long time. "What do you have to do with Touraine?" she protested, "I meant Israel!"

I probably should have, and could have, launched into a long speech explaining what she already knew anyway: that Jews born in France were French and that being Jewish in France was simply about being a member of the Jewish faith, in the same way that other people were Catholic, Protestant, Buddhist or Muslim. That in its own way, what she had said was as offensive to me as when a politician inquires whether a Jewish opponent has double national-ity. I spared myself from having to comment, however, when I re-membered the basic wisdom of a popular French saying:

"Silence is the best expression of contempt."

What would have been gained had I tried to explain? Would she even have listened? I don't think that this woman was anti-Semitic. However, like many people, through ignorance and a lack of strong ethical convictions, she could easily become an anti-Semite in the right climate. This became apparent in 1940, after things in this country had fallen apart. Over ninety percent of the population followed Pétain and his chief henchman, Pierre Laval. They all had their reasons. Even I, a ten-year-old Jewish boy, believed in their rationalizations. You have to remember, Maréchal Pétain had saved France in 1914, he had won the Battle of Verdun against a German army that would later defeat him. France had been bruised and humiliated by its too-rapid defeat. It needed to find a way to believe in itself, to think that not all was lost. In short, France needed a hero and we thought we had found one made-to-measure for the difficult times ahead: Maréchal Pétain.

I'll admit that I also believed in him when I saw his picture hanging over my teacher's desk. But I mistook my heroes. The real hero was waiting in the wings across the British Channel. That person was General de Gaulle, who ran the Resistance from London.

This leads me naturally to yet another question. Are there grounds for concern about a possible resurgence of anti-Semitism in France today? An inevitable question, and I'd say an open-ended one. If we look at Jewish history since the Middle Ages, we find that whenever leaders have needed a scapegoat, Jews have been the convenient sacrificial lamb. They offer a cheap and politically expedient solution. Jews have traditionally been perceived by Christians as the killers of Christ. Jews have historically found their positions even more precarious because of their minority status. And being a minority, they have had few defenses and have succumbed to persecution time and again. The Crusades and the Spanish Inquisition are but two examples.

After the Liberation and the discovery of the concentration camps, it was almost possible to believe that anti-Semitism would finally be eradicated once and for all. Unfortunately, this has not proven to be the case. In Poland, thousands saved from the camps perished after the war under atrocious circumstances. A Jewish community barely exists in Poland today because of the extent of the extermination in that country during the war. And yet anti-Semitism is on the rise in Poland. On television one sees people interviewed on the streets of large Polish cities. People still blame Jews, with complete insouciance, for all their country's ills. They imagine them everywhere, hiding all over the country under assumed names. I still say it was no accident that Auschwitz was in Poland.

I think we must remain vigilant. Anti-Semitism can spread with surprising rapidity, as was the case between 1933 and 1939, a period during which it was impossible to ignore the explicit and official anti-Semitism of Nazi Germany. Despite this, no measures were taken to discourage its spread to France—with the consequences that we all know.

If France were faced with a serious economic crisis, with unemployment in the millions, the game of scapegoating would begin once again—it is a favorite tool for those who preach xenophobia, racism, and anti-Semitism. Just prior to the Gulf War, I stopped at a newsstand in Place Victor-Hugo in the sixteenth arrondissement of Paris. Lo and behold, there I saw a newspaper set up in prominent display. I can't remember which one it was, but I'll never forget its headline: *Who Wants War? The Jews and the Arabs.* When I expressed dismay that this rag should be given such a prominent display, the sales clerk objected, arguing that France was a democracy and that no one was forcing me to buy a paper I didn't like. He then commented that he was sure that it would be a very popular issue. And besides: I was the only one who had complained that the headline was using a racially charged message, a message which I still think was an insult to both Jews and Arabs everywhere.

So what does it mean to be a Jew? Here we are, back to an age-old question. What does it mean to me? Am I proud to be a Jew?

I have often heard Jews say to non-Jews: "I am Jewish and proud of it." It is important to understand that this is not meant to be a provocation. On the contrary. We must understand the nature and the source of this pride, which has too often been derided over the centuries. I'll give just one example, from Hitler's infamous yet widely-read treatise, *Mein Kampf.* He wrote: "The Jew is the archetype of the parasite, a destroyer, which, like a dangerous bacillus, spreads its taint ever further as soon as any opening is presented to it. The effect of its presence is like the spreading of a weed. Wherever Jews take root, in the short run or the long run, they end up destroying the very people that originally took them in."

It has been this way since the Diaspora. But when the pressure subsides, Jewish people have always recovered their dignity and rediscovered their pride. Although I am in no way ashamed of being Jewish, personally I claim no particular credit for it either. I am what I am, and I live by that. Each of us has to recognize that we are only here on Earth due to chance—and a very happy chance; the kind that arises from two people meeting and loving each other. I really believe that human beings, whatever their religion, should only take pride in whatever small or great actions they have contributed to the good of humankind. If we judge ourselves by this standard, we remain humble. We should simply try to live our lives as human beings, which is already a challenge—though a not-impossible one—with as much goodwill as we can muster.

I will say that, for me, being Jewish in France during the twentieth century has meant belonging to a long tradition that stretches back to the time of Abraham and stems from the fact that Judaism was the first great monotheistic religion. It goes back to Moses, who is the only human who ever met God and heard His voice. He even brought back proof of his conversation—the Ten Commandments.

It also means believing in The One God: "The Eternal is our God, the Eternal is One!"

It is also means belonging to the people of the Book, the Old Testament. A propos, I'd like to tell a story for which I take entire responsibility.

An old Jew, who had not committed even the shadow of a sin during his long and pious life, dies a quiet death one night. Instantly, he finds himself in Heaven. God Himself is there to greet him and He seats the old man to His right and showers honors upon him, praising him for his blameless life both as a Jew and as a human being. But somehow the old Jew is full of sorrow, and nothing God does seems to cheer him up. From time to time God actually catches him drying a tear. He finally asks him: "What is wrong, old man? You look careworn. I am God the Eternal, you must tell me everything . . ." But the old man shakes his head . . . it is obvious that he does not want to talk about what ails him. So God insists and then gets angry: "You must tell me what is wrong, I am your God and I can do anything."

Who can refuse God? So the old Jew says: "Listen, Eternal One, I did not dare to admit this before now, but I had a son, an only son, whom I tried to raise as a good Jew as best I could. But it all came to naught. He did not follow, as I did, the faith of our forefathers . . . in fact, I have to admit that . . . he converted."

At that moment God burst out laughing. He laughed so hard that He shook the four corners of the heavens. Then He looked at the old man with compassion and said: "I can assure you that there is nothing to worry about. We must always forgive. Hey! My son converted too."

The old man, encouraged, then asked: "How did You react? How did You punish Him?"

God replied: "Oh! That was easy. I simply drew up a New Testament!"

Being a Jew means having a good sense of humor. It also means never accepting the characterization of a politician, no matter what his stature, describing the Jewish people as "that arrogant and dominant group."

It also means loving your family, respecting it, honoring your father and your mother as it says you should in the Ten Commandments. You should not forget where you came from, no matter how far or how high you climb. You should never forget a place for the poor at the Sabbath meal. It does mean dragging around five thousand years of trouble and tradition, but we should not deny any part of it, because despite everything, despite the persecutions and the genocide, our people have managed to survive.

A last question I have often been asked concerns my life as a writer.

I did not think of this book, *A Bag of Marbles*, as a literary enterprise when I first began writing. My goal was to exorcise some of my childhood demons, to get it out of my system. Of the two choices open to me, I preferred writing to psychoanalysis, and I think I made the right choice.

I also wanted to leave a testimonial of that time for my children, in order to convey to them the essence of my experiences and the values I consider essential: be brave, know how to take care of yourself, don't rely on others, don't let your emotions get the better of you, take responsibility. In short, make yourself as invulnerable as possible. I think these are the qualities one needs in order to face life and its many pitfalls.

The Bible says that a man should perform three tasks in life: get married and have children, build a house, and create something that will survive beyond himself. This book is my attempt to accomplish that final task. I was in no way prepared for the undertaking involved in writing such a book and I had originally expected to publish it at my own expense. The incredible success of *A Bag of Marbles* was totally unexpected. The manuscript was rejected by four publishers before Michel-Claude Jalard and Jean-Claude Lattès accepted it. They then lent me the invaluable editing talents of Claude Klotz to help me polish my work. His contribution even managed to surprise my children, who had already heard these stories countless times before.

Most authors tend to begin their careers with an autobiographical novel. I was no exception. My second novel was also very close to my own life because it was about my mother. Over the years, and mostly due to the letters I received, I understood that many of my readers were curious about what I had been up to since the war. As a result I wrote the sequel to *A Bag of Marbles,* in a book I called *Baby-Foot.* In this book I describe my experiences in the fascinating but very difficult landscape that was Paris after the war. As a result of the crazy things I had lived through during the war, I had passed directly from childhood into adulthood. Sometimes the whole thing still seems unreal to me and I catch myself wondering whether I really lived through those days, or whether they are the residue of some fantastic dream.

The Old Woman of Djerba, my fourth novel, was a real challenge. Certain critics had suggested that once I had exhausted my own life experiences as a source of inspiration, I wouldn't have much left to say. I was convinced they were wrong. The *Old Woman of Djerba* came as the result of a chance encounter. I was only twenty-five at the time and hadn't the slightest notion that one day I would pursue a literary career. I had gone to the Tunisian isles of Djerba with a few friends. Djerba happens to be the world capital of bridge. The hotel was lovely, and lolling on the beach, doing nothing much of anything, was wonderful at first. The only problem was that I did not play bridge and so, after a while, I got a little bored. One morning, as I lounged near the swimming pool, the hotel manager approached me. He said that he could see that I was bored, and he suggested that I might enjoy visiting the rest of the island: "There are markets and bazaars, and if you like old architecture, there is also a synagogue that is over three thousand years old. The synagogue is a monument to an ancient Jewish presence in this part of the world dating back centuries before the Diaspora."

I must admit that the hotel manager had piqued my curiosity. Therefore, the next day, I went off to discover the island. In the morning I visited the souks, the boutiques and the shops. I then enjoyed a typical North African lunch: couscous, mergez sausage and Turkish coffee. By three o'clock I was standing in front of the synagogue. There, I got quite a shock: this synagogue looked exactly like a mosque. And as is the custom in all mosques, one was required to remove one's shoes before entering the building. This was a very potent reminder about just how closely related the three great monotheistic religions are to one another.

Inside, I discovered pre-Roman mosaics as well as stained glass that even Chagall would have been proud to call his own. The rabbi, turbaned in Middle Eastern fashion, personally showed me a Torah that had withstood the tribulations of three millennia.

I was both moved and deeply impressed. For me, this was a return to my roots. When I left the synagogue's protection, the sun beat down upon me and I was surrounded by a crowd of beggars; Arabs who looked like Jews and Jews who looked like Arabs. At a little remove stood an old woman dressed head-to-toe in black. She had clear blue eyes and a mane of perfectly white hair that stretched halfway down her back. Since I was leaving a sacred place, I thought it was probably appropriate to give alms. I approached the old woman and slipped five dinars into her pocket as I passed. She took my hand in hers and said: "No, not you. But if you have a little time, I have a few things to tell you."

I laughed and replied: "What could you possibly have to say to me? I don't know you and you don't know me. Take the money and go enjoy a mint tea."

"You are wrong," she said. "I do know who you are. You are Joseph Joffo."

Because I am by nature skeptical, my friends back at the hotel immediately sprang to mind. I suspected that they had sent this "seer" after me as a joke. I replied impatiently, "Come on! Quit this charade and relax. I know lots of people who perform the same act in music halls. They slip an identity card into an envelope and provide other personal information about a pre-selected subject."

The old woman shook her head and said, "I knew that you wouldn't believe me. But I can see back in time, back even into your distant past. I knew your great-grandmother at Kremarchak in Russia. Her name was Elizabeth Talchinki-Markof."

For a second I thought the ground had opened up and swallowed me whole. There was no way this woman could have known that. I was the only one who knew my great-grandmother's name and the village where she grew up. I immediately took the old woman by the hand and guided her to a café to share the ritual tea of those reunited. For hours, she talked. Liza claimed that she had been on the Earth long before the dawn of humankind, during a time when trees still spoke. She told me a strange story: "When the Tree of Life saw the first lumberjacks walk into the forests, all the other trees began to cry and lament their fates. The Tree of Life, in an attempt to reassure them, observed: 'Do not cry my brothers. Don't you realize that the ax handles are made of wood just like us?'"

She then suggested a parallel between the trees and those Jews who, during the war, waited docilely for the Nazis with their suitcases packed, repeating to themselves: "We have nothing to fear from them. After all, they are human beings . . ."

I will not tell all of Liza's story now. One thing I am sure about however, is that during our entire conversation, I was under a spell. We spoke about everything: life, love, children and so much more . . .

I do not believe to this day that she was a dream. There are moments in life when fiction and reality meet. Now Liza is a part of me and I doubt that I could ever find her again because she has become such an integral part of who I am.

My next book was called *The Tender Summer.* I wrote this book while I was seriously ill. I had seen my daughter Alexandra grow up into a young woman. This book combines that true story with fiction. I realize now, that of all my books, this is the one teenage girls like best. I think it is because the heroes, Alexandra and Jean-Pierre, are very much like young people today.

The Horseman from the Promised Land tells the story of a young man who is an officer both before and after the Russian Revolution in 1917. His many trials and tribulations gradually lead him to embrace Zionism. His activism on this front results in his imprisonment and exile. True to his dreams and ideals, he eventually manages to escape to Palestine. This book follows our hero from Poland, Russia and Turkey, through the Middle East, all the way to the Promised Land.

Simon and the Child tells a story that has some parallels with *A Bag of Marbles.* It is the story of a ten-year-old boy whose mother has begun a new life with a man who is not his father. At first he hates the man and is full of resentment because he thinks this man is stealing his mother's love. Over time, however, they become a true son and father to each other. This story takes place against the backdrop of the war. It is 1942. The little boy is Christian, but his stepfather is Jewish. The book recounts their escape across France and their liberation from the infamous concentration camp of Drancy. I have been particularly satisfied with this book's reception. It was translated into German and was later integrated into the German national scholastic curriculum.

Abraham Levy, a Country Curate is a very simple story. I just imagined what would have happened to Mgr. Lustiger if he had not been made into the Bishop of Paris and had instead remained a country priest. When, at a town council meeting, the announcement is made that the new priest, a Father Abraham Levy, will be arriving the next day, an uproar ensues. Everyone knows that it's not easy being Jewish . . . but being a Christian Jew is harder still. But Abraham Levy has lived through other challenges, including the war, and nothing will deter him from exercising his vocation.

I also wrote two children's books: *The Thousand-Flavored Fruit* and *The Carp.*

I would like to conclude with an anecdote a school principal told me when I was visiting his school. He said that one morning, on his watch, he suddenly heard a loud disturbance in the school yard. When he intervened to find out what was going on, he discovered several students fighting rather savagely. They were flushed and panting, and yelled insults to one another. "Kike! Dirty Jew! Why don't you go back to your own country! You are taking bread out of the mouths of true Frenchmen!" The principal ran to break it up. He was shocked. "What do you think you're doing!? Do you have any idea what in the world you are saying?" After a minute of silence, one of the boys smiled and explained: "Sir, we were only having a little game. We are only pretending to be Joffo. We were playing *A Bag of Marbles.*"

The principal commented: "The most surprising thing about it was that the ones who were yelling out 'dirty Jew' were in fact Jews themselves . . . It was the other children, the non-Jews, who were the ones playing the Jewish characters. I wondered what you would think of this story . . ."

What *do* I think? Perhaps those children were trying to understand something through this game. Perhaps they were trying to understand what it was like for us. I also think that no one can really put himself in another person's shoes. Trying to act out, or recreate, a situation inevitably falsifies it in some ways.

318

But I would add the one thing that is of utmost importance to me. It was not a bad thing to see my adventure transformed into a children's game. I'd be happy if only it would stay that way and adults were never tempted to play it again.

At the time of this printing, M. Joffo's other books, with the exception of *Anna and Her Orchestra*, are not available in English. *Editor.*